REFORMING
KOREA'S
Industrial Conglomerates

REFORMING KOREA'S

Industrial Conglomerates

Edward M. Graham

Institute for International Economics
Washington, DC
January 2003

Edward M. Graham, senior fellow, was associate professor in the Fuqua School of Business at Duke University (1988-90), associate professor at the University of North Carolina (1983-88), principal administrator of the Planning and Evaluation Unit at the OECD (1981-82), international economist in the Office of International Investment Affairs at the US Treasury (1979-80), and assistant professor at the Massachusetts Institute of Technology (1974-78). He is author or coauthor of the following IIE publications: *Fighting the Wrong Enemy: Antiglobal Activists and Multinational Enterprises* (2000), *Competition Policies in the Global Economy* (1997) with J. David Richardson, *Global Corporations and National Governments* (1996), and *Foreign Direct Investment in the United States* (3d ed. 1995) with Paul R. Krugman. He is the coeditor of *Global Competition Policy* (1997) with J. David Richardson.

INSTITUTE FOR INTERNATIONAL ECONOMICS
1750 Massachusetts Avenue, NW
Washington, DC 20036-1903
(202) 328-9000 FAX: (202) 659-3225
http://www.iie.com

C. Fred Bergsten, *Director*
Brigitte Coulton, *Director of Publications and Web Development*
Brett Kitchen, *Director of Marketing and Foreign Rights*

Typesetting by Sandra F. Watts
Printing by Kirby Lithographic Company, Inc.
Cover photo: Grant V. Faint/Getty Images

Printed in the United States of America
05 04 03   5 4 3 2 1

Library of Congress Cataloging-in-Publication Data

Graham, Edward M.
    (Edward Montgomery), 1944-
    The unfinished task of industrial restructuring in Korea / Edward M. Graham.
        p. cm.
    ISBN 0-88132-337-3
    1. Industrial organization—Korea (South).   2. Industrial concentration—Korea (South).   3. Industrial policy—Korea (South).   I. Title.

HD2908.G72 2002
338.95195—dc21   2002017273

The views expressed in this publication are those of the author. This publication is part of the overall program of the Institute, as endorsed by its Board of Directors, but does not necessarily reflect the views of individual members of the Board or the Advisory Committee.

For

Kathryn A. Park
without whose support publication of this book
would have been even more delayed than it was

and

Paul S. Spiegler, M.D.,
and **Thomas G. Zorc, M.D.**
without whose quick intervention the book
might never have been published at all

Contents

Preface

When the "baht crisis" broke out in Thailand during the summer of 1997, few analysts predicted that within months the crisis would spread to South Korea. Korea had been one of the "Asian miracle economies" of the past 25 years and had just joined the Organization for Economic Cooperation and Development (OECD), the "rich nation's club." However, the crisis did envelop Korea and a team from the International Monetary Fund was sent to Seoul to negotiate a standby agreement—effectively, a bailout—in the face of the inability of the Bank of Korea to stand behind the short-term debts of Korean institutions (both banks and private firms). In 1998, the Korean economy went into its deepest recession since the Korean War.

Korea's dilemma arose in part because Korean banks had lent heavily to other nations mired in the 1997 crisis, especially Indonesia, while borrowing funds internationally. But, to a much greater extent, the problem in Korea was home-grown. In particular, huge amounts of debt had been amassed by Korea's large industrial conglomerates (the "chaebol"), most of it owed to Korean banks. In many cases, the funds had been invested in undertakings that were not earning satisfactory rates of return; this was signaled in early 1997 when a number of the smaller chaebol went into bankruptcy. As the year progressed, it became clear that those chaebol in financial difficulty were not limited to the smaller groups; at least one of the top five (Daewoo) was in serious trouble and several others were far from financial health. Indeed, much of the reason why foreign lenders to Korean banks sought to pull funds out of Korea was fear that many of the domestic loans of Korean banks were effectively nonperforming.

In this study, Edward M. Graham examines in detail how this situation arose, tracing its roots to the aggressive industrial policy pursued by Korean president Park Chung-hee during which time the chaebol began to take form. He notes that a major failing of Korea during the "miracle economy" years was that the financial sector in Korea remained underdeveloped and thus never was able to develop a counterweight to the economic (and political) power that, over time, the chaebol acquired. To a large extent, the crisis of 1997 can be seen as the culminating event of that asymmetry that was created by Korean industrial policy, i.e., very powerful industrial groups that operated without the countervailing power of financial institutions.

Graham then looks at the efforts at reform that have transpired since 1997, including reform of the financial sector and of the chaebol themselves. He concludes that much progress has been made but also that this progress has been uneven and that the process of reform is far from complete. In particular, reform of the financial sector has progressed further than reform of the industrial sector. Graham concludes by suggesting what steps remain to be taken in Korea to ensure that a repeat of the 1997 crisis does not occur.

The Institute for International Economics is a private nonprofit institution for the study and discussion of international economic policy. Its purpose is to analyze important issues in that area and to develop and communicate practical new approaches for dealing with them. The Institute is completely nonpartisan.

The Institute is funded largely by philanthropic foundations. Major institutional grants are now being received from the William M. Keck, Jr. Foundation and the Starr Foundation. A number of other foundations and private corporations contribute to the highly diversified financial resources of the Institute. About 31 percent of the Institute's resources in our latest fiscal year were provided by contributors outside the United States, including about 18 percent from Japan. The Korea Foundation supported this study.

The Board of Directors bears overall responsibility for the Institute and gives general guidance and approval to its research program, including the identification of topics that are likely to become important over the medium run (one to three years), and which should be addressed by the Institute. The Director, working closely with the staff and outside Advisory Committee, is responsible for the development of particular projects and makes the final decision to publish an individual study.

The Institute hopes that its studies and other activities will contribute to building a stronger foundation for international economic policy around the world. We invite readers of these publications to let us know how they think we can best accomplish this objective.

C. Fred Bergsten
Director
January 2003

Acknowledgments

A full list of individuals who have provided me with assistance in the preparation of this book would be too lengthy to print and, thus, a partial list must suffice. In thanking the following individuals, I am aware that my debts to all go quite deep. I owe "borrowed inspiration" for the main themes of this book to certain of these individuals, and I also owe the discovery and correction of many errors to those who read early drafts of the text.

In particular, Professor Taeho Bark of Seoul National University first pointed out to me that often hidden problems lurked within many of the large industrial groups of Korea, and he did so during the spring of 1997, when these problems were not yet readily apparent. I was visiting professor at Seoul National University at that time, at the invitation of Professor Bark and on short leave of absence from the Institute for International Economics. That visit awakened me both to the incredible dynamism of South Korea and to the looming problems that the country would soon have to face.

Contributing to my awakening were many people of Korean nationality whom I will not list here as the list would be too long and, moreover, certain people talked to me on condition of confidentiality; but they are to be found, among other institutions, at Seoul National, Ewha, and Yonsei Universities; Korea Institute for International Economic Policy; Korea Development Institute; and several ministries of the Korean government.

Individuals who read early versions of the text and contributed valuable comments include Professors Larry Krause and Stephen Haggard, both at the University of California at San Diego; Dr. Marcus Noland of the Institute for International Economics; Dr. William Zeile at the Bureau of Economic Analysis of the US Commerce Department (but who did so on his own time); Dr. Inbom Choi, now at the Federation of Korean Industries but at the time visiting fellow at the Institute for International Economics; and Professor Hugh Patrick of Columbia University, to whom I owe a special thanks for his very detailed comments. I also owe thanks to several anonymous reviewers who gave valuable suggestions.

I wish to thank individuals at the International Monetary Fund and the World Bank who also gave valuable advice on condition of anonymity. Several individuals at the Korea Economic Institute of America, on whose Advisory Board I serve, provided assistance for which I am grateful; in this regard, let me thank all of you, but especially Dr. Peter Beck, whose assistance often went above any call of duty.

The support staff of the Institute for International Economics, as always, did a very good job bringing this book into print; in this matter, let me thank Brigitte Coulton, former director of publications, as well as Marla Banov, Madona Devasahayam, and Katie Sweetman.

My writing of this book was made possible by a grant to the Institute for International Economics from the Korea Foundation, to whom I extend special thanks (and an apology for not meeting their deadline!). And, of course, I owe gratitude to Institute Director C. Fred Bergsten for allowing me more time than perhaps I really was entitled in order to complete this project.

There doubtlessly remain errors in the book, both great and small. Blame for these must rest on my shoulders; the errors exist in spite of the good efforts of the individuals listed above.

EDWARD M. GRAHAM
January 2003

Introduction

Among those countries that were seen, beginning in the early 1970s and lasting through the 1990s, as the "miracle economies" of Asia, perhaps none performed quite as miraculously as South Korea (or, more formally, the Republic of Korea). As recently as the mid-1960s, South Korea (henceforth simply "Korea" except when confusion with North Korea is possible) could be counted among the poorest of the world's nations. Indeed, in the years immediately following World War II, after Korea had been liberated from the repressive rule of Japan, the nation suffered a brutal war during which perhaps 10 percent of its population perished and per capita income, already low, fell further (see chapter 2). In the aftermath of this war, many analysts felt that Korea was a hopeless economic basket case whose people were destined to be perpetually dependent on foreign aid—and, even with that aid, consigned to live at the edge of poverty.[1] In 1962, in fact, real per capita GDP in Korea was less than that in Thailand, the Philippines, Malaysia, or even Ghana. The average person in Korea in 1962 could claim less than half the income of the average person in Malaysia, then the richest of these four other countries by this measure.

The analysts—and there were many of them—could not have been more wrong. Barely thirty years later, Korea had risen to become a candidate

---

1. See, e.g., United Nations (1952); in 1952, Korean relief programs were largely under the aegis of the United Nations, and military units sent to South Korea to fight the invasion from the North were nominally UN agents. However, both the relief and the military efforts were in fact almost exclusively conducted by the United States.

for membership in the Organization for Economic Cooperation and Development (OECD), the intergovernmental organization headquartered in a posh chateau in Paris once owned by the Rothschild family that is viewed by nonmember governments as a "club" that restricts membership to rich nations. Between the mid-1960s and mid-1990s, Korea, the nation whose economy once was seen as hopeless, experienced one of the most rapid compound rates of prolonged economic growth ever sustained by any nation. By 1988, real per capita GDP in Korea had more than quintupled, making the average Korean richer than the average Malaysian—even though Malaysia was also a high-performance economy whose per capita GDP had increased two and a half times since 1962. In 1988 Korea could in fact boast a per capita income more than two and a half times that of the Philippines and almost twice that of Thailand. Furthermore, rapid rates of growth would continue for almost another decade before Korea would experience a major setback in its economic fortunes.

Underlying the impressive economic growth of Korea since the 1960s have been important changes in the structure of output of the country's economy and, indeed, in its society. In the mid-1960s, when the "economic miracle" began to take hold, Korea's leadership deliberately chose to stress the manufacture of goods for export rather than primarily for domestic consumption. At that time, all that Korea could export were relatively simple goods embodying rather low-skill labor: footwear, apparel, and the like. However, beginning in the late 1960s and continuing through the 1970s, Korean firms, responding to policies undertaken by the government, began to enter new sectors in which it was thought the firms could build international competitiveness (and hence were by definition sectors in which Korea held latent comparative advantage). Most of these sectors could be characterized as "capital intensive"—that is, they required as a condition for entry large front-end capital expenditure. But in comparison to those industries that developed the fastest during the earlier decade of growth, these also required higher levels of technology, demanding, as economists like to put it, higher inputs of "human capital" (i.e., workers with higher levels of educational attainment, where "workers" include technical and managerial personnel). During the period 1971-79, in particular, Korean President Park Chung-hee put particular stress on the heavy and chemical industries, in an effort to build an industrial base designed to turn Korea into a military power. The 1970s in Korea thus is often termed the "HCI period."

This large-scale experiment in industrial policy doubtless should be rated an overall success, given the impressive rate at which per capita income grew in Korea. At the same time, however, major imbalances developed in the economy, cumulatively leading to serious difficulties that manifested themselves toward the end of that decade. These difficulties notwithstanding, during the 1980s and 1990s Korean firms continued to enter into new sectors; as a result, by the mid-1990s Korea was exporting a very wide range of products. These included highly technology- or human capital-intensive products such as semiconductors and electronics. Indeed, Korea became the leading producer of large-scale dynamic random access memory chips (DRAMs), one of the most technically sophisticated products of the modern age (albeit one that, as we shall see, had become a mass-produced commodity by the late 1990s). Korea ranked as well as one of the world's top exporters of automobiles, ships, machinery, steel, and many other goods.[2]

One consequence of the imbalances of the late 1970s was that economics experts inside the Korean government recognized that an industrial policy-driven strategy for development could take the country only so far; they saw that as the Korean economy advanced, the government should get out of the business of guiding the economy and instead allow market forces to hold sway. Thus, starting in the mid-1980s and continuing through the 1990s, many aspects of industrial policy were phased out in Korea. However, as I shall soon argue, some key aspects of industrial policy were retained—ones that indeed were to spell big trouble. Furthermore, during the period of activist industrial policy, many of the private institutions necessary for a market-driven economy to prosper were never developed as fully as they should have been. In particular, during the early days of industrial policy, the focus in Korea was on manufacturing industries, and thus the development of the financial sector lagged that of the industrial sector. This disparity continued even after the government moved toward a more market-driven policy. The earlier single-minded focus on industrial development, with no concurrent focus on financial development, was arguably a mistake. Economic research has consistently shown that a well-developed financial sector is absolutely essential if an economy is to maintain long-term growth (surveys of this research are provided by Levine 1997 and Levine and Zervos 1998). Thus, one major shortcoming of Korea as a miracle economy has been a relatively underdeveloped financial sector, whose consistent lagging behind the industrial sector helps to explain some of the economic difficulties Korea has experienced in recent years.

In late 1997, Korea became caught up in what now is termed the "Asian financial crisis." To put this into some perspective, in 1996 and early 1997 some Korean economists were concerned that a significant economic downturn was imminent, perhaps at worst a nosedive to 4 percent positive growth—about the same rate of growth as the US economy was experiencing at that same time. But while Americans were toasting the robustness of their economy and attributing it to the miracle of the information age, Koreans worried that 4 percent growth would constitute a "growth recession." As it happened, however, performance did not simply

---

2. Detailed descriptions and analyses of Korea's export performance from the middle 1960s to the early 1990s are provided by SaKong (1993) and Cho S. (1994).

fall to a level comparable to that of the United States; instead, the bottom fell out of the Korean economy. Growth in 1998 was *negative* 8 percent, a full-blown recession by any standard. Had this contraction continued for very long, 1998 would have been recorded as the beginning of an out-and-out depression.

But then, almost as rapidly as the economy had plunged into severe recession, in the early months of 1999 the situation began to reverse itself. Recovery was swift, and from the middle of 1999 to well into 2000 the Korean economy grew at a 10 percent rate.

Even during this rapid recovery, however, not everything was proceeding smoothly. In particular, in mid-1999 one of Korea's largest groups of business firms (or, to use the Korean term for these groups, *chaebol*), the Daewoo group, failed. Also, as 1999 faded into 2000, it became increasingly clear that the largest of the chaebol, the Hyundai group, was teetering on the edge of bankruptcy. Moreover, this group was beset by barely disguised internal conflict as several of the sons of the group's founder, Chung Ju-yung, maneuvered for control as the health of their elderly father began to fail. As will be discussed in more detail in chapter 4, after Chung Ju-yung's death in April 2001 the Hyundai group was split into three entities, each controlled by one of the sons, and several of these successor groups continued to experience financial difficulty.[3]

The chaebol had in fact been the main engines of the economic growth of Korea from the HCI period up through the 1997 crisis, and the weaknesses revealed in these groups came as a shock to many Koreans. "Chaebol" is actually something of a junk term, used to designate any of the large nonfinancial groups of firms that are headquartered in Korea. These include specialized groups such as Lotte, which is (mostly) a retailing and hotel chain but also holds some industrial affiliates, and Pohang Iron and Steel Company (POSCO), created as a state-owned firm but now privatized, which largely specializes in primary steel production and indeed ranks as the world's second-largest and most efficient steel producer. However, when Koreans talk about the chaebol, they generally are referring to a rather small number of very large and highly diversified groups of firms that have come to dominate most of the industrial sectors that make up the core of the Korean economy.[4] Some of these groups have

---

3. In this text, Korean names follow the Korean convention: i.e., the family name precedes the "first name," except for those individuals who are widely known internationally by names written in the Western fashion (e.g., Syngman Rhee). Also, as a rule given names (which generally consist of two parts) are hyphenated: thus, "Park Chung-hee," not "Chunghee Park" or "Park Chung Hee." Finally, because transliteration from Korean has not been standardized, I have tried to use the spelling favored by the person him- or herself when this is known: thus, "Chung Ju-yung," as it appears in Hyundai's annual reports, and not "Chung Ju-young" or "Chung Ju-yun," as the same name has appeared in newspapers.

4. For a discussion of various aspects of the chaebol issue, see Yoo S. (1995).

names that by 1997 had become recognized throughout the world, while others were relatively unknown outside of Korea.

The five biggest chaebol at the onset of the 1997 financial crisis were Hyundai, Samsung, Daewoo, LG (formerly Lucky Goldstar), and SK (formerly Sun Kyung). At that time each, had it issued consolidated financial statements, would likely have been included among the world's two hundred or so largest business enterprises ranked by total sales (but not by total profits). Combined sales of individual firms listed on the Korean Stock Exchange constituting each of the three largest groups (Hyundai, Samsung, and Daewoo)[5] were then all over $50 billion, according to published income statements. (Because some of these sales were to other members of the same group, these figures reflect some element of double-counting that cannot be determined from the published data.) To a very large extent, the story of the miracle of Korea is the story of the rise of these five groups and a handful of similar but smaller groups.

Conversely, the story of the Korean crisis of 1997 and of the still not fully resolved problems lying deep within the Korean economy that came to light as a result of the crisis is also largely the story of these same groups. The harsh fact is that even today, many of the affiliates of these groups are experiencing difficulties, to varying degrees and for varying reasons. Only two groups, Pohang and Samsung, are in good financial condition overall. Most of the groups share the same symptoms: some combination of lack of profitability, excessive debt, and overstaffing.

This does not mean that all affiliates of these groups—even those groups that are troubled—are themselves in difficulty. In fact, one characteristic of most of the chaebol is that as diversified groups of firms, they typically hold operations that are by most measures very healthy and profitable; indeed, some are considered to be "world-class" firms, such as Samsung Electrical Company and SK Telecommunications. But each group except Pohang also holds affiliates that are in quite bad shape. The overall health of each of the groups thus is largely a function of which dominate, the healthy member firms or the unhealthy ones.

A major issue for the groups, and for the Korean government (as we shall see, the chaebol and the government in Korea have been, since the beginning of the miracle, deeply intertwined), is whether unhealthy firms and operations within the chaebol can be nursed back to health. Arguably, one strong feature of the chaebol form of organization has been that profits from healthy firms could be used to revive the feeble. The risk is that such a course of action could be ineffective and indeed put the healthy companies at risk. Alternatively, the unhealthy firms could simply be forced to stand on their own, though in many cases they would

---

5. Although the Daewoo group was bankrupt and a ward of the state, most of the firms in it were still in business in 2000. This situation will be discussed in greater detail in the pages that follow.

then fail completely. As noted above, this is the course that the Hyundai group has followed, although its response has been determined more by fate and the passing of its founder than by deliberate plan.

One problem that Korea faces and has to date largely failed to resolve is that the restructuring of unhealthy firms would in many instances lead to large numbers of jobs being lost. Indeed, the avoidance of job loss is arguably the main reason why a large number of unhealthy firms have been allowed to remain in business without restructuring and thus to consume resources that might otherwise be available for other (and almost surely, in the long run, better) uses. Thus, significant labor shedding might still be required in Korea. This thorny problem is one of the main issues addressed in this book.

The histories of the chaebol are usually rather short, as most began to become important institutions only in the 1970s. Although one of them, Samsung, has a pedigree extending before World War II, the others were founded after the war: of the top five, the ancestral firm of Samsung dates to 1938 (but the current mother firm only to 1951), LG and Hyundai both to 1947, SK to 1953, and Daewoo to 1967. As a result, the founders of many of the groups are still alive or have died quite recently; in some cases they are even still actively involved in management. The founders and their families are typically the largest (and controlling) shareholders of the groups. The short histories of the chaebol are in contrast to the history of Korea itself, which spans at least 2,400 years if one counts precursor states that unified to form what was to become modern Korea.

For the most part, these groups were relatively small, family-owned enterprises until the 1970s growth driven by industrial policy. To be sure, as the next chapter details, at least two, Samsung and Hyundai, were quite large by local standards even before 1970, but they remained small by world standards. Their growth into the behemoths that they are today came about largely under the nurture of the government and began at about the same time as the commencement of the HCI drive.

Indeed, the meteoric rise of the chaebol as institutions leads many Koreans to question their legitimacy. To understand this complex issue, one needs to know something about the recent history of economic development and the role of the chaebol in this development in Korea, background that will be supplied in the pages that follow. In brief, some Koreans are suspicious of the chaebol because their growth was financed largely via debt: funds were borrowed from abroad or from banks that intermediated savings generated by private households in Korea. Early on, foreign debt predominated, but as time passed and savings in Korea rose, domestic loans overtook foreign loans as the main source of funding. There is nothing unusual in this intermediation per se; but during the period of Korea's most extraordinary development, lasting from the late 1960s until about the end of the 1980s, the recipients of funds were not determined by market forces. Especially after 1972, intermediation

Table 1.1   The 10 largest chaebol in Korea, 1983

Chaebol	Total assets, 1971 (billions of won)[a]	Total assets, 1983 (billions of won)[a]	Average annual growth of assets, 1971-83 (percent)
Hyundai	158	4,469	32.1
Samsung	416	3,372	19.1
Daewoo	35	3,340	46.3
LG (formerly Lucky Goldstar)	437	2,715	16.4
Ssangyong	310	1.712	15.3
SK (formerly Sun Kyung)	40	1,478	35.1
Hanjin	84	1,340	26.0
Korea Explosives	256	1,173	13.5
Daelim	65	943	25.1
Kukje	153	896	15.8

a. Valued in constant 1980 won.

Source: Kim E. (1996, table 1).

was instead largely by government fiat. Favored enterprises received credit at subsidized rates and numerous other forms of preferential treatment, including all-important government permission to borrow from abroad. When, in the 1970s, overseas borrowings rose markedly, the government often guaranteed the loans extended by foreign banks to private Korean enterprises, and such guarantees were granted on a preferential basis.

The result was the phenomenal growth of certain firms: table 1.1, taken from Kim Eun-mee (1996), demonstrates exactly how fast they grew. Although all of these top ten groups grew very quickly, some clearly did better than others. The very fastest growing groups were Hyundai, Daewoo, SK, Hanjin, and Daelim. Analysts believe that they all had special ties of one sort or another to President Park (see chapter 2). Samsung by contrast was largely seen as out of favor with Park throughout the 1960s and early 1970s. However, beginning in 1976, Samsung began expanding rapidly in the HCI sectors favored by Park, in part by taking over ventures founded by other firms that were failing.

Thus, the many Koreans who doubt the legitimacy of the chaebol credit their success to cronyism or worse. But this interpretation is by no means universally held in Korea. Defenders of the chaebol argue that competence and willingness to take risks were the hallmarks of the owners and managers of these groups during their periods of rapid growth. And whereas in most countries with rampant cronyism the locally favored enterprises tend to be noncompetitive in world markets, at least some operations of the chaebol have emerged as world-class firms in very competition-driven sectors. Thus, when a customer in any advanced country walks into a store selling products that embody advanced technology, such as computers, DVD players, cellular telephones, and the like, he or she sees products made by the chaebol, often under the name of the group—and not, typically, products made by firms based in other developing nations. As Alice Amsden explains in her classic work on Korea:

> Reciprocity (between business firms and the government) in Korea was in no way free of corruption. No business in Korea could survive the last forty years if it challenged the government politically. None could make it big if it did not support the government financially. Yet for all the venality the evidence…suggests that beginning in the 1960s the government's favorite pets—the big business firms that came to account for so large a share of GNP—were outstanding performers from the production and operations perspective. (Amsden 1989, 146)

In the pages that follow, we examine the rise of the chaebol, and find that the facts do not rule out either of the above stories. On the one hand, much evidence points to the chaebol as products of a rather corrupt system that, one way or another, supported ventures that would not have prospered without favoritism in the form of significant injections of explicit and implicit subsidies. One problem faced today by the Korean government, headed by a president who definitely was not himself part of past cronyism and indeed was for many years among the most prominent critics of the system in Korea, is what to do about enterprises that almost surely would collapse without government aid continuing in some form.

On the other hand, as already noted, there is also much evidence that the chaebol are entrepreneurial ventures that battled against fierce odds to establish themselves as world-class competitors in advanced industrial sectors. Whatever might be the truth about the chaebol, it is unquestionably very complex.

To understand how these groups came to be world-class competitors after starting as virtual nonentities in what had been a very poor nation, it is necessary to explore Korea's rise from almost hopeless poverty to the relative wealth of an advanced nation in barely more than one generation. This larger context is also key to understanding why many of these same groups have fallen into serious trouble. Thus, in chapters 2 and 3, we examine the economic history of Korea in order to determine how the chaebol came to be as they are. Chapter 4 then examines the years that preceded the 1997 crisis, beginning with the last half of the presidency of Roh Tae-woo (which lasted from 1987 to 1992); it attempts to pinpoint exactly what was going wrong in the chaebol and what efforts the Korean government made (and did not make) to deal with a situation that clearly, by late 1996, had a large potential to go wrong.

One of the main themes that emerges is that for a variety of reasons, when rates of return on capital began to fall (as was natural for capital accumulated during the transformation of an economy from less-developed status to that befitting an advanced industrialized nation), neither the Korean government nor, more important, Korean firms adjusted as necessary. Instead, Korean firms continued to seek growth opportunities via new capital investment even when returns on this investment were low. Furthermore, this expansion was financed, as before, largely in the form of debt. Such failure to adjust for changing circumstance largely explains why Korea experienced a meltdown in 1997: a combination of high leverage (use of debt financing) and low returns created widespread financial weakness throughout the Korean economy, which ultimately erupted into crisis. Chapter 5 examines the crisis itself and its aftermath, including efforts to resolve the problems that it revealed—problems that were compounded by the deep recession that followed. The main conclusion is that some of the weaknesses of the chaebol—in particular, the vulnerabilities created by the structure of these groups and their dominance in the economy —persist despite efforts at pervasive reform. Chapter 6 concludes by recommending where Korea should go from here.

2

The Miracle with a Dark Side: Korean Economic Development under Park Chung-hee

Prologue to the Miracle

South Korea came into being as the result of the partition of what had been, prior to the early twentieth century, the ancient kingdom of Chosun.[1] This partition into a communist North and a noncommunist South occurred shortly after the defeat of Japan in World War II in late 1945. Korea had been involuntarily absorbed into Japan in 1910, following more than a decade of Japanese domination after the slow collapse of the long-lasting but static Yi dynasty of Chosun. This dynasty had ruled Korea for more than half a millennium, from 1392 until 1910, but to a large extent as a vassal of Chinese rulers, first to the Ming dynasty and later to the Qing dynasty. From 1910 until 1945, Korea was effectively a colony of Japan.

During this period, though some might argue that Japan helped to lay the foundations for future Korean economic development, many Koreans experienced absolute declines in standard of living; and almost all detested the Japanese dominance (Mason et al. 1980). During the 1930s, as the Korean people and Korean resources were increasingly mobilized to serve Japanese war preparations, this detestation deepened. Thus, the

---

1. Chosun is one of several historical names for what is today known in the West as Korea, and the period of the Yi dynasty is now often termed the "Chosun period." It was preceded by the kingdom of Koryon, from which comes the name "Korea." Koreans today in fact call their nation "Hanguk," which is a shortened version of the official name of South Korea, Dae Han Min Kook (Great Democratic Nation of Han).

liberation of Korea from Japan in 1945 should have occasioned joy among the Korean people—and, for a few months at least, it did. But alas, Korea quickly became a focal point of the rivalry between the United States and the Soviet Union, which had emerged from their rather tense alliance to defeat the Axis powers during World War II as opposing superpowers.

During 1946 to 1948, the United States and the Soviet Union each tried to create a government in Korea to its liking, but neither was able to rally a majority of Koreans around its favored candidate for national leader.[2] These were the right-leaning nationalist Syngman Rhee, supported by the United States (and by right-wing Koreans, many of whom had cooperated with the Japanese), and the Communist Kim Il-sung, supported by the Soviet Union. By 1947, it was clear that the majority of the people in the south were not particularly sympathetic to the Communist cause, despite their lack of enthusiasm for the right-wing elements so strongly supported by the Americans. At the same time, during 1946 and 1947 Kim Il-sung and Kim Tu-bong worked with Soviet troops occupying the north to build a strong Communist Party, formally called the Korean Workers' Party, out of what had been the resistance movement.[3] The Communists quickly acted to eliminate moderate and right-wing elements and to establish the Korean Workers' Party as the effective governing organization in the north. To resolve an impasse that was created by the north being effectively governed by Communists and the south by rightists, a formal partition at the 38th parallel—meant to be temporary—was agreed on in 1948.

At the time of the partition, the south was the poorer of the two newly created Korean states, and its poverty was compounded by the arrival of refugees from the north. During the first years of its existence, moreover, almost everything went downhill in South Korea. Although its fledgling government was created as a democracy, the first election in 1948, which elected Syngman Rhee as president, was boycotted by leftists and hence lacked legitimacy in the eyes of many Koreans (and, indeed, many international observers). Rhee, although born in Korea, had spent most of his life on US soil. He held degrees from George Washington, Harvard, and Princeton Universities, and from 1919 until 1941, to the annoyance of Japan, he had been head of a self-proclaimed Korean government-in-exile based in Hawaii that captured the admiration of many Koreans at home. But by 1948, his support in Korea was waning, and what support he had came largely from those elements of Korean society that had collaborated with the Japanese.

---

2. For a detailed analysis of the situation in Korea between the liberation from Japan in 1945 and the onset of the Korean War, see Hastings (1987).

3. In classic Communist style, during the late 1950s Kim Il-sung eliminated Kim Tu-bong as a rival for power.

In June 1950, South Korea was invaded by North Korea. In the ensuing war, the early victories went to North Korea, whose armies overran most of the territory of the South within months (for a detailed analysis, see Hastings 1987). Only the intervention of UN troops, composed mostly but not entirely of US forces, kept the South from yielding completely. They at first were unable to repulse the northern invaders. Only the south-eastern Korean port city of Pusan did not fall to the North Koreans. But UN forces under US General Douglas MacArthur then launched a suc-cessful amphibious landing at Inchon, near Seoul, effectively cutting the northern army in half. The UN forces then pushed the North Koreans back to the border with China, overrunning in turn virtually all of the territory of the North. But North Korea itself was saved by outside intervention: Chinese forces, in a bold winter offensive, drove the UN back south. A stalemate ensued until 1953, when active hostilities were concluded with an armistice that left the Korean states legally at war with each other but de facto at peace and separated by a narrow no-man's-land at the 38th parallel, barely 50 kilometers from Seoul.

Before the war the Communist movement held some appeal to at least a substantial minority of South Korea's population, but the savagery of the North Korean army during its brief occupation of South Korea caused most of its supporters to change their minds. Thus, by the end of the war a much larger majority of the South Korean people was resolved not to be governed by the North. A leftist (and, at times, vocal) minority did remain, but it was small. Under these circumstances, in 1956, although the economy of South Korea was largely still in ruins, Rhee handily won reelection to the presi-dency as the man who had pushed back the North Korean invasion.

South Korea nonetheless remained a poor and largely underdeveloped nation for more than a decade after the war concluded. Large amounts of US aid enabled South Korea both to maintain its military and to keep its population from starving, but one intended goal of the aid, to create a light industrial base, went largely unrealized.[4] One reason was wide-spread corruption: a significant amount of the aid was appropriated for private use, thereby creating a new class of wealthy Koreans and failing to reach the rank-and-file Korean people for whom it was intended. Some of these newly wealthy Koreans went on to found several of the large chaebol that were to become the backbone of the later Korean economic miracle (Jones and SaKong 1980). But the fact that they had, in the eyes of many of their fellow Koreans, obtained their initial wealth illicitly was to taint their many later accomplishments.

Another related reason for the lack of economic development was that the government encouraged import-substitution policies. Such policies

---

4. Numerous analyses were done at that time and later to probe why US aid was so ineffective. Cho S. (1994) reviews some of this material, drawing heavily from Steinberg (1985).

were attempted in much of the developing world, usually without creating significant economic growth. But they often did succeed in creating a class of wealthy entrepreneurs with a vested interest in keeping the failed policies in place. By the late 1950s, such a class existed in Korea. In addition, US policy, prompted by protectionist sentiment in the US Congress, was deliberately to discourage those Korean firms that might have become successful exporters from selling outside of Korea, especially in the textile industry. This is an issue discussed in more detail below.

Although Syngman Rhee again won reelection in 1960, popular dissatisfaction with both extensive election fraud and the poor state of the economy was widespread. In particular, most Koreans believed that cronies of Rhee were beneficiaries of corrupt government practices. Student riots erupted in April of that year, and during their suppression by Korean police at least 142 students died. This calamity in turn led to widespread calls for Rhee's resignation. The US government took the unusual step of issuing a statement that recognized the "legitimate grievances" of the Korean people. The Korean military subsequently let Rhee know that it too sided with the protesters.

Thus, confronted both with intense domestic pressure to resign and with loss of support from the United States, Rhee chose to step down. An interim government headed by Chung Huh was formed until elections could be held. Chang My-on (known in the United States as John Chang) was then elected prime minister and Yun Po-sun president. Chang initiated a series of major liberalizing economic reforms designed to reverse the economic stagnation. Unfortunately, the economy did not respond quickly to these reforms, and popular unrest, rather than subsiding after the resignation of Rhee, actually grew.

Military Coup, and the Miracle Begins

In the face of growing economic and social instability, the Korean military seized power in 1961, effectively ending any pretext of democracy in South Korea. Although many democratic trappings would remain in place, largely at the insistence of the United States (which constantly pressured the Korean government to permit more democracy throughout the period of military leadership), for more than thirty years Korea would effectively be under authoritarian military rule. It was under this rule that the "economic miracle" took shape.

The main organizer of the military coup was Kim Jong-pil, a young lieutenant colonel. But when the military actually took over the government, the leader who emerged was a more senior officer, Major General Park Chung-hee. Park had been a junior officer in the Japanese army during the 1930s and 1940s, and he was strongly influenced by a doctrine—widely held by the Japanese military during that period (Clifford 1994)—characterized by a belief in strong, centralized management of the economy and by a strong nationalism. The first of these beliefs was almost Marxist in its stress on the extent to which the state should engage in centralized planning of the economy; indeed, when Park first took control in Korea, the Kennedy administration in the United States worried that he might be a "closet Communist." However, the second element of this doctrine—intense nationalism—included complete rejection of international communism and the dominance of the Soviet Union in that movement. Park thus in fact proved to be something of an enigma: an intense Korean nationalist who had fought for the Japanese, who believed in the primacy of state power in economics, but who oversaw the creation of what were to become very large, privately owned industrial groups.

Park ruled by fiat for the next two and a half years; he then narrowly won an election held largely at the behest of the United States. He also won reelection in 1967 and again, narrowly, in 1971. In the 1971 election he faced strong opposition from a young firebrand, Kim Dae-jung, who is president of Korea at the time of this writing. Most observers believe that Kim might have won the earlier election had it been truly free. Shaken by nearly being bounced from power, Park ended any pretext of democracy; and from 1972 until his assassination by one of his own protégés in 1979, he ruled effectively as a dictator under the revamped "Yushin" constitution that made him president for life.

Park thus will be remembered by history for a number of reasons, many of them unfavorable. He effectively suppressed dissent in Korea, in the early years by relatively moderate means but with increasing harshness following 1972. Indeed, after 1972 he actively suppressed democracy. But he also placed the highest priority on improving the Korean economy, something that Syngman Rhee had not done. And, almost without question, with the help of a number of very able advisors, Park created what was to become the Korean economic miracle. For this reason, he enjoyed a large measure of popular support by the Korean people until the final years of his rule. Indeed, one reason why the United States, after a period of hand-wringing, recognized the new regime was that the Korean people themselves accepted it. Furthermore, the elections of 1963 and 1967 were legitimately won by Park; there is little evidence that they were rigged. The worst that can be said is that no really effective opposition existed in either year and that Park's government did its best to prevent one from arising (the opposition was to become better organized and much more effective in the 1970s).

One step toward preventing dissent was the founding in 1961 of the Korean Central Intelligence Agency (KCIA), whose first head was Kim Jong-pil, the young officer who had initially led the coup. The mission of the KCIA was as much to keep tabs on potential opposition to the government within South Korea as to gather information about external threats (mostly, of course, from North Korea). Given that North Korea did have agents provocateurs operating in South Korea, the link between the threat from the North and domestic opposition in the South was not fatuous. However, all too often, when dissidence arose in the South that was entirely legitimate and almost surely not instigated from the North, it was treated by the KCIA as though it were purely a product of North Korean provocation.

Though political agencies in the early Park regime were dominated by the military, economic agencies generally were not. Rather, under Park the status of economics experts in the Korean government rose considerably. One of Park's first acts was to elevate the status of economic planning in Korea, placing civilian experts in charge of it. In 1961 he created the Economic Planning Board (EPB), whose head was made deputy prime minister. In spite of the political title and high level of this position, Park insisted that it be filled by a person with superb technical qualifications rather than a political figure or a high-ranking member of the military.

In 1962, the EPB introduced the first of what was to become a series of five-year plans for Korea's development. State-owned banks were created to help implement the government's development plans, and laws were passed to force private banks effectively also to become agents of their implementation. Over the next years, the Korean government became, in the words of former EPB member and Deputy Prime Minister SaKong Il, an "entrepreneur-manager" (SaKong 1993, 27). During the first and second five-year plans, the government itself was involved in industrial undertakings. In the 1960s, more than one-third of government expenditures were for investment, and public investment accounted for close to a third of all fixed capital formation. Thus, between 1963 and 1977, public enterprises in Korea grew at an annual rate of 10 percent and the share of these enterprises in GDP grew from slightly over 6 percent in 1963 to more than 9 percent in 1980 (SaKong 1993, table 3.4). Korea did not consider itself to be a socialist nation but, as SaKong points out, as recently as 1980 the output share of public enterprises in the GDP in Korea was as high as in a number of nations "with socialist intentions," such as India or Pakistan. This emphasis reflected Park's own philosophy, under which the state was meant to be the dominant agent in the economy.

However, as the Park years progressed, the Korean government's role as "entrepreneur-manager" increasingly was manifested not so much in public enterprises, as important as these were, but rather in the government's direction of activities undertaken by the surging private sector. At its core was a policy of subsidizing those private enterprises that were able to achieve increasingly higher levels of export or of substituting domestic production for imports. The subsidies largely took the form of preferential access either to foreign credit or to credit extended by domestic Korean banks. The former was especially important during the early Park years, when domestic Korean savings were low, while the latter become increasingly important during the heavy and chemical industries drive of the 1970s, the topic of the following section.

Some Koreans, at least, tend to see the export orientation of the early Park strategy as the product of pure genius. Though the role of strategic planning cannot be ruled out, it must be recognized that the first five-year plan encouraged both exportation and import substitution (local manufacture of goods that were imported), without explicitly favoring either. Indeed, in the early 1960s, development strategies calling for import substitution were much in vogue among developing nations. Many economists advocated them despite their obvious flaw: such a strategy calls for allocating resources into activities for which the affected nation has revealed comparative *disadvantage*. The classical argument for the gains from trade are based on precisely the opposite approach—that resources should shift, as the result of trade opening, into those activities for which that nation enjoys comparative advantage. In the 1960s, the answer given to this obvious problem was that developing nations might have unrealized comparative advantage in certain sectors that could be exploited if only the right activities could be identified and nurtured.

During such a period of nurture, defenders of these strategies argued, it might be appropriate to grant so-called infant-industry protection from imports. The idea was that the "infants" would grow into robust and healthy "adults" and thus, over time, activities that initially had required protection from imports would transform into being capable of themselves successfully exporting. Whether or not infant-industry protection actually makes practical sense is a question hotly debated among development economists. There are strong arguments against its logic: for example, this protection is likely to promote the development of activities for which no transformation into "adulthood" ever takes place, leaving them perpetually inefficient. Nonetheless, in the first five-year plan, infant-industry protection was one route Korea chose to take, and it arguably had some degree of success. Indeed, the case of Korea is often cited by proponents of infant-industry protection as evidence that this policy can work.[5]

As Korean planners recognized in the early 1960s, if one accepts the logic of infant-industry protection, one faces the significant problem in choosing the right activities—that is, those in which latent comparative advantage does exist. If the choice is incorrect, a protected infant industry might remain an infant indefinitely, requiring state aid in the form of continuing subsidies or protection simply to survive and never prospering. Indeed, the accumulated experience of many countries that have pursued import-substitution policies has been that infants nursed under these policies never grow into robust adults (Noland and Pack 2003).

---

5. In addition to Amsden (1989), see Pack and Westphal (1986).

Rather, they can become voracious infants, consuming vast resources that might otherwise be allocated to more robust activities and thereby retarding development. Furthermore, such "fat infants" typically create significant constituencies for the continuance of state aid, notably in the considerable numbers of workers that they employ. And even if the enterprises never earn acceptable returns on capital invested, their subsidies often make major shareholders wealthy enough to become major contributors to political parties. Thus, these constituencies often can effectively "capture" public policy so as to ensure that the aid is not cut off.

Recognizing these likely pitfalls, Korean planners who worked under Park during the early years developed two unwritten policies. First, export expansion rather than import substitution received higher priority. Thus, those infants given the most nurturance by the state were those that delivered increased exports. Second, complementing the first policy, activities that did not produce the desired result of increased exports were allowed to fail, often with ruthless speed. The unwritten rule in Korea became, in effect, that an entrepreneur who got in tight with the government could become rich, but only if that entrepreneur's export performance was outstanding. By contrast, in many other developing countries, only a close relationship with the government was necessary.

These unwritten policies are evidenced by the export data: although they had accounted for less than 5 percent of Korean GDP at the end of the 1950s, exports had risen to more than 35 percent of a much larger GDP by 1980. Such growth would likely have been impossible had Koreans simply attempted to increase exports of only those goods that were already being exported. Rather, under the unwritten rules, Korean entrepreneurs either took those risks required to succeed in building new areas of comparative advantage for Korea or failed to receive the preferences that were available to firms that met export goals. Under these policies, infants that failed to export were unlikely to achieve capture of government policy—though, as we shall see, the Korean record in this regard was not entirely unblemished.[6]

The antecedents of what became the chaebol, for the most part, were those firms that succeeded under the policies of Park during the 1960s. In fact, as already noted, the entrepreneurs who built these groups often were already quite wealthy by virtue of activities undertaken during the overtly corrupt Rhee years. But many of these same entrepreneurs also succeeded in enlarging their business during the early Park years under policies that demanded performance rather than cronyism.

The instilling of export-oriented values in established companies was facilitated by one of Park's first acts: with great theatrics, in 1962 he

---

6. For various accounts of the export-led growth strategy initiated by Park, see Krueger (1979); Balassa (1988); Papanek (1988); Amsden (1989); SaKong (1993); Cho S. (1994); and Noland (2000).

went after wealthy Koreans who, in his eyes, had illicitly accumulated wealth during the Syngman Rhee period (Jones and SaKong 1980). Most such persons were not subjected to criminal prosecution, as they might have been under laws hastily passed by the Park regime, but rather were forced to pledge to work to build a new Korean economy. Lee Byung-chol of Samsung, then the wealthiest person in Korea, went so far as to pledge to give his entire fortune to the Korean government, and eight other wealthy businessmen followed suit. None of them actually ever did so, though Lee donated land on which he had built a golf course south of the city of Seoul for the construction of a new campus for Seoul National University. What was eventually required of Korea's business leaders was to establish successful operations in new sectors and activities selected by the government. They were obligated in principle to give shares in these new firms to the government (ostensibly to pay back the illicit component of their wealth to the Korean people), but such payments were rarely made. What Park's theatrics succeeded in doing was both to frighten existing wealthy entrepreneurs and to demonstrate that if they played by the new rules that Park set, they could do well under the new regime.[7]

In its first years, the EPB recommended abolishing the multiple exchange rate system that had been in use during the 1950s, under which the Korean currency was persistently overvalued, and replacing multiple rates with a single exchange value for the Korean won that was consistent with export competitiveness. Implementation of this reform proceeded by fits and starts. A unitary fixed rate was introduced in 1961 under which the won was effectively devalued twice against the dollar, but multiple rates were reintroduced in 1963. In 1965 a fluctuating unitary rate was introduced. At the recommendation of the EPB, the Korean government began to ease or remove many import restrictions after 1962, in particular easing or eliminating restrictions on imports of goods or services needed as inputs to exports.

First to benefit from the new policies and engage in export-led development in Korea was the textile and apparel sector. The cotton textile spinning and weaving industry had engaged, as in many countries, the first "modern" industry in Korea even prior to the Park years; indeed, one firm in this sector, Kyongsong Spinning and Weaving, was an important exception to the rule that Korean entrepreneurs did not flourish

---

7. These entrepreneurs included the founders of the SK, LG, Hyundai, and Samsung chaebol. Lee of Samsung in fact in 1962 held a personal fortune estimated to be as high as 19 percent of all wealth in Korea (it must be kept in mind that Korea was a poor country and some part of his fortune consisted of land that had been inherited; but his fortune also was based on corrupt dealings during the Rhee years). In 1963, Lee also paid very large fines to the government. Personal relations between him and Park remained rocky, but even so Lee emerged as one of the major entrepreneurs favored by the Park government. See Jones and SaKong (1980).

under Japanese occupation. Kyongsong was founded in 1919 and had become a major firm before liberation (Amsden 1989). During the 1950s, other firms had entered this sector; by the time of Park's coup d'état, about 15 Korean firms were engaged in cotton spinning and weaving. Despite their number, there was little competition in this sector, for these firms had created a formal cartel. This action was taken partly in response to their having received subsidized loans offered through US aid programs during the 1950s. One condition of the loans was that the recipients not export output to the United States (thus beginning a long tradition by which the US government would lecture Koreans on the virtues of open markets while keeping domestic US markets partly closed to Korean exports). Faced with overcapacity relative to domestic demand, the firms had formed what amounted to a cartel to allocate production quotas. By international standards, labor productivity in this sector was high.

The 1961 devaluations initially hurt the textile firms because they depended on imported cotton and thus had to raise prices of finished goods to pay for the imported input. The instinct of the firms was therefore to seek won revaluation, but the EPB convinced Park that devaluation was ultimately in Korea's best interests. Domestic demand for cotton textile products responded negatively to the higher prices, as would be expected, and even more capacity became idle. The obvious answer to the overcapacity problem facing the industry, and indeed what the EPB sought, was that Korean textile firms begin to export at least some of their output. Were they to do so, the won devaluations would have made Korean products more export competitive. However, a number of obstacles stood in the way. Besides the US policy, just noted, Korean firms simply had not established links with international distributors and other agents necessary to obtain export business.

Park's response, guided by the EPB, was to use a "carrot and stick" approach to encourage these firms to export. As carrots, a large variety of subsidies and other incentives were offered to textile firms—preferential loans conditional upon exporting, tax exemptions (including tariff exemptions for imported inputs), and other measures. Citing Woo K.D. (1978), Alice Amsden (1989, 68) notes that these subsidies were necessary to enable the Korean firms to compete against more-established Japanese exporters, which had noncost incumbency advantages (e.g., established relations with international wholesalers and distributors of textiles and textile products).[8] In terms of comparative advantage, Korean textiles should have been internationally competitive with the Japanese product, and

---

8. SaKong (1993), however, puts a slightly different interpretation on the subsidies; he claims that they largely served to offset price distortions in Korean domestic markets that were created by import-substitution policies and thus enabled Korean exporters to get prices right.

thus perhaps temporary subsidies to offset incumbency advantages held by Japanese firms were warranted. Indeed, their experience in the textile sector taught the Koreans that more than price competitiveness was needed to develop export markets; nonprice incumbency advantages of other producers also had to be identified and overcome.

This approach produced results. In 1961 textiles accounted for about 25 percent of Korean exports totaling $5.7 million. In 1965, four years later, total exports had risen to more than $106 million, of which textiles made up 41 percent.[9] Firms that would eventually become the largest of the chaebol figured in this dramatic growth. For example, one of the star performers was the Cheil Wool Textile Company, founded in 1954 by Lee Byung-chol—who was, as noted above, one of the businessmen cited for corruption by Park in 1963. Cheil became the leading industrial firm in the emergent Samsung group. The name "Samsung" comes from a trading company founded by Lee in 1948, from which Lee made his early fortune deemed "illicit" by Park.

The third largest of the chaebol at the time of the 1997 financial crisis, Daewoo, also began its life in 1967 as a trading company whose major business was the export of textiles and apparel. Specifically, Daewoo rose because it was able to obtain export quota rights to the United States when the United States began to sharply restrict imports of apparel.[10] In the early years, Daewoo's business consisted mostly of selling the right to export clothing to the United States to other firms; its business was simply to collect (to use the economists' term) the rents that accrued to those rights. Over the period 1967-76, Daewoo's exports grew at an annual compound rate of 122 percent. This business was so lucrative that the quota rights were eventually placed in a firm separate from the rest of the group; its sole function was to enrich the original owners but bypass new minority shareholders. But by 1968 Daewoo was engaged in the manufacture as well as the trading of textiles.

Although the export performance of the textile industry and of certain other light industries (e.g., footwear) created the first major spurt of growth of the Korean economy, the development of such industries was not really what Park had in mind for Korea. Rather, he dreamed of a time when Korea would be a major international producer of such products as steel, ships, heavy vehicles, and heavy machinery—products that Park associated with national strength (an association that dated to Park's years with the Japanese military). During the 1960s, however, the EPB was of a

9. In 1964, when Korean exports first reached the $100 million mark, Park established a national "Export Day" at which high export performers received awards handed out by him personally (SaKong 1993).

10. In obtaining these rights, Daewoo chairman Kim Woo-chung doubtless was able to make use of a personal tie to give him access to the president: his own father had been a teacher of Park Chung-hee (see Clifford 1994).

somewhat different mind-set. The EPB experts were all trained (or at least well read) in economics, and they emphasized to Park that if Korea were to succeed as an exporting nation, the government should continue to develop industries in which the Korean economy had at least latent comparative advantage. These, according to the EPB, were in light manufacturing. The EPB agreed with Park that more capital-intensive industries might be built over time, but disagreed that an attempt to develop them should be made early on. Thus, as the EPB prepared a succession of five-year plans for the Korean economy, the experts stressed comparative advantage, while Park continued to push in the direction of heavy industries.

For a time, the EPB held sway. One reason was that the very success of the textile sector in establishing itself as a major exporter served during the 1960s to hold in check Park's ambitions in heavy industry. In addition, the growth of new heavy sectors would require very high rates of capital formation, whose financing in turn necessitates that a nation either generate domestic savings or import large amounts of capital from abroad. During the 1950s, net domestic savings in Korea were close to zero, with the result that capital formation had to be largely financed from abroad (mostly in the form of concessional aid), and this situation was inherited by Park. Consequently, to finance sizable capital formation in the early Park years, Korean firms largely had to look overseas, and the availability of this financing was limited. Foreign lenders simply were unwilling to lend money to build steel mills or shipyards to Korean firms with little or no experience in the heavy industries. For example, whereas the first five-year plan, at Park's insistence, called for the development of an integrated iron and steel complex in Korea, the World Bank nixed that idea. Thus, Korean dependence on foreign finance initially played into the hands of the EPB and constrained Park's ambitions.

Dependence on foreign finance did, however, give the government a potentially powerful method for guiding economic activity, which was to control credit extended by foreign lenders to Korean enterprises by acting as guarantor of that credit. The Park government was very quick to recognize this potential. In 1962, the Foreign Capital Inducement Deliberation Committee was formed within the Economic Planning Board to screen applications by Korean firms for foreign finance. The power to control which firms would receive foreign credit thus came to be used by the government as a tool of industrial policy. This power was used extensively when Korean firms, under government direction, began to invest in highly capital-intensive activities—the heavy sectors of which Park dreamed—during the early 1970s.[11]

---

11. Or, to quote SaKong (1993, 106), "foreign borrowing in Korea has been tightly monitored from the very beginning to make sure that borrowed capital is used productively." Sakong also notes, however, that the government considered all appropriate applications and that the policy was quite liberal, resulting in "excessive" foreign borrowing. This

As growth took off in Korea, national savings rose from essentially zero in the early 1960s to close to 20 percent of GDP in 1970. This jump enabled a growing fraction of domestic capital formation to be financed domestically rather than internationally. Savings as a percentage of GDP continued to grow after 1970, reaching almost 25 percent of GDP in 1980, close to 30 percent in 1985, and more than 35 percent in 1990; Korea thereby transformed itself from a low-savings nation to one of the world's highest savings nations. Although this change enabled Korea to become less dependent on capital from abroad to finance investment, rates of Korean capital formation in most years nonetheless continued to outstrip domestic savings. Thus, Korea continued to be a significant net capital importer, as reflected in a negative balance of payments on the current account, until the middle 1980s. But the greater availability of domestic savings to finance investment implied that those sectors into which this investment was directed could be increasingly determined by the government without being constrained by foreign creditors.

In fact, as domestic savings grew in Korea, control over how to direct those savings fell almost completely in the government's hands, because in 1962 the Park government had brought the financial sector largely under government control. Most banks were nationalized, and a law was passed enabling the government to protect lenders from default risk on at least some loans by means of government loan guarantees. This measure set in motion a process by which banks and other lending institutions became willing to take larger risks than they might otherwise have done. But, at the same time, because they were protected from default, these institutions over time failed to fully develop the capability to assess and manage risk, a failing that was to hurt Korea in the future.

The government's control over loan allocation in fact increased during the Park years. Initially the government made generally available through the banks subsidized loans for working capital to any firm that could demonstrate success in exporting. But in later years subsidized long-term loans increasingly were available only to those firms specifically designated by the government.[12]

"excess" resulted because until the late 1970s, borrowing from abroad carried lower interest costs than borrowing from domestic sources, and exchange rate risk was mitigated by the government's efforts to hold the real rate approximately constant (in fact, as noted later in the text, the real rate's appreciation over that time tended to favor borrowing from abroad even more).

12. During the 1960s, credit (loans for working capital) was granted largely on a nondiscriminatory basis; any firm operating in any sector could qualify if it convinced the government that the result would be increased exports. Later, as will be described below, the EPB began to attempt to "pick winners"—those sectors or activities in which it believed Korean firms could become internationally competitive exporters. But at this time, when allocating long-term credit, the government also frequently favored one firm over another even if both firms participated in the same industry and that industry was among those being promoted by the government.

Because of government control of lending and the preferential terms on which many loans were made, by the late 1960s Korean firms had already become very debt-heavy in their financial structures. The debt-to-equity ratio of the Korean corporate sector was upwards of 400 percent, much higher than in most nations. One consequence was that in 1969 a number of highly indebted companies in Korea were teetering on the edge of bankruptcy, and this number grew in 1970 and 1971. The cumulative result was that Korea faced an international liquidity crisis in 1971 because many of the troubled firms had large foreign loans on the books. In response, the International Monetary Fund forced Korea to devalue the won. This helped exports but also raised the won value of foreign debt held by the troubled corporations, forcing a reduction in foreign borrowing. In 1972, in an effort to ease the financial burden on Korean firms, Park attempted to control the curb market, the largely informal and uncontrolled market for funds that existed outside of the banking system. Lenders in the curb market were told that there would be a three-year moratorium on repayment of debt incurred by firms through this market. This action had the unintended effect of reducing the wealth of the many Korean households that had lent their saving to the curb market. Households reacted by refusing to invest new funds in it. Because many businesses were dependent on the curb market for liquid funds, the overall result proved to be the reverse of what was sought: financial pressures on most firms were increased, not reduced. When this became apparent, Park backed off his efforts to control this market. Even so, with this misstep the popularity of the Park government, which had been very much based on economic successes, began to wane.

As part of the drive to increase exports, the Park government initiated a number of diplomatic moves during its early years. The first, in 1965, was to normalize diplomatic relations with Japan, enabling commercial relationships to develop between Japanese firms and Korean firms. This normalization was highly unpopular, but it bolstered the export capabilities of Korean firms, which in some cases became major suppliers to Japanese firms. As a result, Korean firms gained not only export markets that otherwise would have been unavailable but also a channel by which Japanese technology was transferred to the Korean suppliers. Thus, Korean firms became suppliers to Japanese firms in a number of sectors in which the Korean firms were new entrants, such as the manufacture of electrical and electronic components and other light manufacturing that was more technology intensive than textiles and footwear. For a time, the success of these new ventures further strengthened the hand of the EPB, which continued to argue that Korea's future lay in gradually "deepening" the capital-to-labor ratio of Korean industry and in upgrading Korea's export sectors by advancing skill and knowledge rather than by immediately establishing heavy capital-intensive industry. Knowledge-intensive light and medium industries were seen by the EPB as activities in which Korea held latent comparative advantage, but Park continued to dream of heavy industry.

Other diplomatic moves fed into the drive to transform Korea into an exporting nation. Trade agreements negotiated by the Park government with a number of countries enlarged the number of markets to which Korean firms could sell. Trade-related institutions such as the Korea Trade Promotion Agency (KOTRA), Korea Traders Association (KTA), and the Federation of Korean Industries (FKI), as well as numerous industry-specific trade associations, were created to help facilitate trade. KOTRA was a government agency charged with finding export business opportunities and educating Korean business as to how to avail themselves of those opportunities. (KOTRA also had the power to tax Korean imports, raising revenues that were meant to finance KOTRA's export promotion activities but were also used as political slush funds by Park.) The KTA was a private-sector group that worked with KOTRA to realize overseas market opportunities, and during the Park years it was effectively under KOTRA's control. The FKI was formed by that group of entrepreneurs that had been branded by Park in 1962 as corrupt and who subsequently pledged their personal fortunes to the development of Korea. Even so, the FKI was to become the major vehicle by which the government conveyed its marching orders to Korean industrialists. The new Korean institutions all contributed to the continued rise of Korea as an exporter of light manufactured goods, including final goods as well as intermediate goods such as electronic components. For example, by 1970 Korea had emerged as a major exporter of footwear as well as textile and apparel products, and of a variety of other light manufactured goods such as women's accessories and electronics products.

We can thus summarize the early Park years: Following a disappointing decade after the Korean War, Korea under Park's leadership attempted "export-led growth" policies (intermixed with import-substitution policies). The export-led policies were quite successful, as measured by growth of Korea's exports from sectors in which the country held demonstrated comparative advantage (mostly the textile and apparel sectors). The policies initiated under Park and the EPB simply worked far better than did the earlier policies attempted under Rhee.

However, even in the midst of this reversal of the poor performance of the Rhee era, Korean planners in the EPB worried that the positive results might not be sustainable. In particular, as detailed in the next section, they were concerned that Korea might, over time, lose comparative advantage in those sectors in which Korean firms were currently exporting successfully. They also were under constant pressure from Park to include in their plans the establishment of heavy industry. Thus, in the coming years, the government was to engage in a large-scale experiment in industrial policy, with the aim of creating new sectors in Korea in which domestic firms could become internationally competitive.

The HCI Drive

Beginning in the late 1960s and continuing over the next 10 years or so, the direction of Korea's policies toward the creation of export industries changed, particularly under what has come to be known as the "heavy and chemical industries (HCI) drive" that was formally launched in 1973. As suggested in the previous section, this change of economic strategy was accompanied by a change in the style of Park's leadership, which became increasingly authoritarian during the 1970s—especially after the 1971 election, which was followed by a series of protests. Park's response in 1972 was to declare martial law and then to change the Korean constitution to make himself president for life. In 1973 Kim Dae-jung, who after the 1971 election had become the main leader of what organized opposition to Park existed, was abducted from a Tokyo hotel by Korean security agents who intended to assassinate him. International disapproval of this incident was loud and swift, particularly on the part of the United States and Japan. The Japanese government was especially outraged because the kidnapping had taken place on Japanese soil. Kim was spared death largely because of rapid intervention by the US ambassador to Korea, Philip Habib, who made it clear that the United States would view Kim's death as a serious matter that would affect relations between Korea and the United States.

This incident also caused the popularity of the Park government within Korea itself to drop even further. Indeed, as a result of this failed kidnapping and the increasingly repressive nature of the Korean government, the whole period of the HCI drive, especially its last years, was a time of rising domestic discontent, even though economic growth through much of this period remained positive. Because this was also the period during which the largest of the chaebol began to take shape, there exists in Korea to this day an association of the rise of these firms with the repressive aspects of the last years of Park's rule.

The genesis of the change of economic policy was to be found in the EPB's second five-year plan. This plan, announced in 1967, was meant to cover the period 1971-76. In many ways it mimicked the first five-year plan; for example, it called for specific goals with respect to increased exports and industrial production. However, the plan also suggested that the sectoral composition of exports should change, with the emphasis moving from light manufacturing to heavy manufacturing industries—a shift clearly favored by Park even if not endorsed wholeheartedly by the EPB itself. As early as 1967, some movement in this direction already in fact had begun. But the second five-year plan sought to accelerate the shift. Accordingly, a series of industry-specific acts (detailed below) were passed in the years 1967-70 that signaled exactly what sectors would be promoted by the government.

The second five-year plan was supplanted in 1972 by a third five-year plan, which enunciated three basic goals: the development of agricultural and fishing industries, a major increase in exports, and a further buildup of the heavy and chemical industries. But in 1973, President Park, acting under martial law, announced the Heavy and Chemical Industry Declaration; this marked the official launch of the HCI drive, which shifted priorities still further toward heavy and chemical industries. This declaration was apparently made by Park without consulting the EPB, and it thus marks a takeover of economic as well as political policy by Park. The EPB was not dismantled, but for the next six years, until the assassination of Park, its influence would be much diminished.

Even so, the hand of the EPB was strong in the HCI program. SaKong Il (1993) notes that Park saw such a program as necessary because EPB planners themselves forecast that export growth via the light industries that had grown so impressively during the 1960s and early 1970s could not be sustained. Also, the EPB believed that new protectionist measures were likely to be enacted by those countries that were Korea's major markets in those sectors in which Korean products were already well established, especially textiles, apparel, footwear, and consumer electronics. In fact, a new protectionist measure to benefit the textile and apparel sectors had been introduced in 1964 in the United States (the Short-Term Agreement on Cotton Textiles). Four years later, Richard Nixon waged a successful campaign to become US president in 1968 on a platform that included still more protection for these sectors.

A second concern of the EPB was possible future loss of comparative advantage in many of the sectors in which Korea had become a successful exporter. In particular, in the light manufacturing industries Korea was seen as likely to face rising competition from developing nations in Southeast Asia. Given that these sectors tend to be quite labor intensive, and because Korean wages were rising rapidly, planners at the EPB believed that Korea could rapidly lose comparative advantage to countries where labor costs were considerably lower. Following the 1971 visit of President Nixon to China, fear of loss of comparative advantage to China overtook fear of loss to Southeast Asia.

In addition, although Korea had boosted exports from only 2.4 percent of GDP in 1962 to almost 10 percent of GDP in 1970, imports as a share of GDP also rose, from 18.3 percent to 24.4 percent. Thus, the balance of trade of Korea remained negative. This might be expected: Korea was a rapidly growing economy and, to maintain growth, international import of capital was necessary, causing a current account deficit. Nonetheless, alarm spread when, after the balance of trade had improved during the first couple of years of the Park government, it began to deteriorate in 1966 and subsequent years.

Even so, EPB planners remained skeptical of the idea that to offset potential loss of comparative advantage, Korea should attempt quickly to develop new comparative advantage in heavy capital-intensive sectors. They continued to favor rather a gradual move into more capital- and knowledge-intensive sectors. Park, by contrast, believed in the all-out pursuit of heavy industries. The third five-year plan thus reflected a compromise between Park and his economic advisors. But, as just noted, the HCI Declaration of 1973 superseded the third five-year plan and signaled Park's complete takeover of economic planning.

In fact, even before the HCI drive, differences between Park and the EPB were increasingly being resolved in Park's favor. This tendency is revealed in the sectors targeted in the series of legislative acts that had been passed in conjunction with the second five-year plan (and that thus predated the HCI Declaration). In fact, because these sectors largely coincided with those given priority under the HCI Declaration, the latter did not so much change the direction of Korean policy as change the rate at which the direction changed. The Industrial Machinery Promotion Act of 1967, the Shipbuilding Promotion Act of 1967, the Electrical Industry Promotion Act of 1969, the Steel Industry Promotion Act of 1970, and the Petrochemical Industry Promotion Act of 1970 all called for measures to be taken to grant firms entering into these sectors preferential treatment—easy access to both foreign and domestic credit, tax breaks, public provision of infrastructure, and so on.

The major goals of these acts, with one exception, were to be accomplished by private firms responding to the incentives offered by the government. In the case of the steel industry, whose development required a huge front-end investment (i.e., the resources had to be committed prior to any commercial output being achieved), the plan called for a state-owned firm to be created: the Pohang Iron and Steel Company (POSCO). This venture has arguably been the most successful of all the undertakings to come out of the HCI period; at the time of this writing, in fact, POSCO is the world's second largest and, by most accounts, most efficient steel-making firm. POSCO was established in 1968, and another former general in the Korean army who had been trained in Japan (at the prestigious Waseda University) was put in charge of the firm. This general was Park Tae-joon, who was to run POSCO as though it were a military operation until he retired in 1992. Finance and technical assistance for what was to become a very large integrated steel mill in the then-sleepy fishing town of Pohang, located on the southeastern Korean coast, was obtained from Japan, which had pledged to provide financial assistance to Korea as part of the 1965 normalization of relations (and as compensation for the colonial period). Park Tae-joon's Waseda connections helped to persuade Japanese officials to allow the assistance to be used to create a modern steel complex in Korea, even though some of these officials were concerned that this complex, if successful, could mount serious competition to Japan's steel industry (Amsden 1989; Clifford 1994). What was to become a 9 million ton per year mill was up and running in Pohang in 1972, one year before the HCI Declaration. The output of this mill would provide input for other HCI ventures, most notably a number of entries into large-scale shipbuilding. Twelve years later an even larger complex was opened on an artificial island in Kwangyang Bay, in southwestern Korea.

The ensuing HCI drive had the effect of establishing Korea as a world-class competitor in at least some of the designated heavy industries; but it also created a number of major weaknesses, imbalances, and inequities in the economy (and reinforced certain weaknesses that were already present). Also, the HCI drive propelled the formation of the very large chaebol and the subsequent concentration of economic power in their hands. Moreover, during the HCI drive, development of the financial sector in Korea almost ground to a halt, as all available resources were concentrated into the heavy industries under government direction. As is argued later in this book, the concentration of economic power in a few large groups and the failure to develop a strong financial sector combined to lay the foundation for major problems that would later confront Korea, some of which remain unresolved.

President Park's HCI Declaration of 1973 thus continued to target the sectors enumerated in the earlier acts. The declaration also added non-ferrous metals to the sectors targeted and mentioned a goal of producing 500,000 automobiles annually by 1980. Park subsequently created a Heavy and Chemical Industry Planning Council to implement his grand scheme. Effectively, this council replaced the EPB as his main group of economic advisors. Cho Soon (1994) notes because this new group operated under heavy secrecy, it is difficult to know exactly what it did during the years of its existence. Nonetheless, judging from what is known, the council seems to have been more concerned with solving technical and engineering problems than with evaluating whether the projects being implemented made economic sense, as the EPB might have done. But the Heavy and Chemical Industry Planning Council did at least nominally share authority over planning with the EPB, which continued to devote attention to the economic viability of projects that were undertaken and provided some moderating influence, albeit to an extent not entirely clear.

As part of the HCI drive, in 1973 a law was enacted to create 13 heavy and chemical industry complexes throughout Korea at which facilities in the chosen sectors were to be established. This establishment would be accomplished in part by means of heavy government subsidies. But the nature of the activities required that the policy toward subsidies be revamped. In particular, because these facilities were to be very large in scale, any subsidies for their building would almost necessarily have to be offered selectively and not, as during the earlier period, on a nondiscriminatory basis. The Korean government simply did not have sufficient resources to hand out such large subsidies to all applicants. Likewise, because those projects that continued to be financed overseas would be larger than in the past, overseas lenders would require government guarantees as a condition for granting the loans. During the 1960s, in contrast, although Korean firms had required government permission to borrow abroad, once this permission had been granted the overseas lenders did not require government guarantees. Thus, the government was also forced to become more selective than in the past with respect to which firms were given permission to borrow abroad, as it could guarantee only a small number of large loans. Furthermore, because the creation of the new activities required that resources be sunk on a front-end basis, receipt of subsidies could not be conditioned on performance.

Of course, if subsidies now were to be given to only a few firms—subsidies both large and front-ended—the door was opened to the possibility of cronyism, such that political considerations could effectively determine precisely who received the subsidies. Thus, one story often told about the HCI drive is that an entrepreneur's access to the subsidies was ultimately a function of his relationship with Park Chung-hee. To be sure, Park had always preferred those entrepreneurs who demonstrated that they were capable of meeting the government's goals. But no Korean would deny that of all the entrepreneurs who might have had such a capability, those who actually received subsidies were individuals who found favor one way or another with the Korean president.

Moreover, in the years of the HCI drive it is clear that favored entrepreneurs "followed the subsidies." That is to say, their choice of activity was dictated by what subsidies were available. Thus, William Zeile (1996) demonstrates a significant correlation between the numbers of chaebol-affiliated firms that were established in new sectors during the early years of the HCI drive and the measures of credit preference granted to those sectors. These were the circumstances under which, during the HCI drive, the large chaebol grew out of what had been much smaller groups of firms.

Indeed, as the HCI drive progressed, a pattern of investment undertakings on the part of those firms that were to become the chaebol became discernible. At the outset of the drive, each of the predecessor firms of what were to become the largest of these groups entered into one or a few of the targeted sectors; by and large, they did so successfully, in that they overcame technical barriers to entry. Whether total return on each investment was satisfactory—where the return includes externalities and the underlying investment includes all subsidy components—is another matter. Analysis of the HCI period does show that average returns on capital were high (Hong 1981; Hsieh 1997). This finding, taken together with the rapid growth in per capita income that Korea continued to experience during the HCI period, might suggest that most new undertakings earned positive social returns on investment. However, Yoo Jung-ho (1989) demonstrates that capital invested in the HCI-designated sectors earned average rates of return that were lower than for other sectors.

This conclusion does not imply that returns were inadequate in the HCI sectors, but it might indicate overinvestment in these sectors such that marginal returns on new investments were low. Investors nevertheless made these investments because the available subsidies compensated them for the low returns.

Over time, each of the groups also began to diversify by entering into other "priority" sectors, with two results. First, the groups began to look more and more alike; that is, they all were operating in the same sectors. Second, subsidies continued to flow to these groups even as the positive rationale for granting such subsidies—which rests on the existence of a "wedge" between high social rates of return and lower private rates of return—was diminishing: as the scope of the activities of the chaebol expanded and activities were duplicated, the social rate of return on the investments made by the groups was almost surely declining, to the point that eventually it likely became negative.

We examine further indicators of the success or failure of the HCI drive in the next section of this chapter. First, however, we consider the experiences during this period of several of what were to become the largest chaebol.

One of the priority sectors of the HCI drive was shipbuilding. The largest operation created in the sector prior to the HCI drive was that of Hyundai; Hyundai's main business was construction, carried out through Hyundai Engineering and Construction Company (HECC), which remained the flagship of the Hyundai group until that group was broken into several components in 2001. HECC's first business had been construction work for the US Army, and such work remained important through the mid-1960s. A big break came at that time, when HECC received a contract from the Korean government to construct a highway from Seoul to Pusan. In 1964 Hyundai started its first manufacturing operation, a small cement mill, for which it relied for technical assistance on two US companies, George A. Fuller and Allis-Chalmers. Ten years later Hyundai would export a large-scale cement plant to Saudi Arabia. In 1967 Hyundai established a small-scale car company, about which more shortly.

Through the early HCI years, the construction business of HECC continued to grow; indeed, this business developed into a major export operation in the early 1970s when HECC first won numerous construction contracts in other Asian nations, especially in Southeast Asia and, later, contracts in the then cash-flush oil-exporting nations of the Arabian Gulf. HECC's rising reputation as a major international player in construction was based on the ability of the firm consistently to bid low on major projects, and then to deliver the project on time without cost overruns.

With the onset of the HCI drive, Hyundai began to diversify its activities by entering into the sectors targeted for development by the government. Hyundai's first really big new venture was initiated in 1970, when a shipbuilding division was created within HECC to start a large-scale shipyard at Ulsan, a small town near Pusan.[13] This move was not, of course, driven by dispassionate analysis on the part of Hyundai management indicating that shipbuilding might be a good activity to enter. Rather, Hyundai was responding to the government's 1967 act to promote shipbuilding. Thus, the decision to enter the sector was ultimately determined by the government and, indeed, Hyundai needed the government's blessing to go ahead with its plans.

Korea at the time already did have some shipbuilding capability, in particular that represented by the government-owned Korea Shipbuilding and Engineering Corporation (KSEC). It is unclear why Hyundai was chosen to carry out government plans to enter into the production of very large ships rather than, say, KSEC, whose capacities could have been enlarged. (As it happened, later on during the HCI drive, KSEC was given the go-ahead to create an operation to build large ships—and this project, as we shall see below, proved to be a near disaster.) Indeed, one might wonder why this sector was pursued at all; at the time that the decision to enter shipbuilding was made, there was an emerging worldwide glut of capacity, and few shipyards anywhere were operating profitably. A plausible explanation is simply that President Park had developed a close relationship with Hyundai founder and chairman Chung Ju-yung.

For whatever underlying reasons, Hyundai pressed ahead with its plans with the strong support of the government. In 1972, when the shipyard was beginning to take shape, the operation was incorporated as a separate firm from HECC; the new firm was Hyundai Shipbuilding and Heavy Industries, later renamed simply Hyundai Heavy Industries (HHI). The spin-off apparently had to do mainly with tax treatment of income from the new operation.

The shipyard began building its first ships, two identical very large crude carriers commonly known as "supertankers," in 1973, using steel from the POSCO mill that was by now operating nearby in Pohang. The ships were finished in March 1975, significantly behind schedule. The largest barrier to entry that Hyundai had to overcome was not inadequate finances—with government guarantees behind it, Hyundai was able to raise the needed capital abroad—but rather insufficient human capital: it lacked the knowledge and skills necessary to build large-scale ships. Thus, the start-up of the yard required much technical assistance from abroad. In 1973, about 70 personnel from Hyundai were sent to work at A&P Appledore shipyard in Scotland to learn how to organize and manage a large shipbuilding operation. Appledore itself was in financial distress and welcomed the revenue from Hyundai. Hyundai engineers concurrently learned ship design from the Scottish firm Scotlithgow, which sent personnel to the Ulsan facility to work on the two large crude

---

13. The following paragraphs on Hyundai Heavy Industries rely on information in Amsden (1989) supplemented by information in Hyundai annual reports.

carriers, which were identical in design to ships produced at its own yards. The main benefit to Scotlithgow was the additional revenue; Scotlithgow also was suffering economically. Thus, perhaps because the shipbuilding sector was in a depressed state, Hyundai was able to acquire needed technology on the cheap. Additional technical assistance was soon obtained from Kawasaki's shipyards in Japan, which licensed the Hyundai yards to build two more ships in 1974 of design similar to the Scotlithgow ships, all of which were destined for the Greek oil tanker tycoon George Livanos. Hyundai later won orders for a type of container vessel originally designed by another Scottish firm, Govan, that was going out of business. This order enabled Hyundai to achieve some needed scale economies in production.

As noted by Alice Amsden (1989), the support of the Korean government to HHI has never been publicly documented in any detail but is known to have been very substantial. The creation of the shipyard required a front-end investment of $900 million, which was at the time a very large sum for a single undertaking by a Korean firm. Overseas credit for this investment was arranged by the government, which also guaranteed the loans. The government provided as well the land and infrastructure needed by the shipyard free of charge, a practice that would be repeated many times over for favored projects. Furthermore, the government supplied financial assistance to help HHI to win its first order. Amsden notes that in addition to start-up subsidies, the government gave HHI, and other shipbuilders, continuing financial assistance. Such assistance was probably necessitated by the state of shipbuilding during the 1970s; as already noted, the industry was suffering from excess capacity worldwide.

In addition, the Korean government required that crude oil delivered to Korean oil refineries be carried in Korean-made ships, and Hyundai was given a monopoly in implementing this requirement. Thus, Hyundai Merchant Marine Corporation (HMMC, or Hyundai Marine) was established to take delivery of the oil tankers from Hyundai's shipyard and to operate them. As a consequence, Hyundai became not only a shipmaker but also a shipping line.

In spite of the assistance it received from the government, during the early years of its shipbuilding operation HHI found itself beset with a number of problems. The worst of these were technical. In particular, Hyundai lacked the internal capability to modify ship designs to meet specific needs of individual customers. The firm responded by investing to increase its own technological competence and to wean itself from reliance on the assistance of foreigners. To this end, Hyundai Industrial Research Institute was founded in 1978 to concentrate on ship design. It was eventually staffed with about 900 well-trained technical personnel; through its efforts, HHI was able to stop drawing on foreign design expertise altogether. In 1984 HHI started the Maritime Research Institute, which worked on advanced ship design, enabling HHI to enter into the production of vessels such as liquefied natural gas (LNG) carriers, which commanded higher margins than "commodity" ships such as oil tankers.

Also in 1978, the firm created Hyundai Engine and Heavy Machinery Company to produce ship engines and other heavy components that had previously been sourced from Japan; the new company was intended both to reduce costs and to increase reliability of engine delivery. To be internationally competitive in this industry, a firm's ability to meet delivery deadlines for ships was as important as making a low bid. Hyundai suspected that Japanese producers had both raised prices and intentionally delayed delivery of engines in order to reduce the competitiveness of HHI. Although operating in an industry marked by low or negative profitability worldwide, HHI showed profits in its public statements. Nevertheless, HHI and its associated operations almost surely incurred massive losses (especially if one counts the losses that doubtless were incurred, albeit never reported, by Hyundai Marine). It could report profits only because many if not most of these costs were borne by the government (and thus by the Korean people at large, who also had to pay for some indirect transfers that benefited Hyundai, notably those created by the monopoly right granted to Hyundai Marine to transport crude oil to Korea) and not by the shareholders of the emerging Hyundai group.

Low profits notwithstanding, HHI was not the only large shipbuilding firm that came into existence during the HCI drive. In addition to the new entrant Hyundai and the incumbent (and failing) KSEC, two other of the emerging chaebol, Samsung and Daewoo, created large-scale shipbuilding operations by the end of the HCI drive. But unlike Hyundai, neither Samsung nor Daewoo entered the shipbuilding business from the ground up. Instead, during the late 1970s both took over ailing firms that had attempted to enter the sector but had gone bankrupt doing so. Samsung acquired Daesung Heavy Industry Company, an entrant into shipbuilding by another nascent chaebol, in 1977. Daewoo became a shipbuilder by acquiring KSEC's failing shipyard at Okbo in 1978.

The KSEC shipyard was meant to function on the same scale as Hyundai's Ulsan yard. However, from the beginning it had been dogged by financial and operating difficulties. Reportedly, Daewoo took it over in 1978 with a 51 percent equity share at the insistence of Park Chung-hee, despite the reluctance of its chairman, Kim Woo-chung (the remaining shares were held by the government-owned Korea Development Bank). At the time of the takeover, completion of the Okbo yard was years behind schedule. Over the next several years, Daewoo was to invest more than a quarter billion dollars into this shipyard without the operation ever showing a profit. It would become one of several albatrosses plaguing the Daewoo group that would eventually bring the whole chaebol down.

The KSEC/Daewoo Okbo operation underscores one of the darker aspects of the HCI drive: many of the activities then created encountered from the onset serious difficulties that were never fully resolved. Indeed, one characteristic of the entire HCI period in Korea was that a sizable number of attempted entries into the targeted industries resulted in bankruptcies—or, to use the terminology in favor at the time, created "unsound" firms. The first response of the Korean government to the emergence of "unsound" firms was to assist them by wiping out their debts and allowing them to continue in operation with clean balance sheets (this is in fact how the Korea Development Bank came to be a 49 percent owner of the Okbo shipyard). But to the surprise of few, this approach was not very successful; by 1976 the government found itself forced to broker on a large scale the acquisition of unsound firms by firms (or groups) that were deemed sound.

Cho Soon (1994) notes of such acquisitions during the later years of the HCI drive that the government stepped in with "rescue loans" meant "to avoid the massive layoffs that would accompany bankruptcy." This action established a precedent that would be followed right up to current times: banks would be forced by the government to lend to firms in difficulty in order to keep them from shutting down operations and laying off workers. It could be argued that the earlier policy of allowing nonperforming firms to fail was not entirely abandoned, because the takeover of the unsound firms resulted in the original shareholders losing their stakes in the failing firms. The hope was that the unsound firm would be turned around by the new owner. But, as noted, this did not always happen.

Thus, both Samsung and Daewoo entered shipbuilding by acquiring unsound firms. Such acquisitions would continue to be a major means by which the largest chaebol expanded over the next two decades. But many of the failing firms continued to be unsound even after being taken over by the large chaebol. They were able to remain in business only because their operations were in effect subsidized by better operations within the same group.

Even after the HCI drive ended, a number of other shipbuilding operations were started in Korea. In 2001 nine major shipyards were listed (ones that built large oceangoing ships, i.e., not including facilities that were repair-only or that built smaller vessels for use on inland waterways), owned by eight different firms: Hanjin (the owner of Korean Airlines, which took over KSEC's operations other than Okbo), Samho, Daedong, Shina, and Daesun as well as the three large chaebol listed above. Daesun reentered the business in the late 1980s. In the 1990s the Halla group, controlled by close relatives of Hyundai's founder Chung Ju-yung, also attempted to enter the large shipbuilding sector, with disastrous results for the group (see chapter 4).

What can be said about these other operations? First, they were all on a significantly smaller scale than those of Hyundai. According to the Korean Register of Shipping, the total number of ships delivered by or on order with Hyundai since HHI's inception through year-end 2000 was 1,224. All other shipyards combined have delivered or have on order 1,490 ships. The two largest shipbuilding operations in terms of ships delivered apart from HHI are Daewoo Heavy Industries and Samsung Heavy Industries. The ships delivered by or on order from Daewoo Heavy Industries total 541, and this operation has, as just noted, been heavily money-losing from the outset. (In some years, Daewoo has reported profits on its shipbuilding, but it is difficult to know to what extent these might have derived from subsidies.) In 2002, although the Daewoo group had failed, Daewoo Heavy Industries was still in business. It had a negative net worth, and a market value of close to zero.

Samsung Heavy Industries, which holds the Samsung shipbuilding operation, has compiled a somewhat better record. Although it delivered or has on order 391 ships, significantly fewer than Daewoo, according to statements published by the company it has earned profits in more years than has Daewoo. But losses were reported in 1996, 1997, and 1998. The price of equity shares in the firm has plummeted in recent years, with the result that the market price of the firm is now significantly below book value. Nonetheless, the Samsung group has a reputation for being generally better managed than the other large groups in Korea; one possible indicator of superior management is that Samsung Heavy Industries has in recent years had significantly higher sales per employee than the comparable units of either Daewoo or Hyundai.

Shipbuilding thus stands out as an example of how firms decided to enter into a new sector, following the subsidies rather than evaluating expected total return on investment. This approach almost surely led to overinvestment in the sector reducing average returns on capital invested. The experience of Daewoo suggests that at the margin, these returns were low or even negative.

The same pattern is visible in other sectors. For example, entry into electronics, one of the sectors designated by the HCI drive, was largely driven by the availability of subsidies. Some predecessor firms to the chaebol were already participating in this sector before the drive began—notably Goldstar (the "G" in LG), which was founded in 1959 to assemble radios. By the time of the enactment of the Electrical Industry Promotion Act of 1969, Goldstar was producing a number of electronic and electrical goods, including television receivers, telephones, and home appliances. At least some of Goldstar's production was as a subcontractor to Japanese firms; indeed, Goldstar products were in some cases exported and sold under the brand names of non-Korean firms. Other firms had already entered this sector prior to the 1969 Act, such as the Taihan group, which was in fact the largest electronics firm in Korea prior to the HCI drive but which did not fare well once the drive began.

Still other firms entered electronics following the passage of the Electrical Industry Promotion Act of 1969. Two of these were firms associated with what were to become the "big five" chaebol: Samsung established the Samsung Electronics Company in 1969, and Daewoo created an electronics firm in 1971. Daewoo's electronics operations were later enlarged via acquisition of the Taihan group, which had become "unsound." Both Daewoo and Samsung initially produced television sets, again often acting as subcontractors to foreign firms so that Korean-made products were exported and often ultimately sold under a foreign brand name.[14] The remaining two of the big five entered into the electronics sector well after the conclusion of the HCI drive—Hyundai in 1983, and SK only in 1995 by beginning to produce telecommunications equipment.

During the HCI drive, the Korean government sought to upgrade Korean electronic firms from merely being assemblers of televisions and producers of relatively simple components. Accordingly, ambitious long-term goals were set for these firms to become producers of advanced electronics products, including computers. The usual array of incentives was offered, centering on subsidized loans (including overseas credits). But the government also established an industrial park that would be dedicated to semiconductor and computer manufacture, and founded and placed in this park a government-supported research institute that would work with Korean companies to build technological competencies. The domestic market for targeted products was closed to foreign competition, and foreign direct investment in these products was also forbidden. However, recognizing that the main obstacle to successful entry by Korean firms into electronics, as into shipbuilding, was their lack of relevant technologies, and recognizing also that technology was not as easily bought outright from overseas sources in the electronics sector as in shipbuilding, the government allowed joint ventures to be established between Korean firms and foreign firms that were seen as technological leaders. Three of the five biggest chaebol formed such joint ventures during the HCI period: Samsung, Daewoo, and Goldstar. At a later time, Hyundai did also.

The HCI drive also called for Korea to become a significant producer of automobiles. In this sector, there is some question as to which company was the first entrant. The Hyundai Motor Company was established in 1967 for the purpose of producing cars and, during its early years, assembled Ford Motor Company's Cortina from parts shipped to Korea by Ford. But the goal of the HCI drive was integrated production not assembly of imported components. Hyundai's first truly Korean car—not a foreign-designed car assembled in Korea and sold under a Korean nameplate—was the Pony. Unveiled in 1974, it went into production only in 1976. Although of Korean design, the Pony nonetheless used a substantial number of imported components; the first car with all-Korean content was not built until 1994.

---

14. See Moran (2001) on the role played by contracting to foreign multinationals in the development of the Korean electronics sector.

In the meantime, Hyundai had competition. The most successful was Kia, which had been founded in 1944 to manufacture bicycles but had in the intervening years diversified into motorcycle production (1961) and small trucks (1967). In late 1974, Kia beat Hyundai to the punch by producing the first car of Korean design actually to roll out of a Korean factory (Ford was a minority shareholder in Kia). Another small entrant into the automobile sector, Asia Motors, proved to be an "unsound firm" and was acquired by Kia in 1976. A somewhat more successful new entrant, Shinjin, did well during the 1960s as an assembler of General Motors vehicles but was unable during the HCI period to create a product that could compete successfully with Hyundai's Pony. Shinjin, declared unsound in 1978, was acquired by Daewoo, resulting in the formation of Daewoo Motors, set up originally as a 50-50 joint venture with General Motors. From the beginning, the relationship between Daewoo and General Motors was difficult. In 1992 General Motors relinquished much of its control of Daewoo Motors, becoming a minor shareholder, and Daewoo subsequently went on a major binge of expansion that would help to lead the already troubled group to bankruptcy. But after the bankruptcy of Daewoo in 2000 and following protracted negotiations, General Motors acquired Daewoo Motors in 2002.

The End of the HCI Drive, and an Evaluation

It was apparent by 1976 that the HCI drive was creating major problems in Korea; the fourth five-year plan, issued that year, indicated that of the industries originally designated for development, only three—steel, shipbuilding, and heavy machinery—would be granted continued support (Clifford 1994). Even this decision did not reflect a dispassionate judgment as to which sectors were likely winners. Rather, these were the sectors into which large sums of money had already been sunk, creating gigantic facilities in which thousands of Koreans were already employed (Cho S. 1994). In other designated sectors where significant employment had not been created, projects were scaled back or canceled—for example, in nonferrous metals and fertilizers (which were to have become the backbone of the chemical side of the HCI drive).[15]

Even so, the HCI drive ended not in that year but in 1979, when Park was assassinated. The assassination was linked to riots during October by laborers in the cities of Masan and Pusan. These riots were, at least in part, instigated by President Park's order that Kim Young-sam, later to become Korea's president but then a rising opposition politician in the

---

15. Korea did eventually succeed in establishing a competitive petrochemical industry; unlike most sectors in Korea, however, this one involved very substantial foreign direct investment.

National Assembly who urged moderate democratic reform, be expelled from the Assembly. In the last week of October, in a bizarre twist of events, Park was assassinated by his own head of national intelligence, Kim Jae-kyu, who had become one of Park's closest advisors. Kim apparently acted in fear that Park was about to sack him in favor of another advisor, Cha Chi-chul, who had advocated a tougher position than his own in dealing with the demonstrators. Cha was also killed by Kim. The full story of the assassination will never be known, for the one person who could have supplied it—Kim Jae-kyu—was executed about four months after committing these crimes. Detailed accounts of the assassinations and their aftermath are offered by William Gleysteen (1999) and John Wickham (1999).[16]

At least one reason for the growing popular dissatisfaction was a widespread perception that the HCI drive was concentrating wealth in the hands of a few Koreans. Public resentment was doubtless reinforced by a perception that those Koreans who were getting wealthy were the friends and cronies of Park. This might not have been entirely fair; as already noted, at least some of the founders of the rising chaebol were not particularly close personally to Park. Also, as early as 1974, the government had attempted to rein in the credit granted to the largest chaebol. Responding to the concerns of EPB economists that debt levels of the largest firms were becoming excessive and creating financial risk, it enacted a banking act intended to strengthen their supervision. However, the new requirements in fact did little to check the expansion of these groups or to reduce the amount of credit granted to them.

Nonetheless, there is no question that the HCI drive had the effect of concentrating wealth in the hands of relatively few families. As SaKong Il has shown (1993, table 2.5), income distribution in Korea did become more skewed during the 1970s; the Gini coefficient—a measure of inequality in income distribution—rose from 0.332 in 1970 to 0.391 in 1976, and during those years the proportion of income going to the richest 10 percent increased from 25.4 percent to 29.5 percent. (In contrast, income distribution had become less skewed during the 1960s.) Furthermore, it is almost certain that joined with the trend during the 1970s toward a more inequitable income distribution was an even sharper trend toward more inequitable distribution of wealth. Also significant was the common perception that the growing wealth of an elite group of Korean families was more the result of subsidy than of performance. And the empires of these families did grow: whereas in 1970 the top 30 business groups in Korea controlled a total of 126 subsidiaries, by 1979 that number had risen to 429.

---

16. At the time of the Park assassination, these two authors were the two most senior US officials stationed in Korea: Gleysteen was the US ambassador, and Wickham was commander of US military forces.

Table 2.1 Interest rates, by category, in Korea during the HCI period

Year	General loan[a] nominal rate	Policy loan nominal rate[a] (export)	Curb market loan rate	GDP deflator	Real interest rate on general loan[b]	Real interest rate on export loan[b]
1971	22.0	6.0	46.4	12.9	9.1	−6.9
1972	15.5	6.0	37.0	16.3	−0.8	−10.3
1973	15.5	7.0	33.4	12.1	3.4	−5.1
1974	15.5	9.0	40.6	30.4	−14.9	−21.4
1975	15.5	9.0	41.3	24.6	−9.1	−15.6
1976	18.0	8.0	40.5	21.2	−3.2	−13.2
1977	16.0	8.0	38.1	16.6	−0.6	−8.6
1978	19.0	9.0	39.3	22.8	−3.8	−13.8
1979	19.0	9.0	42.4	19.6	−0.6	−10.6
1980	20.0	15.0	44.9	24.0	−4.0	−9.0

a. Administered loan.
b. Nominal rate minus GDP deflator.

Sources: SaKong (1993, table A18), and author's calculations; data originally from Bank of Korea.

There was a factual basis for the widespread belief in Korea that the HCI drive not only favored the already wealthy but did so by giving select entrepreneurs public money. Interest rates on "policy loans"—those that financed the heavy investments of the HCI drive—were below market rates and, indeed, below the rate of inflation during most of the HCI period. Thus, the real rate of interest on policy loans was generally negative throughout this period, especially for export loans. A real negative rate was of course tantamount to a subsidy (see table 2.1). And, as stressed earlier, policy loans were available only to firms that were selected by the government. Even in 1980—when the HCI drive had ended, Korea was in recession, and the government was implementing stabilization policies—interest rates on policy loans remained negative.

In a recent unpublished paper, Anne O. Krueger and Yoo Jung-ho (2001) provide data on preferential loans as a percentage of total loans outstanding by deposit money banks in Korea from 1963 to 1998.[17] They also estimate the subsidy implicit in policy loans granted to Korean enterprises from 1963 to 1982, where the policy loans include the preferential loans granted by the deposit money banks and loans made through the Korea Development Bank (a "nonbank bank"). Krueger and Yoo show that from 1963 to 1970, preferential loans rose from 5.5 percent to almost 10 percent

---

17. Similar calculations, with roughly consistent findings, are made for just the HCI period by Zeile (1991a).

Table 2.2. Estimated subsidy component in policy loans of Korean banks and ordinary income reported by Korean manufacturing firms, 1963-82 (billions of won)

Year	Total subsidy implicit in policy loans	Ordinary income reported by Korean manufacturing firms	Ratio: Subsidy/income
1963	1.2	4.5	0.27
1964	2.7	5.6	0.48
1965	3.9	6.6	0.59
1966	3.9	11.4	0.34
1967	3.3	13.4	0.25
1968	5.5	20.6	0.27
1969	7.9	24.3	0.33
1970	14.5	22.9	0.63
1971	20.3	11.8	1.72
1972	21.5	56.5	0.38
1973	26.0	62.3	0.42
1974	54.2	176.1	0.31
1975	107.6	169.7	0.63
1976	165.7	313.6	0.53
1977	172.9	390.0	0.44
1978	187.3	615.1	0.30
1979	256.7	573.9	0.45
1980	271.8	−55.7	n.a.
1981	454.1	5.6	81.09
1982	546.6	403.6	1.35

n.a. = not applicable

Sources: Krueger and Yoo (2001, table 4), and author's calculations.

of total loans outstanding, and rose further to around 18 percent of total loans outstanding by 1980. During the HCI years (1973-79), this percentage ranged from 16.4 to about 19 percent. The subsidy component is difficult to calculate because the implicit subsidy is the difference between interest that would be paid under a free-market lending rate and the interest actually paid for the preferential loans, and the former is not available (curb market rates cannot be used to estimate the free-market rate, because so much credit was allocated at nonmarket rates that the curb market was only a fringe market). As just noted, the real rate of interest in Korea during the HCI period on policy loans was often negative, and hence one readily surmises that the subsidy element was indeed large.

Krueger and Yoo thus calculate the free-market rate as a three-year moving average of the sum of the real GDP growth rate and the CPI rate of inflation. Using this estimate, they compare the implicit subsidy that this rate implies with the total ordinary income (earnings) reported by the Korean manufacturing sector for the years 1963-81, as shown in table 2.2. The table also shows the ratio of the estimated subsidy to the ordinary income of this sector. As can be seen, the ratio varies substantially from year to year, because both the estimated subsidy and the reported earnings of the manufacturing sector change; but at no time was the ratio below 0.27, and in some years it was above 1.0. During the pre-HCI years (1963-72), the average ratio was 0.53; but it fell to 0.44 during the HCI years (1973-79). This suggests that although favored firms during the HCI period received very heavy government subsidies, the overall rate of subsidization actually fell somewhat compared to the earlier period.

Zeile (1991a) has derived measures of the relative cost of loans across manufacturing sectors during the HCI period. His main finding, consistent with that of Krueger and Yoo, is that those firms expanding in targeted sectors were in fact recipients of loans on more favorable terms than were available to firms operating in nontargeted sectors. Zeile also shows that the sectors that were "favored" in terms of credit preference tended to achieve larger increases in net exports over the following decade (i.e., the 1980s) than nonfavored sectors.

Yet though it is clear, as previously suggested, that the subsidies largely determined the strategies that were followed by large Korean firms, rates of return on capital were great enough that overall the subsidies were doubtless, in the words of Krueger and Yoo, "intramarginal." That is to say, many and perhaps even most of the projects undertaken were ones that might have earned satisfactory returns on capital even in the absence of subsidies, although some unsound firms were created in the process. Citing W. Hong (1981), Krueger and Yoo (2001) note that overall return on capital invested during the HCI period might have been as great as 35 percent, despite the many business failures during those years.[18] We may thus raise a real question: to achieve the goals of the HCI drive, were subsidies actually required? Alternatively, might not the goals have been met with government intervention that was less heavy-handed, that did not so patently favor certain enterprises (and, in so doing, bestow extraordinary benefits on a small group of families)?

Of course, as John F. Kennedy observed, "a rising tide lifts all boats," and this statement applied to the Korean economy during the 1970s. Yet even if the income of the average Korean was rising, Korean popular dissatisfaction over increasingly inequitable income distribution mounted as the 1970s progressed. Park tried to deal with this dissatisfaction by encouraging sizable wage hikes in 1976 to 1978 (table 2.3), increases that were well in excess of productivity gains and hence put cost-push pressure on the underlying industries. Nevertheless, discontent welled up when the overall economic performance of Korea deteriorated significantly in 1979. Per capita GDP growth during the period 1967-71 (SaKong

---

18. SaKong (1993, table 3.6) cites rates of return in the manufacturing sector during the HCI period ranging from 17 percent to 40 percent, but gives no indication of how these were calculated. No data on these rates of return for years after 1977 are given.

Table 2.3 Real growth rates, nominal wage increases, inflation rates, and real wage increases in Korea during the HCI and Chun periods (percent)

Year	Real GDP growth rate	Nominal rate of wage increase in manufacturing	Rate of inflation	Real rate of wage increase in manufacturing
1972	5.1	13.9	12.0	1.9
1973	13.2	18.0	3.7	14.3
1974	8.1	35.3	16.8	8.5
1975	6.4	27.0	25.5	1.5
1976	13.1	34.7	17.9	16.8
1977	9.8	33.8	12.1	21.7
1978	9.8	34.3	7.0	17.3
1979	7.2	28.6	19.8	8.8
1980	−3.7	22.7	27.3	−4.6
1981	5.9	20.1	21.4	−1.2
1982	7.2	14.7	7.6	7.1
1983	12.6	12.2	3.6	8.6
1984	9.3	8.1	2.1	5.7
1985	7.0	9.9	2.6	7.3
1986	12.9	9.2	3.0	6.2

Sources: GDP data: SaKong (1993, table A.39); wage data: Cho S. (1994, table 5.2); inflation data: Bank of Korea.

1993, table 2.3), before the HCI drive, had averaged 8.7 percent, and it slipped slightly to 7.3 percent during the years 1972-76.

In spite of some slippage in the per capita GDP growth rate, nominal rates of growth of wages in Korean manufacturing rose during the HCI period. Much of the increase in nominal wages was absorbed by inflation (see table 2.3) but, even so, real wage increases (wage increases adjusted for inflation) were quite high during 1976-78, indeed much higher than could be justified by productivity increases. Real wage increases in excess of productivity increases are not, of course, sustainable in the long run, because the long-run result is a rise in unit costs of production, such that the relevant good becomes uncompetitive in world markets. Given this, a likely explanation for government tolerance of the unrealistically large real wage increases in Korea during the late 1970s was that Park hoped that these would serve to mollify rising public discontent with his rule. But when real wage increases began to spiral downward in 1979, the result was to intensify the already strong sentiment in Korea against Park's increasingly strong-handed rule.

Adding to the imbalances, the government had attempted to keep the nominal exchange rate fixed; in dollar terms Korean unit labor costs therefore rose during the late 1970s, reducing the price competitiveness of Korean exports. One result was that beginning in 1976, Korean export growth

Table 2.4 Exports, imports, and trade balance as a percentage of GDP in Korea, 1961-79

Year	Exports as percent of GDP	Imports as percent of GDP	Trade balance as percent of GDP
1962	2.4	−18.3	−15.9
1963	3.3	−20.7	−17.4
1964	4.1	−13.8	−9.7
1965	6.0	−15.3	−9.3
1966	6.8	−19.5	−12.7
1967	7.4	−23.3	−15.9
1968	8.8	−28.1	−19.3
1969	9.4	−27.6	−18.2
1970	9.9	−24.4	−14.5
1971	11.6	−25.5	−13.9
1972	15.0	−23.6	−8.6
1973	23.7	−31.4	−7.7
1974	23.9	−36.4	−12.5
1975	24.4	−34.8	−10.4
1976	26.8	−30.6	−3.8
1977	27.2	−29.4	−2.2
1978	24.7	−29.1	−4.4
1979	24.6	−33.1	−8.5

Sources: SaKong (1993, table 8.4), and author's calculations; from Bank of Korea data.

began to slow—just as HCI projects were coming on line. By 1979 exports as a share of GDP were declining, an indication that growth was coming from nontargeted sectors (see table 2.4). The balance of trade throughout the Park years was negative, reflecting the fact that Korea, as a rapidly growing economy, was a net capital importer. However, the (negative) balance of trade as a percentage of GDP had been reduced throughout the 1970s (with the exception of the 1973-74 "oil shock" years, when a jump in oil prices caused it to rise temporarily). Thus, when in late 1978 and 1979 this balance turned suddenly worse, the change was seen as a warning sign.

In response to the deteriorating economic situation, Park authorized a number of measures to stabilize the economy; these were announced in mid-April of 1979. Their main objective was to bring inflation under control, and to that end both fiscal and monetary policies were tightened. Such tightening required that policy loans granted to the chaebol for large HCI projects be reined in and that loans no longer be given at interest rates that were, in real terms, negative. Thus, the announcement of these measures effectively signaled the end of the HCI drive. In addition, real wage increases were reduced significantly in 1979. Unfortunately, the measures failed to prevent further overall economic deterioration. Later that year, the Korean economy was subjected to the external shock of oil price increases. Unusually cold weather added to the country's woes, as agricultural production slumped. Finally, following the assassination of Park in October 1979, the discontent that was already brewing erupted into a period of political upheaval marked by frequent strikes and protests, which disrupted industrial production.

Indeed, the sorry end of the HCI period, with Korea in recession and in the throes of rampant political turmoil, has led some analysts to conclude that the HCI drive must be judged a failure (see, e.g., Yoo J. 1989; Noland 1993; Clifford 1994; Noland and Pack 2003). But as others have noted (e.g., Amsden 1989; Zeile 1991b; SaKong 1993; Cho 1994), this judgment may be too harsh. In fact, the record is very mixed. The period was one in which Korean firms did successfully enter new industries. Overall rates of return on capital were almost surely positive, although the marginal products of capital (and hence the real rate of return) in the HCI was actually lower than in nonfavored sectors (Yoo J. 1989). William Zeile (1991b) has calculated total factor productivity (TFP) increases by sector in Korea during the years 1972-85, finding that most of the sectors that were created under the HCI drive experienced TFP increases as rapid as those in nontargeted sectors.[19] In some sectors they were in fact much higher than the average for all Korean manufacturing. Such results might be expected for a number of reasons (e.g., achievement of scale economies, implementation of newer and better technologies, and learning by doing).

However, some analysts have calculated that total factor productivity did *not* grow especially fast in Korea during the HCI drive and, indeed, its growth might even have been negative. For example, Park Seung-rok and Jene K. Kwon (1995) argue that TFP experienced a negative growth despite rapid growth of output; in their calculations, the increased output was generated entirely by growth in factor inputs (capital and labor). Lee Jong-wha (1996), by contrast, detects positive TFP during the HCI drive; but unlike Zeile, he finds that the sectors heavily supported by the Korean government experienced less rapid TFP increases than other manufacturing industries. In fact, Zeile (1993) also finds that TFP increases in the sectors dominated by the chaebol, which by and large were the heavily supported sectors, are below average when R&D spending and economies of scale are accounted for. Zeile concludes that this "casts serious doubt on the proposition that the chaebol possess an organizational advantage which has contributed to the rapid advances in productivity observed for the Korean economy" (1993). A number of other

---

19. Total factor productivity measures increase in output that is not accounted for by increase in factor input. For example, if additional investment in a sector doubles all factor inputs (e.g., total plant and equipment and total number of workers), one might expect output to double. In such a case, there would be no increase in total factor productivity. If, however, output more than doubles, the difference is attributed to an increase in total factor productivity.

studies reporting various conclusions regarding TFP growth in Korea are reviewed by Kwack Sung-yeung (2000). A general problem in assessing them is that measurement of TFP growth is extremely sensitive to the exact methodology used (above all else, to choice of production function), leading to results that are not extremely robust—that is, different analyses yield different results even if they are performed rigorously and objectively. This is unfortunate, because more than anything else, an evaluation of the success of industrial policy rests on a determination of whether such policies, when applied, cause rates of TFP to increase or decrease.[20]

Moreover, because inefficient capacity was often created in these industries, a good many of the new ventures proved to be "unsound." Further, rather than closing such operations, the Korean government most often subsidized their takeover by more sound firms. The hope was that the takeover would result in a turnaround in the unsound operation; the reality was sometimes the creation of a much larger unsound firm.

Nevertheless, the process of having sound firms take over unsound ones was instrumental in the growth of the large chaebol. The share of the top 10 groups rose from about 5 percent of Korean GDP at the beginning of the HCI period to more than 10 percent at the end (SaKong 1993, table A.21). Also during this period, these groups created practices and problems that in some cases have continued to the present. These included the creation or acquisition of groups of poorly performing operations, high levels of debt, huge moral hazard problems, and the related emergence of a "too big to fail" mentality in Korea. Moral hazard is discussed in more detail later; in brief, large and well-connected enterprises in Korea have been viewed as likely to be bailed out by the government were things to go seriously wrong for them, thus giving banks an incentive to lend funds to them without any critical review of the process. The problems created by moral hazard finally exploded in 1997, and they still have not been entirely worked out.

---

20. Indeed, the debate over whether the Asian "economic miracle" was real or ephemeral founders on this point. The results of Alwyn Young (1995), cited by Paul Krugman (1994) in a widely read article on Asian growth that claims it resulted almost entirely from nonsustainable growth of factor inputs, are that TFP growth throughout Asia was not particularly high during the era of the "miracle." But these results are contested by a number of credible analysts (e.g., Hsieh 1997).

Appendix 2.1
Might Industrial Policy in a Developing
Country Succeed for Reasons Not
Explained by Classical Economics?

Can a rationale for industrial policy, such as that behind Korea's HCI drive, be developed that does not rely on the infant-industry argument (which, as demonstrated in the text, is flawed on both theoretical and pragmatic grounds)? Novel theoretical insight into this issue—not specific to the case of Korea,[21] but nonetheless providing some basis for explaining why the HCI drive was at least a partial success—is to be found in a very recent book by Ralph Gomory and William Baumol (2000), a prominent mathematician and economist respectively. As the Nobel Prize-winning economist Robert Solow declares in a book-jacket blurb, the reasoning of Gomory and Baumol is innovative; furthermore, while they cannot yet be shown to be correct, neither can their arguments be dismissed out of hand.

Gomory and Baumol argue that at least some aspects of neoclassical trade theory are wrong. In particular, they claim that the revealed comparative advantage of a nation can be determined more by accident of history than by factor endowment, as trade theory asserts. Specifically, if a nation happens to establish a new industry by committing significant resources to creating capacity for a particular type of good or service whose production is characterized by scale economies, then the entry barrier formed by that scale economy gives that nation a created advantage in that good or service. Indeed, the scale economy can follow from a requirement that substantial resources be precommitted before the commercial production of a product has begun, creating a "sunk cost" that must be amortized against future production. In this case, the average cost per unit of production declines constantly as production takes place, so that an incumbent with a history of production can produce at a lower average unit cost than a new entrant. Gomory and Baumol call "retainable" any activity that is characterized by sunk front-end costs and increasing returns to scale (so that average unit costs fall as output increases). Once a firm establishes itself in such activity, it is protected by barriers to entry that bar easy challenges by new entrants.

Gomory and Baumol also note that whereas neoclassical trade theory posits a unique free trade equilibrium that both is more or less predetermined by the factor endowments of nations and is optimal from the point of view of all countries, in an economy where activities are retainable many free trade equilibriums are possible in principle. Furthermore, none among these is optimal for all nations. Some of these equilibriums are such

---

21. Indeed, as is detailed below, the Korean experience exposes some of the limitations of Gomory and Baumol's reasoning.

that all nations might benefit by moving from one particular equilibrium to some other equilibrium. Others are such that one or possibly a group of nations can benefit by changing to another equilibrium, while another nation (or other nations) would suffer reduced welfare from such a shift. Thus, in the world of Gomory and Baumol, to maintain a free trade equilibrium that enables each nation to continue, ad infinitum, specializing in those sectors in which it currently holds comparative advantage does not necessarily produce the best outcome for all nations. Rather, in this world, under some circumstances it can be advantageous to all nations for some industries to move from one country to another. Generally, such shifts will benefit everyone if relatively rich countries (i.e., ones with high per capita incomes) yield activities to relatively poor ones. But some such moves can, under other circumstances, create income losses for those nations that lose activities. These losses tend to occur, for example, if activities move from countries that already are relatively rich to other countries that are also relatively rich.

Any such movement implies that new entry must be made into the industry: for example, a new entrant in a relatively poor country displaces (or at least takes market share away from) an incumbent producer in the relatively rich country. Given that incumbent firms operating in retainable industries are protected from challengers by scale economies, how can such new entry hope to succeed?

One possible answer is that the migration of the activity is accomplished via foreign direct investment, so that the incumbent firm itself is the agent of the transfer (presumably thus avoiding many of the costs associated with creating the activity). In this case, managerial control is retained by the incumbent (and foreign) firm, a potentially undesirable circumstance from the viewpoint of the residents or the government of the country to which the activity has migrated. Objections might arise even if very substantial benefits to the local economy are created by this migration.

There are other alternatives. In a case in which the scale economy derives from costs that must be sunk before entry, the government may grant subsidies to cover these costs, so that they are not fully borne by the producer but rather are assumed in part society at large.[22] According to economists, however, a subsidy is warranted only if any undertaking that is subsidized creates some sort of external benefit—that is, a benefit that is not captured either by producers or users of the product or service created by the undertaking, so these benefits are themselves captured by society at large (though not necessarily enjoyed by each member of this society in proportion to the costs borne by that member). The total of

---

22. A subsidy must be financed by the government that grants the subsidy, and government finances come ultimately from taxes paid by the citizens whom the government serves.

such benefits must exceed, or at least equal, the cost of the subsidy. Gomory and Baumol argue that this condition might be met if the economy, by incurring the sunk costs of entry, gains activities that offer higher per worker productivity than is available elsewhere in the economy. Benefits to the public (or at least some members of it) would then be created in the form of higher wages in the new activity than could be achieved in other activities.[23]

In the framework of Gomory and Baumol, the HCI drive and other industrial policy initiatives can be seen as deliberate efforts to create retainable industries in Korea. Indeed, we have already seen that EPB planners believed that the sectors in which Korea had achieved export success during the 1960s were nonretainable. Gomory and Baumol note that the characteristics of a nonretainable industry include constant or decreasing returns to scale, low costs of entry (implying, as noted, lack of one source of scale economy), and no extremely specialized knowledge associated with the industry—that is, the required knowledge is available from a number of sources and is relatively easy to grasp. For example, the cutting and sewing of garments corresponds to their definition of a nonretainable activity. This industry might indeed be expected to migrate to whatever nation is able to offer the lowest wages (even if, after the activity has landed there, its effect might be to drive up the marginal product of labor and hence to put upward pressure on wages).

Thus, by the reasoning of Gomory and Baumol, the EPB was correct in its assessment in the late 1960s that Korea would not be able to long retain its revealed comparative advantage in textiles and apparel and in other light industries. But the EPB did not urge that Korea move quickly into retainable activities, such as those in the heavy industrial sector. Gomory and Baumol might therefore have agreed with Park Chung-hee that it was appropriate for Korea to seek to enter sectors requiring large up-front investments in which scale economies were significant, though the list as actually drawn up might not have been entirely to these scholars' liking.[24]

---

23. Strictly speaking, the wage rate is equal to the marginal productivity of labor; that equality is, in fact, a condition for profit maximization in a firm. If labor mobility is high (i.e., labor markets are efficient) and labor is homogenous, the creation of an activity that raises marginal productivity in an economy should cause all wages to rise to a new level. Practically speaking, however, the conditions are unlikely to be fulfilled. Nonetheless, the new activities are likely to offer new job opportunities for skilled workers, enabling workers who possess the requisite skills to command wage premiums and thus earn higher than average wages. Over time, as new activities are created and labor markets respond to the new demands generated by these activities (i.e., workers learn the required skills), the net result should be rising wages over a broad swath of the labor force.

24. On this matter, however, I have not consulted either Gomory or Baumol and do not claim to speak for them!

Do Gomory and Baumol endorse Korean industrial policy? The answer is "not explicitly." But they nonetheless do provide some new ammunition that is sure to benefit those analysts who claim that industrial policy can play a useful role in economic development. And, as noted above, while their theories are not proven, they should not be rejected out of hand either.

3

The Miracle with a Dark Side:
The Chun and Roh Years, 1980-92

Chun Doo-hwan Takes Over

Following the assassination of Park and a short interim of power struggles within Korea, the country came under the leadership of two more military generals: first Chun Doo-hwan (1980-87) and next Roh Tae-woo (1987-92). Chun was self-appointed, as Park himself initially had been. Roh was elected but his presidency is nonetheless generally seen as essentially a continuation of military rule. During the almost 12 years in which these two generals held power, the Korean economy generally prospered, albeit with some hiccups that turned into coughs during Roh's last years. These were also years in which the large chaebol continued, by and large, to grow and, in some cases at least, to prosper. Much in Korea thus went right during this time, and the period ended with a restoration of democracy. Nonetheless, the two generals to this day are generally reviled rather than revered in Korea. To understand why, it is necessary to understand the circumstances under which they came to power.

When he was assassinated in October 1979, Park Chung-hee had done nothing to prepare Korea for a change of leadership. He had named no successor and established no method of choosing one in the event that he should be unable to carry out his functions as head of state, beyond a provision that made the prime minister acting president if he were incapacitated. When he was assassinated, after all, Park was president of Korea for life, and his clear intention was to keep living and ruling for a very long time.

But at the time of the assassination, there was widespread discontent in Korea that had both economic and political overtones; indeed, as explained in the previous chapter, it indirectly led to the assassination. Popular dissatisfaction was to erupt in large demonstrations in the months that followed Park's death, and these were used in turn as an excuse for a military crackdown and the continuation of military rule.

The military took power despite the presence in Korea of individuals who enjoyed widespread support and were prepared to lead the country. During the last years of Park's rule new figures arose (or perhaps more accurately, were reinvented) who served as leaders of a de facto opposition to Park that existed in spite of the oppressive nature of the Yushin regime. Three persons in particular had emerged, any one of whom might have become president had free and open elections been held in Korea. All had the family name "Kim," and hence they were collectively known as "the three Kims."

All three have already been mentioned. The first, Kim Jong-pil, had as a young officer led the coup that ultimately resulted in Park becoming head of state; he subsequently served as prime minister and first head of the Korean Central Intelligence Agency in the early Park years. He later had a major falling-out with Park. Although he went public with his complaints, he stayed within the government party. But in 1979, as leader of the party, he probably destroyed his chances for becoming Park's successor by playing his hand too early. Because he saw himself as the only one of the three Kims who might be acceptable to the military as president, he attempted to get himself named as interim president in the immediate aftermath of the assassination. However, it soon became clear that he in fact had very little support from within the military, and his bid failed.

The second Kim, Kim Young-sam, was the advocate of democracy whom Park had thrown out of the National Assembly in early 1979. At that time, he had been the leader of the opposition party in the Assembly that Park had tolerated, if just barely. Kim Young-sam was in fact generally seen as a moderate and his rather weak opposition to Park may explain why his party had been allowed to exist under the Yushin regime. In 1979, perhaps because of his moderation but certainly also because he had been recently singled out for abuse by Park, he quite possibly enjoyed the most widespread popularity of the three Kims.

The third was Kim Dae-jung, the opposition leader who had run against Park in 1967 and 1971, nearly winning in his second attempt, and whose 1973 abduction from a Tokyo hotel by Korean security agents had triggered a storm of international disapproval (which almost surely saved his life). As noted in chapter 2, Kim had been subsequently imprisoned but then released in 1978 in a move designed by Park Chung-hee to convince US President Jimmy Carter that Korea was making progress on issues of human rights. Kim's main constituency was in his home province, economically backward South Cholla, where discontent with the Park government was the highest anywhere in Korea. People in this province tended to believe that they were distinct from other Koreans (Cholla had been a separate kingdom before Silla, the first unified Korean kingdom, was created), and they also believed that the relative underdevelopment of their province was the result of deliberate policies by the Park government to keep them down. Their suspicions had some justification (Jones and SaKong 1980; see also Wickham 1999). During the HCI drive, Park had clearly favored locating new industrial complexes in the southeastern areas of Korea and especially in Kyongsang province, the area of his birth. Few activities were located in the southwest region that encompassed the two Cholla provinces, even though one explicit objective of the HCI drive was to locate heavy industry, seen by Park as vital to Korea's defense, as far from the North Korean border as possible. Cholla is in fact as far as Kyongsang from the border.

Thus, in 1979, Kim Dae-jung and Kim Young-sam were increasingly rivals claiming the leadership of the opposition. Both would, in the future, become president of Korea (Kim Young-sam was president at the time of the onset of the financial crisis, and Kim Dae-jung is president at the time of this writing). But both of them in 1979 were deeply distrusted by the Korean military. The events following the assassination of Park were a product of this distrust; in retrospect, it is clear that the leaders of Korea's army simply did not wish either of these two Kims to become head of state, and the army had the power to enforce its wish.

The prime minister of South Korea under Park at the time of his death, Choi Kyu-ha, became acting president as per the Yushin constitution. One of Choi's first moves, after proclaiming martial law, was to name Major General Chun Doo-hwan of the Korean army as chief investigator to learn the full truth of Park's assassination.

Almost immediately after the assassination, the US government issued a warning to the government of North Korea not to try in any way to take advantage of the lack of a leader in Seoul. In the weeks that followed, US naval forces were dispatched to the area, and US-staffed air defenses in South Korea were bolstered.[1]

Also in the weeks that followed the assassination, a group of officers of the South Korean military plotted to take control of the army away from chief of staff General Chung Sung-hwa, using as pretexts a supposed threat from the North and an alleged complicity of Chung in the assassination of Park, in which at least some of the plotters saw the hand of North Korea despite the lack of any evidence whatsoever. They subsequently took action in what is now commonly referred to as the "12/12 Incident." Under the command of General Roh Tae-woo (the future president), units

---

1. As noted by both Wickham (1999) and Gleysteen (1999), there was in fact no imminent threat posed by North Korea; the US actions were purely precautionary.

of the South Korean army known to be loyal to the group were moved into Seoul on December 12 to arrest Chung and to give effective command of the South Korean army to the plotters. Their leader was Chun Doo-hwan, the person who had been put in charge of investigation of the assassination and who then became chief of staff of the army in place of Chung (and thus administrator of martial law in Korea).

Following the 12/12 Incident, for several months there was relative quiet in Korea; but during the spring of 1980 a new round of student protests and workers' strikes erupted. Both Kim Young-sam and Kim Dae-jung figured in these actions. There is little evidence that they actually fomented them and, indeed, both urged calm on the part of the agitators. But because they were leaders of the opposition, the strikers and protesters looked to them for leadership. For his part, General Chun tended to see the protests and strikes as the product of hidden actions by North Korea (Wickham 1999).

In mid-April, in what surely ranks as one of the most ill-considered actions imaginable, President Choi named Chun as acting head of the KCIA in addition to his position as acting chief of staff of the army. The groundswell of negative popular reaction rose swiftly. Kim Young-sam, at a press conference held on May 9, called for an end to martial law and for power to be turned over to an elected government under a new constitution that had been hastily drafted in the National Assembly following the assassination of Park. Matters reached a head later that month.

First, students and other protesters clashed with police in Seoul and elsewhere. On May 17 a major crackdown was initiated, over US objections, following the killing of a policeman in Seoul. At Chung's instigation, President Choi issued a new emergency martial law decree: it enabled the arrest of student leaders, the detention of all three Kims, the shutdown of university campuses, and the indefinite postponement of a meeting of the National Assembly scheduled for May 20. Furthermore, it became clear that President Choi under the new decree was effectively stripped of almost all power as head of state, which reverted to the military.

In Kwangju—the main city of South Cholla province, which had historically been the region's capital—protesters refused to heed the decree and end their protest. On May 18 students from Chonnam and Chosun Universities, both located in Kwangju, staged a large-scale but peaceful demonstration, which was broken up forcefully by riot police. Members of Korea's Special Warfare Command—an elite army unit trained to fight North Korean commandos—then entered the city and sought out any young people who looked like students in order to beat them up. In some cases, however, soldiers actually bayoneted their victims.

Citizens reacted by storming government buildings and seizing firearms and ammunition. The army units withdrew to a perimeter around the city. The military issued a statement blaming Kim Dae-jung for the insurrection in Kwangju, though at the time the insurrection began he was in detention. On May 27, after talks between the government and leaders of the insurrection broke down, upwards of six thousand army troops entered Kwangju and secured the city; in the process, about 200 people were killed.

In August, Kim Dae-jung was put on trial by the Chun government and found guilty of fomenting the unrest in Kwangju. He was then sentenced to death. International outcry was immediate, including from the United States. President Carter in December 1980 sent Secretary of Defense Harold Brown to Seoul to plea for clemency for Kim, to no avail. But Richard Allen, an advisor to US president-elect Ronald Reagan, sent word to Chun that the American reaction to the execution of Kim Dae-jung would be "like a lightning bolt from heaven striking you" (Gleysteen 1999). In a deal struck in December 1982, Kim agreed to go into exile in the United States; there, while a visiting fellow at Harvard University, he wrote a book titled *Mass Participatory Economy: Korea's Road to World Economic Power* (1996). He returned to Korea in 1985 in order to run for the National Assembly. It was reported that Chun was reluctant to allow Kim to enter the country but, in the end, nothing was done to stop him.

More than ten years later, in 1996, Chun was tried and convicted for complicity in the murder of the 200 or so citizens who died during the suppression of the Kwangju insurrection. His death sentence was commuted to life in prison on appeal in December 1996, and he was pardoned in December 1997 by President Kim Young-sam after consulting with Kim Dae-jung who had just won election as Korea's next president.

But those events lay in the future: in early 1981, Chun became head of state of Korea. At the time, the Korean economy was going through its worst period since the 1950s; indeed, for the first time in many years, in 1980 growth turned sharply negative. Thus, Chun's urgent task was to restore economic health to Korea. A first priority was to tackle inflation. Excessive growth of money supply—caused by policy loans to chaebol during the HCI drive, where the real interest rates on these loans were often negative, and remittances from construction projects in the Middle East that were not sterilized by the central bank—had caused inflation to surge. The excesses of the HCI drive had also led to a serious structural problem of imbalance of supply and demand. As a consequence, some sectors had so much excess capacity that the market for the relevant product could not clear at any price that yielded positive returns on the capital employed by suppliers operating in that sector. The situation was especially dire in the chemicals sector, where capacity had been added in anticipation of rising exports that failed to materialize because Korean firms were not competitive. In contrast, in other sectors there was excess demand, but because the government in effect rationed all bank credit to favored projects and firms, no financing was available to fund expanded supply to meet this demand. Also, import restrictions often prevented the inflow of imports that could have alleviated the imbalance. As might be expected, relative prices of goods for which excess demand existed rose. In addition, the Korean economy had to absorb the second oil shock in 1979. And, of course, the protests and strikes of 1980 had resulted in much lost output—though the economic consequences of this turmoil were probably the last thing on the minds of either the protestors or the government authorities at the time.

Economic Reform under Chun

Chun Doo-hwan fully recognized that getting the Korean economy on a better footing was one of his most pressing tasks as president. To accomplish this, he took a leaf from the book of Park Chung-hee and appointed a superb group of well-trained economists to advise him. It was headed by Kim Jae-ik, who first served as director general of the planning board of the EPB and later as secretary for economic affairs in the Blue House (the presidential residence). Noting that economic stabilization measures (fiscal and monetary restraint) that had been implemented in April 1979 by the Park government had had little success, the group advised additional stabilization measures. In addition, it recommended long-term structural adjustment and reform, including liberalization of the import regime. During 1981, interest rates were cut in an effort to stimulate the economy; at the same time, at Kim Jae-ik's urging, Chun attempted to jawbone Korean industry not to raise prices and labor leaders not to press for wage increases. Also, special tax breaks were enacted to benefit those HCI industries in the most difficulty. In 1982 these tax breaks were rescinded as part of a package that lowered overall corporate tax rates.

Over the next year or two, Chun's measures, as recommended by Kim Jae-ik and his team, met with considerable success. GDP growth resumed in 1981, albeit at an initial rate that was anemic by the standards of the Park years. But then, in 1982 and following years, real growth rates rose back to "miracle economy" levels. Growth made it possible to grant real wage increases in 1982, offsetting the real wage declines of 1980 and 1981 (see table 2.3).

Ironically, after taking power in what had amounted to a coup d'état, Chun promoted his government as one of "social justice." By this, he seemed to mean "economic justice." He hoped to reduce the economic inequities that had arisen in Korea, which were at the root of much of the nation's popular discontent. However, at the end of the day, little was actually done. Thus, in December 1980, before Chun officially assumed power but with his approval, an antitrust law went into effect, called in English the Monopoly Regulation and Fair Trade Act but commonly known as the Korean Antitrust Act or KAA (Chang 1996). To implement it, a new regulatory agency, the Korea Fair Trade Commission or KFTC, was created. The law was amended in 1986 to toughen the provisions pertaining to economic concentration, a move that was clearly aimed at the chaebol. The law contained the normal provisions of antimonopoly laws, addressing cartels and cartel-like behavior (e.g., collaborative acts among sellers to fix prices, restricting output or shipments, or allocating territories among sellers), mergers, and abuse of a dominant market position by a seller. The last provision, modeled more after European than US law, was directly itself aimed at chaebol: under the law, monopoly was not per se illegal; but in markets in which one company (or more) was deemed to hold a dominant position, certain practices were labeled abusive and subject to sanction.

Under the new law, a dominant position was deemed to exist if either (a) one firm held more than 50 percent of the market or (b) the combined share of the top three firms was greater than 75 percent, where the market share of any firm holding less than 10 percent of the market was excluded from the calculation. In 1990, 135 markets in Korea were considered to be characterized by market dominance, and almost 80 percent of these were associated with the top 30 chaebol. Any of the following conduct was considered to be abuse of a dominant position: unreasonably determining, maintaining, or altering the price of a good or service; unreasonably restricting the sale of a good or service; or unreasonably interfering with the business activities of other firms (Chang 1996). This list reflects the belief of Kim Jae-ik's advisory team that the price inflation of the late 1970s resulted at least in part from arbitrary price increases by large firms holding dominant market positions.

The law also contained provisions aimed at vertical restraints; for example, it proscribed on a per se basis almost all retail price maintenance (again reflecting concern at the time of the law's passage with price inflation) and a number of unfair trade practices such as unreasonable refusal to deal, false or deceptive advertising, coercive tactics to force another firm's customer to switch suppliers, and unreasonable or coercive use of asymmetric bargaining power. An amendment to the KAA in 1984 covered subcontracting practices designed to promote fairness in sectors in which large contractors (i.e., chaebol-affiliated firms) held market power over smaller supplier firms.

In addition to these features more or less standard for antitrust law, the KAA contained some provisions that were idiosyncratic and meant to cover certain practices of the chaebol unique to Korea. These included a prohibition on the establishment of holding companies, a measure intended to inhibit new activities entered into by the chaebol being incorporated into separate companies under the control of a common chairman. The prohibition seems to have been meant mostly to limit the power of what came to be known as the "office of the chairman" in each of the large groups, but by most accounts it failed to achieve that goal.

Another provision required the KFTC to identify the 30 largest business groups in Korea, ranking them by the total assets of all affiliated companies; a company was considered to be an affiliate of a group if it was under the control of the same single person or entity as other firms within the designated group. Foreign-owned firms were not, for these purposes, considered to be group members or controlling entities (thus, if a foreign firm owned several subsidiaries in Korea, these would not be counted as one of the largest groups even if the value of their assets would otherwise have qualified them for inclusion). Furthermore, subject to exceptions, the following held:

- There was to be no direct cross-ownership; for example, if firm A held shares in firm B, where A and B were members of the same group, then B could not hold shares in A.

- No member firm of a group could increase its holdings in the equity of another domestic Korean firm (not a member of the group) above 25 percent. This provision was designed not just to prevent the largest groups from entering new businesses by acquisition (as Samsung had done in shipbuilding) but to prevent them in principle from entering any new activities. However, as we shall see, this prohibition was subject to exceptions that rendered it all but useless.

- No firm in such a group was allowed to guarantee the debt of another firm in the group by an amount more than 20 percent of the net assets of the guaranteeing firm.

- Finance and insurance companies belonging to a group were not allowed to exercise voting rights in shares held in affiliated firms.

These were tough provisions in principle (some of the toughest did not come into effect until 1986), and the KAA was a law with the potential to check the power of the chaebol considerably. However, from the beginning, this power was sharply circumscribed. To begin with, the KFTC was made subordinate to the Economic Planning Board, and thus competition policy was made subordinate to industrial or trade policy. (The KFTC did become an independent agency in 1994.) Furthermore, especially during the early 1980s, when the priority was to get a stagnant economy moving again, neither the EPB nor anyone else in the Chun administration paid very much attention to fostering competition. Rather, as already suggested, the new law was seen more as a vehicle for regulating price increases (Chang 1996) than regulating competition. During the period 1981-90, though the KFTC investigated a total of more than 5,000 cases of conduct alleged to be in violation of the KAA (Yoo S. 2000, from data reported in KFTC annual reports), little action was taken beyond issuing warnings to the putative offenders.

Moreover, major exemptions to the provisions directed against the power of the chaebol reduced the potency of the law. For example, the limitation on the acquisition of equity ownership in nonaffiliated firms did not apply if a "large business group" (one of the 30 designated groups) acquired shares of other firms under certain laws (e.g., the Manufacturing Development Law or the Tax Exemption Law). Also, if a capital investment were made to maintain a technological cooperation relationship or if the KFTC were to determine that a capital investment by a large business group was necessary to strengthen the international competitiveness of a "priority sector" as designated by presidential decree, the investment would be permitted. Thus, the provision in the KFTC designed to keep the chaebol from entering new activities was all but neutralized if any of these exceptions could be invoked. Also, most practices that might violate the KAA were exempt from the law if they were carried out in response to other regulatory statutes. Finally, some sectors were exempt from coverage by the KAA.

More generally, the law failed to address a core aspect of the chaebol issue—that by virtue of their size and family connections, these groups wielded influence beyond that created by market dominance. In other words, the power of the groups derived not from market power so much as political power. The KAA, even had it been more rigorously enforced to reduce market power, would not necessarily have been effective in reducing the power of the groups exercised through political channels.

A second major reform undertaken during the early Chun years at the recommendation of Kim Jae-ik was privatization of the banking system, whereby almost all banks that had been put under government ownership in 1962 were returned to private ownership. A major justification for this action was to end what had become financial dualism in Korea: favored enterprises could receive credit on preferential and even subsidized terms while other firms had to go to so-called curb markets for financing, where loans typically bore very high rates of interest. But this reform did not achieve this goal, as financial dualism persisted; indeed, curb market finance seemed to be playing an increasingly important role in channeling savings into investment even after the banks were privatized (SaKong 1993). According to some sources (e.g., Kim Dae-jung 1996), even though the banks were privatized, they remained during the Chun years under effective government control in that they lent only to firms in favor with the government. In fact, the government continued after privatization to control the appointment of the top officers and directors of the banks. But the government did take steps to ensure that the banks did not come under chaebol control: no shareholder was allowed to own more than 8 percent of the equity of a bank, and measures were taken to disperse bank ownership widely.

Thus, the potential impact of the KAA and of banking privatization was blunted. Doubtless part of the reason was that as growth resumed, pressure for reform diminished. Alas for Chun, however, three events kept him from receiving much credit for the economic turnaround. They also brought to an end his efforts to instigate reform that might lead to greater economic fairness in Korea.

The first episode was a scandal in 1982 involving his friends and in-laws. The scandal centered around Chang Yong-ja, a female socialite, and her husband Lee Chol-hi, who was related to Chun's wife. Chang and Lee were found to have been operating in the curb market by lending to large groups and taking promissory notes from them. The two then sold the notes into the securities markets, so that the notes were not retired when the loans were repaid. This proved to be fraud on a large scale: the total value of the promissory notes they sold equaled about 13 percent of the total currency in circulation (Clifford 1994). When the scam was revealed, it was also found that Chang and Lee had used their relationship with Chun and his wife as their main selling point to induce firms to borrow from them. Although no hard evidence ever was uncovered to suggest that Chun or his wife were directly involved in the scandal, parties to the fraud did include a number of close relatives of Chun's wife as well as senior officials at banks who had been appointed by Chun and who were found to have been bribed by Chang to advance funds to companies to which Chang and Lee had made loans. The scandal created a widespread feeling within Korea that the Chun government was using its power in order to enrich cronies and relatives, and it brought to a halt (and made a mockery of) efforts by Chun and his economic advisors to launch an anticorruption drive.

The second event that undermined Chun was a tragedy that almost claimed his own life. In late 1983, in Rangoon, Myanmar, there was an assassination attempt against Chun, who was visiting with a number of top officials of his administration. The attempt was carried out by North Korean commandos, who planted a claymore mine near where Chun was to have sat during a welcoming ceremony. When the explosive was detonated, Chun in fact had not yet been seated and thus escaped unscathed. But Kim Jae-ik and sixteen others were killed, including Deputy Prime Minister So Sok-jun, an ally of Kim Jae-ik in seeking economic reform. Without this team, Chun had little sense of what economic strategy to pursue. Indeed, following the death of Kim Jae-ik, the movement for economic reform largely lost momentum and direction (Noland 2000). The public perception of Chun thereafter increasingly became one of a man who lacked both vision and principle.

Third was the bankruptcy of the Kukje group, which was at the time the sixth largest of the chaebol. The group was liquidated in 1985—a move that might, under different circumstances, have been positive both for Korea's economy and for Chun's political fortunes. One reason for the complications, as Kim Dae-jung has suggested (1996), was that the bankruptcy might have been caused at least in part by banks' unwillingness to advance funds to the group because its owners were in political disfavor. Kukje's chairman, Yang Chung-mo, in fact had openly supported the opposition party leader Kim Young-sam in National Assembly elections held earlier in that year. But the group was unquestionably in serious trouble. Like the other large chaebol, it had become a sprawling, diversified empire during the Park years, and some of its growth had resulted from taking over firms that were in difficulty. And also like other groups, in making these acquisitions it had relied on debt to an extent excessive even by Korean standards. Indeed, the group's inability to pay finance charges that were significantly in excess of cash flow was the main reason why it fell into distress in 1985. Although this type of problem was widespread among many groups, the Kukje group had a higher debt-to-equity ratio than any other chaebol in that year. Kukje was also notoriously poorly managed (Clifford 1994). For example, even as it was having trouble servicing its existing debt, it built an expensive headquarters building in downtown Seoul with financing obtained in the curb market. The office building neither created new revenue nor reduced costs, but the curb market financing added to what was already a suffocating level of debt service costs. Also, at a time when professional management skills were badly needed, high management positions in the group had been given to the chairman's several sons-in-law, none of whom was especially qualified to hold these jobs.

The shutting down of this group thus might also have been meant to send a signal to other chaebol that there were limits to the government's willingness to back the debt of a highly leveraged group. Indeed, following the closure of Kukje, the finance minister, Kim Mahn-je, summoned home Kim Woo-chung, the chairman of Daewoo, from a trip to Japan to warn him about what was regarded as excessive debt buildup at Daewoo. However, Kim Mahn-je also reportedly offered assurances to Kim Woo-chung that Kukje was the only group that would be forced into bankruptcy. Thus, the warning might have been perceived as hollow; Daewoo continued to rely as heavily as before on debt to finance expansion.

Even so, had Kukje been dismantled in an orderly fashion, the bankruptcy might have restored some of the credibility of the Chun government by sending a signal that the government was serious in seeking reform of the chaebol. Instead, Kukje's liquidation sent another strong whiff of scandal through Korea. In particular, the public strongly believed that the liquidation was designed to benefit cronies of Chun, notably the Hanil and Dongkuk groups whose chairmen were close to Chun. The liquidation was carried out largely in secret, and the process by which one group or another was awarded a piece of Kukje was not at all transparent. Prices paid by the Hanil and Dongkuk groups were apparently below what would have been realized in open transactions (Kirk 1999). Whatever the circumstances of the liquidation, in 1993 the Korean Constitutional Tribunal found that it had been unconstitutional.

Further Efforts to Reform the Chaebol

In spite of the setback created by the assassination of Kim Jae-ik, some carryover of the reform movement persisted into the later Chun years. Yet bad luck continued to follow Chun, as much of what reform as did take place was to have little effect—or, worse, unintended ill effects. For example, efforts were made in 1984 to carry out the recommendations of Kim Jae-ik's team about strengthening the system of credit supervision for large chaebol. Kim had advised the full implementation of measures first undertaken in 1974 to tighten credit to the largest groups by supervising the financial activities of these groups more strictly than those of other businesses. As had been the case earlier, the main concern in 1984 was that the debt levels of the largest chaebol were creating undue bankruptcy risk. The new measures were intended to freeze the total bank credit available to the largest 5 groups and to set ceilings on additional credit extended to the next 25 groups. Also, interest rates were deregulated on nonpolicy loans.

But, as in 1974, the new measures proved inadequate to achieve the stated goals. One main reason was that chaebol, especially the largest groups, began to raise funds from nonbank sources, often by establishing, acquiring, or expanding their own financial subsidiaries. By law, these had to be nonbank operations, because control of banks by the top chaebol was illegal (a group could hold up to but no more than a 5 percent share of the equity in a bank). However, during the 1980s the chaebol, and especially the top five groups, became increasingly adept at using nonbank financial subsidiaries to intermediate private savings into investment. Indeed, these subsidiaries began to act very much like banks regardless of their legal status. For example, six life insurance companies were then operating in Korea, three of which were under the control of a chaebol. These companies were subject to no financial disclosure requirements, but it can be assumed that in Korea, as in all countries, the life insurance business was characterized by low profitability and enormous cash flow. But, in most countries, low returns are accompanied by low risks, as life insurance firms hold highly diversified portfolios. In the case of the Korean chaebol-affiliated life insurance firms, about 60 to 70 percent of the products sold (their liabilities) were "endowment products"—financial instruments with perpetual market value more akin to savings accounts than to term insurance products, which pay off only on the death of the policyholder (and which can expire prior to his or her death). Moreover, almost half the assets of Korean life insurance companies were loans to corporations within the group that owned the life insurance company. Thus, Korea's life insurance companies came to be seen as private piggy banks for the chaebol that borrowed from the public in order to fund activities within the group.

In addition, during the 1980s the chaebol acquired or created merchant banks that engaged in underwriting primary capital market security issues, leasing operations, and short-term lending. These operations, like those of the life insurance companies, were not subject to prudential supervision by the Bank of Korea; and also like the life insurance companies, merchant bank lending was concentrated within the groups that owned them. Furthermore, the chaebol established or acquired other nonbank financial institutions that could serve as captive sources of finance. These included securities companies, whose function was to issue and guarantee bond issues by affiliated firms. The large chaebol also created investment trust companies (ITCs). The role of the latter somewhat resembled that of banks, in that both types of institutions take deposits and make loans. But unlike a bank, an ITC also operates somewhat like a mutual fund; in principle, it helps small investors to hold diversified portfolios of securities. In practice, chaebol-affiliated ITCs held stock only in other chaebol-affiliated firms. In later years, these ITCs would be associated with some of the worst abuses of funds invested by minority shareholders of these groups.

Some of these institutions had been acquired before the 1984 measures were enacted. For example, in 1963 Samsung had acquired a small life insurance company, the Dongbang Life Insurance Company. But after 1984 this company's activities were expanded significantly; in 1989 it was renamed Samsung Life Insurance. Likewise, a small fire and marine insurance company that had been acquired in 1958 by Samsung was enlarged following the 1984 measures. Symbolizing the growing role of finance in the Samsung group, during the mid-1980s both these companies moved into new office buildings in downtown Seoul designed to accommodate their increased business activities. In 1988 Samsung further enlarged its financial empire by acquiring a credit card company. And in 1992, what had been the Kukje Securities Company was acquired and subsequently enlarged and renamed Samsung Securities. Thus, by 1992 Samsung had emerged as a major supplier of nonbank financial services.

This pattern was repeated at most of the largest chaebol. By the early 1990s, for example, the Hyundai group had established or acquired no fewer than eight financial affiliates, including all the kinds described above. Likewise, Daewoo held affiliates corresponding to each of these types of institutions. In 1980 the LG group acquired Pusan Investment and Finance, a merchant bank that was later renamed LG Merchant Bank, and then in 1982 established Goldstar Investment and Finance, which was built into an investment bank. This group had already acquired insurance operations as well as a security firm in the 1970s, and during the 1980s the activities of these affiliates were enlarged. In 1985 the same group acquired Donghae Mutual Savings and Finance Corporation, and in 1987 Korean Express, a credit card issuer. In 1988 LG established LG Investment Trust Advisors.

In contrast to the other big five, the SK group was somewhat slow to get into the supply of financial services. This group established a life

Table 3.1 Share of assets of nonbank financial institutions owned by chaebol in Korea, 1990 (percent)

Type of institution	Share of top 5	Share of top 10	Share of top 30
Life insurance company	36.5	36.5	38.4
Marine and casualty insurance	28.0	41.4	44.5
Securities firm	26.3	36.5	63.1
Merchant bank	12.8	23.3	23.3
Short-term finance firm (ITC)	7.2	10.1	29.9

Source: Yoo S. and Lim (1997).

insurance company in 1988 and a securities firm only in 1995. It doubtless took these actions after observing the success of the other groups in obtaining finance for expansion from their subsidiaries.

Not all of the nonbank financial corporations in Korea were, however, under control of the chaebol. Table 3.1 reproduces estimates by Yoo Seongmin and Lim Young-jae (1997) of the total assets of each type of nonbank financial corporation held by the top 5, top 10, and top 30 chaebol respectively in 1990.

During the 1980s, as might be expected as a consequence of the expansion of nonbanking financial activities by chaebol, the shares of nonbanking financial institutions in Korea of both loans and deposits increased; the shares of deposit money banks correspondingly decreased, as did the shares of government financial development institutions (the Korea Development Bank, the Export-Import Bank of Korea, and the Long Term Credit Bank of Korea; see table 3.2). The share of both deposits and loans of life insurance companies grew especially quickly as the chaebol expanded these activities.

Samsung, Hyundai, and Daewoo became particularly adept at converting these firms into quasi-banks. Thus, the chaebol were able to use what amounted to captive nonbank financial firms to circumvent, or at least minimize the impact of, restrictions placed on bank lending that were intended to keep these groups from further dominating the Korean economy. For this reason, and also because the privatized banks exhibited clear preferences for lending to the chaebol despite the 1984 measures, the growth of the chaebol was hardly checked during the Chun period and the succeeding presidency of Roh Tae-woo. In fact, by some measures, the shares of the largest 5 and 30 groups in the Korean economy actually increased during the Chun years, though by other measures they decreased slightly. For example, the shares of Korean value added of the top 5 and top 30 groups in 1983 in the mining and manufacturing sectors (1983 is the first year for which such data are available, pursuant to passage of the Korean Monopoly Regulation and Fair Trade Act; see

Table 3.2 Shares of deposits and loans in Korean institutions, 1980, 1985, and 1990 (percent)

	1980	1985	1990
Deposit shares			
Deposit money banks	68.4	53.5	52.5
Development institutions	3.8	4.1	3.1
Nonbank financial institutions	27.8	42.4	44.4
(life insurance companies)	4.8	11.1	12.6
Loan shares			
Deposit money banks	63.3	58.4	59.0
Development institutions	14.8	10.8	8.3
Nonbank financial institutions	21.9	30.2	32.7
(life insurance companies)	3.1	5.9	10.0

Source: OECD, *OECD Economic Surveys: Korea 1998,* table 9; from Bank of Korea data.

above) were 16.7 and 32.4 percent. In 1987, at the end of the Chun presidency, these shares were 19.1 and 32.6 percent; thus, the big 5 groups increased their share of value added, but the share of the next 25 groups fell somewhat. But share of value of shipments of the big 5 between 1980 and 1988 fell slightly, from 22.6 to 22.0 percent, and the share of value of shipments of the top 30 groups fell from 40.4 to 38.2 percent. By the end of the Roh presidency in 1993, the share in value added of the big 5 chaebol had further increased to 20.3 percent, and the share of the top 30 had also increased, to 33.5 percent (implying that both the top 5 and the next 25 groups increased their share of GDP). These increases in the relative size of the chaebol indicate very substantial increases in the absolute size of the groups (Yoo S. and Lim 1997, from Korea Fair Trade Commission data).

One important role of nonbank financial institutions was to reinforce family control over the chaebol during this period of rapid expansion. These institutions became major shareholders in the nonfinancial affiliates of the groups, while themselves remaining under the firm control of the founding chairmen of the groups (or, in some cases, their descendants, when founders had died or had given up active control). To be sure, the chaebol-affiliated firms also had minority shareholders and, as the chaebol expanded, equity financing helped to underwrite the expansion; as a result, by the late 1980s total voting shares held by minority shareholders significantly exceeded those held by the founding families. But in no way did dilution of their share of ownership weaken the control of the founding families over their expanding empires. In fact, what the dilution often implied was that nonfamily shareholders bore risks for new ventures of the chaebol but did not enjoy the returns if they succeeded, because new ventures often were financed by debt that was guaranteed by more established subsidiaries. The established subsidiaries were, in part, owned by minority shareholders, but not the new ventures, which were family-owned. If the new venture panned out, all return on investment went to the family. If the new venture failed, loan guarantees would kick in, ensuring that part of the loss was borne by nonfamily shareholders.

In 1990, according to the KFTC, in the top 30 chaebol the total equity share of the founding families was 14.7 percent; internal shareholdings controlled by the families accounted for another 36.3 percent, giving the founding families an effective share of 45.4 percent.[2] This share would not change much over the next six years. The founding families' shares, direct or indirect, were higher in the top five chaebol: in 1990 the average direct equity share of the families averaged 13.3 percent but internal shareholdings were 36.3 percent, for a total share of 49.6 percent. Among the top five, however, the founding families' total (direct and indirect) shares varied substantially from group to group. At the top of the list, this combined share was 60.2 percent for Hyundai's Chung family; on the bottom, LG's Koo family held a combined share of only 35.2 percent.

In all of the large chaebol, in fact, and in spite of the provision of the KAA designed to prevent this, during the 1980s power became increasingly centralized in the office of the chairman or, as these offices were known formally, the "planning and coordination offices." The offices of the chairmen (in Korean, the *chongsu*) informally fulfilled the role of determining overall policy (see Yoo S. 1999, 2000). They typically employed small but well-trained teams of professional managers (many with MBAs from major US business schools) who assisted the chairman. According to the Organization for Economic Cooperation and Development (*OECD Economic Surveys: Korea 1998*), in all of the largest five groups, this office directly controlled the top management of affiliated firms. In principle, those firms each had a board of directors that was legally required to be independent and to report to all shareholders, not just the founding family shareholders.[3] In practice, the offices of the chairmen greatly impinged on the independence of these boards of directors; indeed, the boards typically acted almost as agents rubber-stamping the decisions taken by the chairmen.

---

2. Also, Yoon (1998) notes that these figures represent only the interests of family members in stock exchange-listed affiliates of the chaebol. Family control of unlisted nonaffiliates was considerably higher (upward of 65 percent), and these unlisted affiliates often held significant shares in listed affiliates. Thus the effect of this "pyramiding" (holding of shares of one company by another) gave the families greater control than might appear at first glance.

3. In the aftermath of the 1997 crisis, steps were taken to try to make directors of chaebol affiliates more independent of the offices of the chairmen, in particular requiring that "outside" directors be named who would in principle represent minority shareholders. See chapter 4.

In addition, in each of the large chaebol, there could be identified at least one affiliate (sometimes more) that held large blocks of shares of other affiliates (Yoo S. 2000). These "core" affiliates acted something like holding companies, even if they also engaged in other activities and therefore did not qualify as pure holding companies (as would have been illegal under the KAA). The type of subsidiary serving as the core varied from group to group; in most cases it was the oldest or at least one of the oldest subsidiaries. Thus, at Hyundai it was the original firm, the Hyundai Construction and Engineering Company; at Samsung it was the Samsung Corporation, the trading affiliate. Daewoo also used its trading affiliate— the Daewoo Corporation, the firm that had started as a textile trading operation—as the core subsidiary.

Vestiges of Industrial Policy Remain During the Chun and Roh Eras

Although the general philosophy of the Chun presidency and, even more overtly, the succeeding Roh presidency was to try to move Korea away from government planning toward the adoption of market-oriented policies, government planning was by no means wholly abandoned. Indeed, in what was one of the last of the major industrial policy initiatives, the drive to develop a Korean capacity to produce advanced semiconductor products (the Very Large Scale Integral Circuit or VLSIC project), we can see something of a reversion to the policies of the HCI drive. This project in fact arguably (and ironically) represented the most successful implementation of such policies.

The genesis of this project was in the first years of the Chun presidency. Chun himself had a strong interest in science and high technology, and he believed that Korea's future lay with the high-tech and science-based industries (see Kim Y. 1995). The Science and Technology Advisory Council was thus created as an office within the Blue House in 1980. Funds were increased for Koreans to study science and technology abroad at the graduate level, and more support was given science and technology at Korean universities as well. Between 1977 and 1988, the number of Koreans involved in research and development quintupled, rising from 11,700 to 56,500 (Kim Y. 1995). The government funded the establishment of an industrial park to be devoted to semiconductors and computers in 1982, contributing $60 million to help to create the Electronics and Telecommunications Research Institute in this park. In 1983, laws were passed restricting the importation of computers and related equipment at the low end of the market. They also restricted foreign direct investment in this sector unless the direct investment was in the form of a joint venture with a Korean firm. Joint ventures by foreign computer firms subsequently were created with Samsung, LG, Hyundai, and Daewoo. A 1985 law (the Industrial Development Law) had the intent of replacing policy loans with direct support of R&D as the main tool of industrial policy. In 1983 the Korean government helped to fund R&D projects involving more than 100 firms, by no means all of them chaebol affiliates.

The VLSIC project, when it got into full swing in 1987, came to take on many of the characteristics of the HCI drive. The goal was to enable Korean firms to become internationally competitive suppliers of a product embodying advanced technologies; for this to succeed, there had to be major front-end investment in developing the necessary technical capabilities as well as in building the necessary plant and equipment. Thus, as with earlier HCI projects, the government was involved in the creation of both human and physical capital.

As with the HCI projects, the VLSIC project did not actually represent the first entry by Korean firms into a new sector. The Samsung Semiconductor and Telecommunications Company had in fact begun to produce 64 kilobyte (64K) DRAMs in 1983. Samsung Semiconductor and Telecommunications Company had been created in 1974 when Samsung acquired Korea Semiconductor Company, a start-up venture by Dr. Kang Ki-dong, a Korean American scientist-entrepreneur who had gained experience at Motorola (Kim L. 1997). But until the early 1980s, Samsung produced relatively unsophisticated products.

Its entrance into the 64K DRAM market required a substantial leap forward in the underlying technology. Samsung at first sought to license the needed technology from foreign firms, but found no willing partners. Samsung then set up a task force in 1982, which ultimately identified small (and mostly struggling) US firms that possessed the technology it required. It proceeded to obtain that technology either by buying or licensing it from these companies or by buying the companies outright. A subsidiary was set up in California that successfully hired talent from several US firms. In 1984, Samsung introduced its first 64K chips to the market (Kim L. 1997). Hyundai and LG quickly followed; both were able to license the needed technology.

On the one hand, this manufacture represented a substantial accomplishment, because 64K DRAMs were very sophisticated items. On the other hand, at the time of their first production by Samsung, the world standard was no longer the 64K DRAM but rather the 256K DRAM, which had been introduced in 1982. Korean firms thus were producing an obsolete, albeit very sophisticated, product when they entered the sector in 1983. This continued to be the case when Samsung began to produce 256K DRAMs in 1984, shortly after the introduction of 1 megabyte (1000K, or 1M) DRAMs by the internationally leading firms in Japan and the United States. And when Samsung, followed by Hyundai, did introduce 1M DRAMs in 1986, the foreign competition had gone on to 4M DRAMs. Furthermore, foreign sources of technology had by then all but dried up. In addition, in 1986 Korean firms lost a series of lawsuits brought by US firms charging patent infringement for DRAM design. In response, the Korean government that year created a research consortium (the Electronics and Telecommunications Research Institute, or ETRI) made up of the three Korean DRAM producers—Samsung, Hyundai, and LG—and six Korean universities. The objective was to develop technologies to enable the Korean firms to produce 4M DRAMs (and beyond) without infringing foreign patents.

Thus, the ETRI-VLSIC project was meant not to launch Korean firms into a new market but rather to bring them up to speed relative to their international rivals. In this objective, the program succeeded; by late 1992, when international competitors introduced 64M DRAMs, Korean firms were able match them with chips of the same capacity. Likewise, in 1994 Korean firms were among the first to introduce 256M DRAMs—though not without outside help. By then Korean firms were involved in strategic alliances with international producers. Korean market leader Samsung, for example, participated in such alliances with eight US firms and six Japanese firms, among them industry leaders including Micron, Intel, Texas Instruments, IBM, AT&T, Toshiba, Sharp, NTT, and Fujitsu. LG and Hyundai also were in alliances with some of these same firms, albeit not as many as Samsung (a difference that helps to explain why Samsung was the industry leader). The interest of the foreign firms was not simply access to the Korean market, for which it was necessary to form alliances with Korean firms. They also wished to gain new sources of supply for vital components, thereby protecting their own production networks should existing suppliers be unable to meet delivery schedules or should other disruptions occur.

Exactly how much government assistance was involved in the ETRI-VLSIC project is not easily ascertained. One possible indicator of assistance was that in the years after 1985, the volume of preferential loans classified as "for equipment of export industry" rose dramatically (see table 3.3). This increase came as the total volume of preferential loans peaked in 1987 and then declined sharply in 1988, when interest rates were partially deregulated. Whether the former loans were largely directed toward the VLSIC project is not something that I have been able to verify, but it is a reasonable surmise (and, if correct, would seem to belie the claim of at least certain Korean authors—e.g., Sohn, Yang, and Yim 1998—that the development of the semiconductor sector in Korea was funded completely privately).

Again, government assistance necessarily was selective, because of the scale of the undertaking. The major beneficiaries of this program were three of the largest chaebol: Hyundai, Samsung, and LG. Ultimately Samsung emerged as the world's largest producer of DRAMs. For a time, Hyundai became number one after it took over the semiconductor division of LG following the 1997 financial crisis. At that time, Hyundai could in fact

Table 3.3 Preferential loans in Korea for "equipment of export industry" and total preferential loans, 1985-90
(billions of won)

	Preferential loans for equipment of export industry	Total preferential loans	Ratio of loans for equipment of export industry to total preferential loans
1985	595.2	4,690.7	0.13
1986	1,866.9	6,366.4	0.29
1987	2,416.5	5,904.0	0.41
1988	2,725.8	5,003.5	0.54
1989	2,905.0	5,340.5	0.54
1990	3,015.0	5,986.1	0.50

Sources: Krueger and Yoo (2001, table 3), and author's calculations; from Bank of Korea data.

claim to be the world's largest builder of both ships and chips; unfortunately, these operations came close to bankrupting the group, which goes to show that being number one is not always what it is cracked up to be.

Although the VLSIC project was in some ways like the earlier HCI drive, there were differences as well. As already noted, the main initiative for the undertaking came from the three principal firms and not the government. Indeed, according to Sohn Chan-hyun, Yang Jun-sok, and Yim Hyo-sung (1998), government planners in the EPB were initially reluctant to support a venture by Korean firms into the DRAM business, which the planners saw as excessively risky given that production was then dominated by a few large American and Japanese firms (indeed, in the United States there was much hand-wringing over what was then perceived as growing Japanese preeminence in this area; some American analysts in the 1980s described these devices as "technology drivers," meaning that dominance in producing DRAMs was key to further technological progress in the semiconductor sector).[4] Thus, no subsidies other than those for R&D were given to semiconductors in the early years of the Chun presidency. It was only after these firms had demonstrated some measure of success that further government backing came. Furthermore, once the VLSIC project did get under way, by most accounts private money was put at risk, unlike during the HCI period.[5]

---

4. In the United States a government-sponsored consortium, SEMATECH, was therefore organized to reassert US dominance in the manufacture of DRAMs.

5. On this point, however, there is some conflict in published accounts of the project, which in fact tend to be a bit sketchy. Amsden (1989) claims that this undertaking had subsidies, some of them nontransparent; Sohn, Yang, and Yim (1998) emphasize the role of private capital and claim that government assistance was minimal. Neither account

But even though Korean firms did succeed in becoming large producers of DRAMs, they never became dominant producers. Indeed, by the time they achieved full-scale operations and had caught up technologically with rivals in Japan and the United States, there were numerous international competitors supplying state-of-the-art DRAMs, including some based in other Asian markets (notably Taiwan and Malaysia). Also, by the early 1990s it was becoming clear that claims for a pivotal role of DRAMs as so-called technology drivers were quite exaggerated. Instead, DRAMs were fast evolving into a high-tech commodity item that would increasingly be sold on the basis of price rather than advanced technological features—even though the product was upgraded during the 1990s, with individual microchips packing more and more memory.

Notwithstanding these unforeseen events, Korea's venture into semiconductors must be rated a qualified success. By 1993, only a decade after Korean firms entered the market for DRAMs and just six years after the VLSIC project began, Korea was exporting more than $7.7 billion of DRAMs, and Korea's share of the DRAM market was close to 20 percent in both the United States and Europe (Sohn, Yang, and Yim 1998). In this growth, a 1991 agreement between the United States and Japan on DRAMs, whereby a floor price was set on Japanese DRAMs exported to the United States, benefited Korean firms significantly. Korean producers were able to gain US market share by selling below the floor price.

One of the firms in the VLSIC project, Samsung, has garnered very high profits throughout the 1990s from semiconductor sales, especially during periods when demand was growing faster than supply. Some analysts believe that most of Samsung's profits during the 1990s came from electronics, relying largely on semiconductor manufacture or manufacture of products employing semiconductors. Samsung has emerged as one of the world's technological leaders in this sector, and profits from its electronics business doubtless were instrumental in enabling the group to remain financially sound during the 1997-98 crisis, unlike several other of the large groups. Hyundai and LG never were to experience similar success. Indeed, when the semiconductor operations of these two firms were merged following the 1997 crisis, the resulting firm (now named Hynix) quickly became a problem child; in an earlier time, it would have been termed an "unsound firm." (The story of Hynix is taken up further in chapter 5.)

---

offers quantitative estimates of either the amount of private capital involved or the amount of public subsidy.

On the basis of the indirect evidence (the rise in preferential loans for equipment of export industry noted in the text and table 3.3), I find Amsden's version most credible (otherwise, where did these loans go?), but the extent of government sponsorship of the VLSIC project can never be fully known.

Despite the problems of Hyundai and LG, the semiconductor venture was indicative of Korea's emergence as a center of high technology activity during the 1980s and 1990s. Between the early years of the Chun presidency and the final years of the Roh presidency, the amount of research and development done in Korea increased dramatically: R&D as a percentage of GDP rose from 0.81 percent in 1981 to 2.17 percent in 1992. Also, the number of Korean students acquiring foreign graduate degrees in technical subjects shot up. During this time, real GDP more than quintupled, so that R&D in fact increased more than 15-fold. Furthermore, whereas in 1981 R&D in Korea was about 55 percent government funded, by 1992 it was 82 percent funded by private firms.

One consequence of these transformations has been that in 2002, one of the most positive aspects of Korea is prowess in information technology, not only because Korean firms are at the forefront in producing it but also because Koreans are leaders in using it. This prowess owes much to the turn toward high technology and science-based activity favored by Chun Doo-hwan during his years as president and advanced further by his successor (and co-conspirator) Roh Tae-woo.

In matters other than the VLSIC project, the Korean government was still in the industrial policy business during the Chun and Roh years; in fact, some projects persisted into Kim Young-sam's presidency, when industrial policy was formally ended. For example, responding to large losses being incurred by Korean motor vehicle manufacturers (despite heavy protection from imports) following the second oil shock of 1979, the government in the early 1980s attempted to create mergers among what were then six manufacturers. The idea was to create companies producing at the minimum efficient scale, which no Korean manufacturer had achieved by 1980. To this end, the government announced in late 1981 a program whereby Hyundai Motor Company was to acquire the troubled automotive division of Daewoo and, in exchange, Hyundai was to yield its power generation business to Daewoo. (This type of "big deal" that forced trading of operations among the chaebol would be attempted again following the 1997 crisis.) At the same time, Kia was to acquire Dong-A, a manufacturer of light trucks, buses, and minivans. In both cases, the firms would be given national monopolies—Hyundai's for passenger cars and Kia's for light trucks, buses, and minivans—which were meant to last until 1989. The first of these deals fell through because Daewoo believed that its automotive operation was more valuable than Hyundai's power generation business, and no scheme of compensation for the difference in value could be agreed on. Kia did acquire Dong-A and Hyundai exited the truck business, leaving it as a monopoly to Kia. Thus, the passenger car business was a duopoly, while light trucks was a monopoly. Sohn, Yang, and Yim (1998) note that the outcome was doubtless favorable in the passenger car market, which in Korea was subject to heavy import protection; they surmise that with no effective competition in this market, Hyundai likely would have produced an inferior product at an exorbitant price.

As it happened, even facing some domestic competition Hyundai was able to establish a high-volume manufacturing operation for subcompact cars. This enabled Hyundai, with limited success, to begin exporting to the United States, where incumbent US firms largely had exited the subcompact market (as indeed had Japanese exporters). Thus, the intended goal of the policy—that Hyundai create the scale and efficiency seen as necessary to become an effective international competitor—was achieved without a monopoly ever being created. Furthermore, Hyundai's success actually served as something of a shot in the arm to Daewoo Motors, which implemented measures personally supervised by chairman Kim Woo-chung to increase its own scale of operation, improve its efficiency, and improve the quality of its product (Kim L. 1997).

In 1987, the 1981 policy measures were revised to increase competition in the Korean motor vehicle industry. The monopoly granted Kia was allowed to expire, and Hyundai reentered the light commercial vehicle market and by 1993 had overtaken Kia to become the market leader. Kia in turn introduced the Sephia automobile in 1992, thus reentering the passenger car business.

In 1992, the final year of the Roh presidency, the government announced the XC-5 project, intended to put Korean firms into the ranks of top international car manufacturers. In 1994 this program was extended under what was known as the XC-5 program, which was designed to help Korean companies develop the expertise needed to independently develop automotive technology. Korean firms were still relying on foreign technology and imported components to some significant degree at that time, although in 1994 Hyundai introduced an "all-Korean" car—that is, one that contained no foreign components and had an engine of Korean design.

Also in 1992, Samsung was given permission to enter the passenger car business under authority granted to the KFTC the year before. This move was to prove to be a mistake for Samsung, as is detailed later, but the permission was very welcome to the chairman of the Samsung group, Lee Kung-hee, who had taken over in 1987 following the death of his father, Samsung founding chairman Lee Byung-chol. Lee Kung-hee had sought for several years to enter this sector and had been frustrated by the government's refusal. Success in creating capacity in the automotive sector is not, however, the same as creating demand; demand for cars in Korea during the late 1980s and early 1990s did grow rapidly—but not as fast as supply. This might have been a warning signal, but it went unheeded. Indeed, Samsung executives whom I interviewed told me that chairman Lee Kung-hee's own advisors counseled against Samsung's entry into the automotive sector, but he overruled them.

In fact, as Korea entered into the 1990s, some wrong turns were taken and a number of warning signals went unheeded. We turn to this matter next.

Mistakes Mount in the Second Half
of Roh Tae-woo's Presidency

For all of the heavy-handedness of the Chun years, they were marked by generally good macroeconomic management and a rising performance of the Korean economy, once growth resumed in 1982. This trend seemed to continue into the first years of the Roh presidency. Investment continued to be high and savings also rose, enabling a current account surplus. But as time progressed, this administration began to display economic mismanagement and increasingly poor economic performance, especially in its final three years. The main economic problems were that both inflation and a trade deficit reemerged. These were associated with an easing of credit in 1990 that was urged by the leaders of the chaebol but also was necessitated by large wage increases that were granted during the first years of Roh's presidency. In addition, the late Roh years, like those of his predecessor, were tainted by a number of scandals involving corruption; these would later lead to criminal charges being brought against Roh personally. The ultimate consequence was that Roh left office largely in disgrace.

While the GDP deflator was 16.4 percent during Chun's first year, that rate declined steadily, reaching a low of 2.8 percent in 1986. In 1987, Chun's final year, there was a slight rise in this deflator to 3.5 percent, which was worrying but not yet a problem. In the first year of the Roh presidency, 1988, the deflator rose further to 5.9 percent. Rising inflation arguably was indirectly one result of moves toward democracy undertaken in Korea in the late 1980s. When it was announced in 1987 that presidential elections would be held, only slightly more than 15 percent of all Korean workers belonged to unions, and there was much feeling across the country that unions were not effective in securing wage increases. But under a more democratic government, union leaders suddenly felt emboldened to make wage demands without risking reprisal. Thus, whereas in 1984-86 there had been slightly more than 200 labor disputes per year, the number jumped above 3,700 in 1987. Furthermore, whereas in the earlier years less than 23 percent of the disputes had been over wage increases, in 1987 this percentage surged to more than 70 percent. In a word, the Korean labor movement became militant as Korea democratized. In 1988 the number of disputes decline somewhat, to 1,873, about half over wage increases; but many of these resulted in strikes, some of which turned violent. The average real wage increase in manufacturing began to creep upward, from 6.2 percent in 1986 to 8.3 percent in 1987 and to 11.7 percent in 1988. At the same time, however, the marginal productivity of labor in manufacturing dropped from 8.8 percent in 1986 to 5.4 percent in 1987, and then to barely more than 1 percent in 1988, so that cost push inflation was now arguably occurring in Korea. Meanwhile, the unionization rate in Korea increased, rising to 17.3 percent in 1987 and 22.0 percent in 1988.

These developments alarmed Roh's highly competent deputy prime minister and head of the EPB, Cho Soon. Cho's priority became tackling the inflation problem by contracting the rate of credit expansion and cutting back on most preferential loans; as a result, all such loans except those to acquire export machinery were eliminated. These measures had some positive effect: the GDP deflator fell to 5.2 percent in 1989, despite continuing real wage increases that now were greatly outstripping marginal productivity increases in the manufacturing sector (the real wage increase was 18.3 percent in 1989, whereas the marginal productivity of labor actually fell by about 0.5 percent). But real growth also fell, from more than 12 percent in 1988 to slightly under 7 percent in 1989.

Cho's plan also called for interest rate deregulation and for expansion of money and bond markets at unregulated interest rates. Had the plan been implemented, one likely outcome would have been some short-term pain (e.g., unemployment increases and possibly bankruptcies of some firms). It might also have resulted in more responsible demands from unions than those that were voiced at the time (and were to reemerge in the aftermath of the financial crisis in 1998). But the credit squeeze cut into the expansionary aspirations of the large chaebol, whose leaders heavily backed Roh's Democratic Liberal Party, as well as into the aspirations of the labor leaders, and in April 1990 both business and labor leaders persuaded Roh to oust Cho and most of his economic team. Thereafter, the emphasis was on "growth first," meaning mostly that rapid credit expansion resumed. Plans to deregulate interest rates were put on hold. Interest rates fell on nonpreferential credit, including curb rates, which went from 23.7 percent in 1989 to 20.6 percent in 1990, while the GDP deflator rose during the same period from 5.2 to 10.6 percent (and thus the real rate of interest on curb loans fell). However, on most outstanding loans to the chaebol, nominal interest rates were held constant, so that for them the real rate of interest actually fell less. Inflation continued to be high in 1991, with the GDP deflator reaching 10.9 percent; and according to an estimate by the Lucky Goldstar Research Institute (affiliated with the LG Group, and cited in Kim Dae-jung 1996), the rate of inflation on the consumer goods bought most often by low- to middle-income Koreans rose to almost 17 percent in that year.

Most of the credit expansion between 1990 and 1992 took place in nonbank financial institutions. This was enabled by an infusion in 1991 of 3 trillion won into investment trust companies, which as we have seen were to a large extent captive financial arms of the chaebol.[6] The

---

6. Cho Soon in the meantime had been named as governor of the Bank of Korea, a demotion from his previous position. He resisted the infusion to the ITCs, which was in fact illegal, and was sacked soon thereafter. Cho's removal from the governorship of the Bank of Korea resulted in renewed calls for central bank independence. He subsequently became mayor of Seoul.

share of nonbank financial institutions of deposits in Korea rose from 59 percent at the beginning of Roh's presidency in 1987 to 64.6 percent in 1989 and to 65.9 percent in 1991, while banks' share of deposits fell from 41 percent in 1987 to 34.1 percent in 1991 (data from Bank of Korea, *Monthly Bulletin*, various issues). This trend toward the rise of nonbank financial institutions had started however before the policy change of 1990.

Whereas during the Chun presidency Korea's balance of trade had improved markedly as inflation came down, leading in 1986 to a significant balance of trade surplus, in 1989 this surplus dropped to just over $5 billion. Then, in the following year, the current account turned negative by more than $2 billion. Belatedly, the wor exchange rate began to depreciate, stabilizing at about 790 won to the dollar in 1992. The deterioration of the Korean current account might have been exacerbated somewhat by what Kim Dae-jung calls "a silly effort to please the American government" (1996, 150), whereby the Korean government called for Korean trading companies to increase imports of American-made and other foreign-made goods, mostly luxury items.

As a consequence of the easing of credit, real growth at first rose to 9.3 percent in 1990; but as inflationary pressures continued to mount, it declined to 8.4 percent in 1991 and then dropped to 4.7 percent in 1992 (Bank of Korea, *Monthly Bulletin*, various issues). The slowdown in 1992 was termed in Korea a "growth recession." The overall effects of the policies followed by Roh thus proved to be a spurt of growth, accompanied by problems of rising inflation and a growing trade deficit that made the growth spurt extremely short-lived.

Throughout the Roh years there also occurred a land and real estate bubble, with land prices rising by an average of almost 25 percent per year between 1987 and 1991 but stabilizing in 1992 (data from Ministry of Construction, as reported in Kim Dae-jung 1996, table 7.1). The winners during the upswing were the large chaebol that owned large amounts of land in Korea, particularly in urban areas. Some chaebol were actively involved in speculation, and some spectacular capital gains were made by certain of these groups. For example, the Lotte group bought land in Seoul for 80 billion won in 1988 and sold it for more than 1,000 billion won three years later. Much of the gains by other groups came simply from selling at high prices land that they had previously held. In May 1992, Roh made a gesture toward cracking down on land speculation by the large business groups by enacting a measure requiring the chaebol to sell all land not used for business purposes. Yet this measure backfired, at least as far as public opinion was concerned, because it induced the top 30 chaebol to sell upwards of 60,000 acres of land at large capital gains, with some of this land bought by government agencies.

Adding to Roh's mounting unpopularity was the performance of the Korean stock market and the government's efforts to stabilize it. In the first year of his presidency, the Korean stock market index rose from 630.1 to over 1000, during which time many ordinary Koreans bought stocks. But the market subsequently crashed down to the mid-600s, where it stayed for the remainder of his term. Over the five years of his presidency, the market thus was stagnant in nominal terms—but stagnation of course implied substantial real losses even to investors that held stocks at the beginning of the 1987 bubble, not to mention those that acquired stocks after prices began to rise. In late 1989, in a failed bid to reverse a falling market, the government ordered investment trust companies to borrow money to buy stocks. The government subsequently used public money to partially compensate those ITCs that had taken losses in an arrangement that excluded small investors. When word of this spread, crowds ransacked the Korean stock exchange and the offices of some large brokers. Despite the partial bailout, the balance sheets of the ITCs were severely damaged.

As if matters were not bad enough for the Roh Tae-woo administration, beginning in late 1991, as the administration was about to enter its fifth year (with the next presidential election only a year away), a number of corruption scandals became public that further tainted what had already become a widely unpopular presidency. The biggest of these involved Hyundai, whose chairman, Chung Ju-yung, disclosed that he had contributed 25 billion won—then worth about $30 million—to Roh for political favors. This disclosure was apparently in retaliation for the Roh government's having assessed Chung some $180 million in taxes when he began to pass some of his assets to his sons. Stories of further corruption then multiplied. It was alleged in the press, for example, that the Hanbo group had used a slush fund held in bank accounts under false names to buy favor with the Korea Land Development Corporation, a state-owned enterprise. Journalists also published allegations of kickbacks to the president associated with the 1989 stock market bailout.

Corruption had of course long been one of the darker sides of the whole Korean economic miracle, and Korea had already been through a number of scandals including the Chang/Lee scam of the early 1980s. What made the corruption scandals of the early 1990s different was that with newfound freedom of the press on the rise and the military dictatorship now four years in the past, stories about corruption were spreading more openly. Also, at least in some cases, these stories were better corroborated than those told earlier. Whether Roh was actually significantly more corrupt than his predecessors is not clear.[7] Perceptions that the Park Chung-hee regime was corrupt had been behind at least some of the unrest in 1979, and scandals had plagued Chun throughout his tenure as president. But during the Park and Chun years, news of scandals

---

7. Chun and Roh were both convicted of corruption charges in 1997; see chapter 4.

spread mostly by word of mouth, with open criticism of corrupt behavior largely off-limits to the Korean press. In his final years in office, in contrast, Roh was subject to constant criticism in the press.[8]

In 1991, the earlier plan to deregulate interest rates was resurrected, as part of a four-phase program that also included other financial liberalization measures. However, the first phase was a modest one, covering the deregulation of only certain short-term rates. A second phase, mandating the deregulation of rates on all loans (except policy loans), as well as rates on corporate bonds and long-term deposits, was scheduled for 1993, after the presidential elections. The third and fourth phases were slated for 1996 and 1999, and their implementation was conditional on certain goals having been met (e.g., price stability). Monetary expansion was reined in to bring inflation under control, but arguably this restriction led to the "growth recession" of 1992 that turned public opinion against Roh. Had Roh simply allowed the policies of Cho to run their course, the case is strong that inflation would have been contained by 1990 so that growth could have resumed; but this is not what Roh chose to do.

In 1991 a number of measures meant to rein in the chaebol were also introduced. In an effort to contain the continuing diversification of these groups, each group was required to designate core companies and sectors, which had to be approved by the KFTC. Bank lending to noncore subsidiaries was subject to restrictions meant to discourage the chaebol from creating new subsidiaries operating in new sectors. However, in spite of these policies, the chaebol continued to diversify, not least because the KFTC was quite generous in what industries and sectors it allowed to be designated as "core" and permitted the list to be expanded every three years. Also, as described earlier in this chapter, the chaebol held nonbank financial subsidiaries from which loans could be raised; hence the restriction of bank credit to noncore chaebol affiliates did not necessarily prevent these affiliates from obtaining financing. Between 1991 and 1997, the total number of subsidiaries of the top 30 chaebol in fact increased from 557 to 819.

Moreover, the chaebol continued to use debt financing as they continued to increase capacity. Indeed, what was to be a long streak of expansion by these groups was launched with the easing of credit in early 1990 following the departure of Cho Soon from the government. Roh cannot be entirely blamed for this, of course, because most of this expansion took place during the presidency of Kim Young-sam; but it did begin under Roh.

---

8. Also, popular books were being published that were highly critical of Roh; for example, Kim T. (1991), which is cited by Kim Dae-jung (1996).

Taking Stock, to See the Forest Through the Trees

This book is not really meant to be an economic history of Korea. Rather, its focus is a specific problem: especially in the wake of the 1997 crisis and subsequent recession, and in spite of the reforms and growth of the economy that followed the period of crisis and recession, some of Korea's largest groups of firms remain quite unhealthy. This is an appropriate point to step slightly back and ask what has been revealed about this problem thus far.

In brief: the largest chaebol expanded at a rapid pace, largely financing the expansion with what was essentially other people's money (i.e., not the money of the families that controlled the groups). Because some of this money was advanced on preferential terms (i.e., there were elements of subsidy), this expansion, even though it created much benefit for the Korean people, also created much dissatisfaction. Discontent erupted because so much favoritism was shown to a small group of people—the owners of the chaebol. But beyond fomenting discontent, as events were to prove, this expansion also created enormous risk.

As has already been mentioned, some of the expansion resulted in overcapacity. But what precisely does "overcapacity" mean? On the most fundamental level, it occurs when the return on capital (the plant, equipment, and financial working capital needed to create economic undertakings) is not sufficiently large to warrant incurring the cost of that capital. Elementary economic theory holds that all other things being equal, if capacity is added to increase the supply of a good or service offered in a market, a point will eventually be reached at which there is a diminishing marginal return on the capital invested to create that capacity. The capital to be invested is optimal when the marginal return on capital equals the marginal cost of the capital. If we take as a working assumption that the supply of funds for investment is large relative to the funds required to finance a single undertaking, this cost is not affected by the undertaking and can be assumed to be constant. And if the return to capital declines as capital accumulates but the cost is constant, the optimum in fact will eventually be reached as capacity is expanded. Furthermore, because of diminishing marginal returns, if capital continues to be added once this optimum is reached, adding yet more capacity will result in the marginal return falling below the cost of capital, making the net return on this additional capital (marginal return on the capital minus its cost) negative. At this point, capacity can be termed "excess."[9]

---

9. How do supply and demand of the goods or services produced using this capital fit into the story? As capital is added, supply is increased: all other things being equal, this increase in supply drives down the price of the good or service so that the unit profit realized on selling the good or service is reduced. It is primarily for this reason that there is a diminishing marginal return on capital.

The above statements apply to one market. As a practical matter, of course, there might be excess capacity in one market but inadequate capacity in some other market, as apparently happened in Korea in the later years of the HCI drive.[10] In principle, an efficient capital market would prevent such imbalances from arising, because if the return on capital in one market (or, more precisely, on capital invested in the sector that supplies that market) were to be higher than in some other market, the capital market should stop advancing funds for expansion of capacity in the former and direct these funds toward the latter. Indeed, if capital markets were globally efficient (in the sense that financial institutions held complete and accurate information about marginal rates of return on capital in all markets globally), there never would be a differential between marginal rates of return on capital in different markets. For Korea during the 1960s, 1970s, and 1980s, there were new markets into which Korean firms could enter and earn higher returns than on existing operations. That they actually did so was a function of both capital market efficiency and at least some intelligent government planning.

But the emerging problem in Korea in 1992, when Roh Tae-woo stepped down and was replaced by a new president, Kim Young-sam, was not simply one of overcapacity per se. Overcapacity creates difficulties irrespective of how it has been financed. But in the case of the chaebol, as we have already seen, the bulk of new capital formation was financed by debt, and debt financing can create additional problems. The reason has to do with the cyclical nature of demand for many products and services. Debt financing results in a recurring interest cost being incurred by the debt holder—the firm that must be paid whether or not the capital financed by the debt generates enough cash to pay that cost. In fact, the recurring cost may be somewhat greater than that of interest charges alone, because the lender might demand some repayment of principle on the loan; the total charges that must be repaid on a recurring basis are termed the "service costs" of the debt. Obviously, the service costs of debt increase with the amount of debt that is incurred. If the interest rate is fixed, the service cost is invariant when the amount of debt is held constant. But even if the rate of interest is adjustable, the service cost of debt does not necessarily adjust to the firm's rising or falling revenue.

From a corporate point of view, the use of debt to finance capacity expansion can be attractive largely because debt service costs, or at least the interest component of these costs, receive favorable tax treatment. For tax purposes, interests costs are deductible, and that deductibility enables part of the cost to be borne in essence by the public treasury.

---

10. Such imbalance occurs because the capital used to create supply in one market—e.g., steel—is specialized and cannot be used to supply a different market, such as that for petrochemicals.

The same is not true if capacity is financed, say, entirely through equity. Rather than being tax deductible, dividend payments to shareholders, which represent the "costs" of equity from the corporation's point of view, are taxable. From the viewpoint of existing shareholders, it can thus be preferable for new capacity to be financed by debt rather than by new equity,[11] if this equity is raised from persons other than the existing shareholders. This preference was especially strong in Korea, where the costs of debt were in effect doubly subsidized by the government (interest rates were below market, and interest payments were tax deductible as well).

However, because of the cyclical nature of earnings, the argument in favor of debt over equity finance has certain limits. If, in a cyclical downturn, return on capital temporarily diminishes because income falls, dividend payments on equity can be reduced or even eliminated if necessary to preserve the financial health of the firm. But service costs of debt must still be paid. Thus, in a prolonged downturn, if debt levels are too high the costs of servicing the debt can endanger the financial health of the firm or indeed drive it into bankruptcy, even if the firm is viable in the long run.

What level of debt is too high? There is really no absolute answer to this question (see Krueger and Yoo 2002). But a partial answer is that it depends both on how high is the firm's overall rate of return to capital and on how cyclical is the underlying market. As the overall rate of return on capital declines, the level of debt that is "too high," in the sense that it creates unacceptable risks to the firm, also declines; thus, other things being equal, a firm whose overall return on capital is low should not be as leveraged (i.e., have as high a debt-to-equity ratio) as a firm whose overall rate of return on capital is high. Also, the greater the fluctuation of demand (i.e., statistically speaking, the greater the variance of demand at any given price), the greater becomes the riskiness to the firm of high levels of debt.

Given these definitions, were the debt levels of the chaebol in the early 1990s too high? Again, this is a question that is difficult to answer in an absolute sense. But what can be said with certainty is that by 1993, Korea was no longer a developing country (where return on capital for almost any undertaking would by high) but rather was rapidly becoming an advanced country in which rates of return on capital almost surely were, at the margin, diminishing. Thus, conditions were such that the risks of debt financing were rising.[12] Indeed, this danger had been recognized by

---

11. Assuming that the marginal return on that capital exceeds the after-tax cost of the debt!

12. Hsieh (1997) has econometrically estimated trends in the real rental price of capital in Korea between 1966 and 1990; he finds that this price has declined at an average annual rate of –5.3 percent over that time. The real rental price of capital is the marginal product on capital, and this decline indicates a falling rate of return on capital.

the Chun regime 10 years earlier, when efforts had been made to force the chaebol to reduce leverage.

Furthermore, as the chaebol grew during the 1980s and 1990s, it became a common practice for one affiliate within a group to guarantee the debt of other affiliates. Under some circumstances, this might have been rational. For example, a group might have wanted to enter a new undertaking with expected positive return but where entry was subject to considerable start-up risk—that is, uncertainties were such that there was significant probability that costs might be larger than expected or revenues lower than expected. In such a case, even if the expected rate of return on the undertaking was positive, the variance around this positive expectation would be large. Thus, risk of bankruptcy might be significant even if expected returns were positive. Under these circumstances, a guarantee by a subsidiary in the same group acting as a cash cow might have been required by banks as a condition for loans to the new undertaking. In effect, the guarantee was a financial option by which the banks mitigated bankruptcy risk by transferring it to owners.[13]

From the owner's point of view, this could be perfectly rational. Theory and empirical evidence suggest that a rational decision maker's (or investor's) aversion to risk should decrease as a function of the net wealth of the decision maker or, equivalently, that willingness to take risks should increase with the wealth of the decision makers.[14] The reasoning is simple: given a choice as to whether to commit a sum of money to a risky undertaking where that sum is a significant portion of the decision maker's net worth, the decision maker might be well advised to walk away from the undertaking, even if the expected value of the undertaking is positive, because an unfavorable outcome would be ruinous even if the probability of such an outcome is low.

But, by contrast, if the decision maker were to have a higher net worth, so that failure would not be ruinous, then he or she is better placed to take a chance on the favorable outcome. Thus, by this reasoning, as the chaebol and their owners accumulated wealth, they indeed should have become more willing to take risks that were not subject to any sort of government guarantee, a conclusion that in turn suggests that cross-guarantees could be useful instruments. This willingness should nonetheless have been bounded; chaebol owners should have been willing to take risks on new undertakings where the probabilities favored outcomes that would increase the wealth of the group and owner, but not have been willing to

---

13. This option can create a problem of moral hazard, as explained later in this chapter. Banks might, if given such guarantees, advance loans to projects that are fundamentally unsound.

14. The classic work expounding both the theory and empirical evidence pertaining to the relationship between wealth and a decision maker's risk aversion is Raiffa and Schlaiffer (1968).

enter into undertakings that risked bankrupting the whole group. In fact, however, the owners did take such risks—for example, by using listed affiliates to guarantee loans of riskier unlisted affiliates. The effect was to transfer risk from the owners to minority shareholders of the listed affiliates, while ensuring that these minority shareholders did not share in the returns of the unlisted affiliates, when and if such returns were realized (see Friedman, Johnson, and Mitton 2002).

In practice, this bound often seemed to be ignored. Yoon Bong-joon (1998) argues that debt guarantees became so pervasive that if any affiliate of a chaebol were to have become bankrupt, the whole group would be in danger of being brought down by that bankruptcy. One consequence was that as bankruptcy risks mounted during the 1990s, the banks in some cases made what were in effect policy loans to weak affiliates of chaebol, fearing that if these weren't advanced, the whole of the loans to the chaebol were at risk and not simply the loans of the weak affiliates. Moreover, the banks in Korea were thus "evergreening" their loans to at least some chaebol affiliates (Krueger and Yoo 2001, 2002): that is, the banks were advancing loans where the proceeds were used for nothing more than paying debt-servicing charges. In effect, the subsidiary was "borrowing from Peter to pay Paul" or, even more accurately, "borrowing from Peter to pay Peter." In the aftermath of the 1997 crisis, the difference between a sound and a shaky group (e.g., between Samsung and Hyundai) was which dominated in the ensemble, the weak subsidiaries or the strong.

According to published statistics, the major chaebol did not actually increase their debt-to-equity ratios during the 1990s, but they maintained this ratio at levels that were very high by international standards while they continued to expand their operations. The average debt-to-equity ratio for the top 30 groups in 1989 was 4.21; this average rose slightly to 4.26 in 1993 but fell to 3.97 in 1994, according to KFTC reports. Moreover, there might have been additional debt in some of the groups that went unreported, so these figures may understate the true average ratios. Because the groups did expand, total debt held by them also expanded. According to KFTC data, the gross assets of the top 30 groups were 96.7 trillion won at the end of 1990; but these assets grew by more than 50 percent, to 156.7 trillion won, by the end of 1992 and to 199.5 trillion won by the end of 1994. By the time the crisis hit in 1997, the gross assets of these groups totaled 348.4 trillion won. Apparently, the chairmen of the chaebol figured that they could expand via debt financing indefinitely.

Thus, when Kim Young-sam was elected president in 1992, taking office in 1993, there was in fact a mounting problem in Korea: major business groups, already highly leveraged, were taking no steps to reduce their leverage but indeed were continuing to expand, with the result that rates of return on capital were almost surely, at the margin, diminishing. The clear implication was that the bankruptcy risk of the chaebol was, with time, rising. From the perspective of hindsight, this should have been seen as a major problem. But in 1993, it was a problem that few leaders in Korea took very seriously.

Why did the banks allow this to happen? The answer to this question does not seem to be, as some observers have suggested, that the banks were too small to be able to stand up to their borrowers. Stijn Claessens (1999) argues that the banking system in Korea was in fact quite concentrated, with six large banks controlling more than 50 percent of banking assets. Assets of each of these banks accounted for 10 percent or more of GDP; in other OECD nations, the very largest of banks has assets equal to no more than 5 percent of GDP.

One answer might simply be "habit." After all, by the mid-1980s the banks had been lending, massively, to the large chaebol for more than 15 years at the direction of the government. The accumulated experience of doing so was not wholly positive; loans often did go bad, and from the 1970s onward Korea's banks held significant portfolios of nonperforming loans. Rather than being cleaned up, the bad loans were kept on the books for years; and in the 1990s, those loans that should have been classified as nonperforming began to rise markedly.[15] For many Korean banks, revenues from banking barely covered costs because of interest rate regulation.[16] Bank owners might therefore have been expected to demand better performance from the banks, and policy reforms that would enable better performance. However, because the law prohibited any one shareholder from holding more than 4 percent of the equity of the bank, and because shareholders were not well organized, there was no strong constituency on the shareholders' side demanding either better performance or policy reform.

Furthermore, bank presidents and other top executives were appointed by the government and not by shareholders. As a result, according to Kim Dae-jung (1996, 100), "bank officers are not evaluated objectively—according to their managerial performance—but by their demonstrated sycophancy with government officials." Supporting the notion that habit figured in the behavior of Korean banks, and that there was very little incentive for them to improve themselves, is evidence that Korea's banks experienced *negative* total factor productivity growth during the 1980s

---

15. According to Kim Dae-jung (1996, table 8.1), the percentage of "abnormal" loans—i.e., those that probably should have been considered nonperforming or at least highly problematic but were carried on the books as though they were performing—was upwards of 25 percent of the total loans of the eight largest Korean banks even in 1988; the loans actually carried as "nonperforming" constituted 5.7 percent of all loans of these banks, a figure that was little changed as late as fall 1997.

16. To compensate for their losses, banks received special loans (at 3 percent nominal interest rates).

and 1990s (Nam 1999): that is, the output of the banks per unit of input actually declined.

But habit alone, however, does not satisfactorily explain the banks' behavior; after all, we are still left wondering how the bad habits began. To answer this last question, considerations of "moral hazard" must be introduced.[17] In the context of the banks in Korea (as well as elsewhere in the recent international finance literature), the idea of moral hazard is as follows: a bank or other financial institution makes loans to projects where the risk of default is unacceptably high, except that there exists a contract (which itself may or may not be "hidden") with the government to the effect that the government will bail the bank out in the event of default. If such a contract exists, the banks hold what amounts to a financial option that is given to them free of charge. If the loan proves to be performing, the bank collects the interest and other fees and eventually is repaid the principal. If the loan proves to be nonperforming, the bank recovers the principal. Thus, default risk is transferred to the government. Such an option, because it is granted free of charge but has value, is a government subsidy.[18] Like any subsidy, it can distort outcomes, because funds flow to projects subject to the subsidy, and these projects might not represent the best available use of the funds. In this context, the "moral hazard" is essentially the perverse incentive that is created by the implicit contract (or option) that gives rise to the implicit subsidy.

Closely related to this notion is the idea of being "too big to fail." Some firms or groups of firms might be deemed too big and important to fail, because failure would generate substantial unemployment and other undesirable outcomes that the government would prefer to avoid. Fear of contagion also played into this scenario: if one big group were to fail, others might follow. "Too big to fail" creates a problem of moral hazard if banks believe that the firms that are too big to be allowed to fail by the government are those that will be bailed out in the event of bankruptcy. The government thus gives the firm an implicit insurance policy against bankruptcy, at no cost to the firms' owners. Effectively, the bankruptcy risk is passed on to society at large—the risk is "socialized."

Danny Leipziger (1998) notes that moral hazard as specific to Korea manifests itself in the propensity of Korean economic agents to take on undue amounts of risk on the expectation that losses, if these are actually realized, will be covered by someone else (i.e., the state).[19] We have seen

---

17. The classical work on moral hazard is Arrow (1964); see Guesnerie (1992) for a survey of the theory of moral hazard.

18. Note that this option is not the same as that created by a loan guarantee by another member of the same group, as discussed in the previous section.

19. Krugman (1998) offers a theory of how moral hazard as described here caused overinvestment in Asia.

that this is not quite true: during the 1960s, failure to achieve export performance resulted (in some cases at least) in withdrawal of subsidies and almost certain failure for a firm (there was no socialization of risk); and even during the 1970s the equity investment by entrepreneurs in firms that became "unsound" was lost (though arguably, because the state granted preferential credits to these firms, the state held a quasi-equity position in them and could be seen as enacting partial socialization of risk). Nonetheless, there arose during the HCI period something like a "too big to fail" doctrine that took the following form: If a venture was undertaken but failed, it would be transferred under government management from one owner to some other owner (usually one, it would seem, in special favor with the Korean administration), thereby ensuring that the liabilities of the original owner were limited (i.e., that owner would not be liable for shutdown costs of the undertaking). The hope, of course, was that the new owner could turn the undertaking around and make it profitable.

At the time of the HCI drive, such a doctrine may have made a modicum of sense. The risks that the government was then seeking for entrepreneurs to take were large relative to the wealth of the entrepreneurs (or, in other words, the risks were such that entrepreneurs who undertook large undertakings and failed stood to lose everything). Thus, by implementing the "too big to fail" doctrine as described above, and socializing bankruptcy risk, the disincentive to risk-taking created by wealth constraints was removed (or made less binding).

The problem is that this doctrine remained in place long after it ceased to be relevant. Thus, both firms and banks in Korea behaved as though such a doctrine was in force in the 1980s and 1990s, right up until the crisis broke out. But by the late 1980s, whatever rationale it might have enjoyed earlier had ceased to exist. All of the top 30 groups in Korea— and certainly the top 5—had amassed huge amounts of assets, and these firms should have been able to underwrite reasonable risks of entering new activities without any need for government assistance, implicit or otherwise.

All said, then, the banks in Korea simply did not play the roles that financial institutions are supposed to play in modern market economies— to act to efficiently allocate resources via loan decisions and to effectively monitor the performance of borrowers. In particular, Korean banks seemed to have neither the will nor capacity to take corrective action when poor performance might have warranted such action. They did not develop the analytical skills (e.g., those of credit and risk analysis) needed to properly evaluate and monitor firms to which they lent, relying instead on government guidance. Relative to Korean industry, Korean banks and other financial institutions were simply underdeveloped. Indeed, one of the failings of early industrial policy was a failure by government leaders, especially the military leaders, to realize that a modern and efficient financial sector is as important, or is indeed more important, than a modern and efficient steelmaking industry or even information technology sector.[20] Had this fact been fully recognized, Korea might have developed its financial sector the same way it developed its industrial sector, taking care to learn what is best practice, to master this practice, and to take steps to ensure that Korean bankers and other financial executives were as well trained and well motivated as its engineers. But this was not the course that Korea took.[21]

---

20. In recent years, in fact, a powerful literature has emerged indicating that the level of development of the financial sector of a nation is correlated closely with measures of economic performance, including growth. Given the relative underdevelopment of the financial sector in Korea and the high growth rate, Korea must be something of an outlier in this regard: i.e., Korea's economic performance seems to have occurred in spite of the underdevelopment of the financial sector. For reviews of the relevant literature, see Levine (1997) and Levine and Zervos (1998).

21. As Cargill (1999) points out, the Korean government was urged for years by the World Bank and other outside advisors to pay more attention to developing a strong and effective financial sector. Many of Korea's top economic leaders recognized that this should be a priority. It was the leaders at the very top who were deaf to this advice. And, of course, as already observed, there were powerful constituencies in Korea whose interests were to make sure that the advice went unheeded. See also Noland (1996).

4

From Full-Blown Democracy to Disaster: The Kim Young-sam Years, 1993-97

Reform and Growth in the Early Years of the Presidency of Kim Young-sam

In what was the first truly democratic and fully contested election since the early Park Chung-hee years, one of the three Kims, Kim Young-sam, was elected president in 1992 as the candidate of the Democratic Liberal Party (DLP), which had been created by Roh. The election was not pretty. Kim was seen by much of the Korean population as a sellout for joining with Roh to form the DLP in 1990. The spring of 1992 saw student rioting (this in fact had become something of an annual event), and many Koreans feared that the riots might be used by Roh as an excuse for a return to martial law. Kim Dae-jung headed the main opposition party. But there was another opposition party, created and headed by Chung Ju-yung, the chairman of the Hyundai chaebol. In 1992, this party controlled 10 percent of the seats in the National Assembly. Chung's motivation, other than sheer ambition, was to get even for taxes assessed on portions of his estate passed as "gifts" to his children.

A bitter campaign ensued in which Chung accused Roh of creating an economic crisis while Kim Young-sam countered that there indeed had been economic mismanagement but that he was not Roh and would correct it. Chung responded by publicly denouncing Kim Young-sam as a person of limited intelligence. In the end, Chung ruined Kim Dae-jung's chances of election by splitting the opposition vote. Kim Young-sam was elected with 44 percent of the vote, while Kim Dae-jung received 36 percent and Chung only 20 percent. Chung one year later was tried and convicted of illegally using funds from the Hyundai group to finance his election bid. Relations between the Hyundai group and the Kim Young-sam government thus became somewhat frosty during the five years Kim was in office.

Kim Young-sam had answered Chung's charges by campaigning as a candidate who, in spite of the admitted economic mismanagement during the previous administration of his own party, would put things right. Thus, with Kim's blessing, under the five-year plan announced in July 1993 a "Blueprint for Financial Liberalization and Internationalization" was unrolled: it would decontrol interest rates, revise monetary tools, create short-term money markets, and liberalize capital accounts and foreign exchange transactions (see Kwon 1994). This plan was really just the second phase of the four-phase interest rate deregulation plan announced in 1991, and thus it was actually a product of the Roh period. Nonetheless, Kim readily claimed credit for it, especially when the chaebol chairmen united to speak out against it. These chairmen believed that the "Blueprint" would cause interest rates to go up and thereby squelch the growth of their groups. Kim did not entirely discount this possibility, and hence he acted cautiously in implementing the deregulation. However, he also saw that by carrying out the "Blueprint" he could restore some of the public credibility as a reformer that he had lost when he aligned himself with Roh, because its changes went against the publicly stated preferences of the chaebol chairmen. Indeed, in 1993 the chaebol were again out of favor with much of the Korean public because they were seen as responsible for the 1992 "growth recession."

Out of caution, only one element of the second-phase deregulation, the decontrol of interest rates, was executed in July 1993. But when no negative effect on growth was observed, the remaining elements were implemented in November of that year, decontrolling all lending rates except those on policy loans. Deposit rates except for demand deposits were to be decontrolled by 1996, as per the earlier plan, and demand deposit rates were to be "liberalized" (i.e., possibly not fully decontrolled, but nonetheless allowed to respond to changes in other market rates) by 1997; but the 1993 plan left the details of this liberalization unspecified. The plan also called for the "streamlining" of policy loans—which then accounted for about 35 percent of all bank lending—by 1997, again without specifying exactly what this meant.

In October the band of exchange rate fluctuation that was allowed without intervention was widened, and the plan called for its further widening in increments until by 1997 the won would freely float. Also, ceilings on foreign investment in the Korean stock market were to be lifted and gradually eliminated, bond markets gradually opened to foreign investors, and other measures taken to encourage (or at least to reduce impediments to) foreign investment, especially foreign direct investment, in Korea.

Kim Young-sam subsequently announced a series of anticorruption measures that proved to be very popular with the Korean people. In particular, a "real name" system for holding accounts in Korea was adopted, banning accounts established under fictitious names for nefarious purposes. Furthermore, the real owners of such accounts were required to be identified.[1] This was the key element in an effort to end what had become a common practice in Korea: chaebol executives seeking government favor would deposit funds into anonymous accounts held by politicians and senior government officials. Also, politicians and senior officials were required to disclose their personal assets, on the theory that questions raised about outsized assets would help curb the worst abuses (indeed, in the coming months disclosures raised questions that forced the resignations of a number of officials, including the mayor of Seoul). A particularly important result of implementing the real name system was that an account held in the name of Kim Woo-chung (the chairman of Daewoo) containing the equivalent of several million dollars was discovered to be in fact under the control of Roh Tae-woo, the former president. This disclosure paved the way for bringing charges of corruption against Roh; Roh's conviction on these charges is discussed below.

There was intense feeling in Korea that Kim Woo-chung (and other chaebol chairmen found to have been making payments to senior government leaders) should also be brought to trial. Charges indeed were brought against Kim and Samsung chairman Lee Kun-hee as well as eight other chairmen. All were found guilty and sentenced to jail terms—but all the sentences were suspended either by the presiding judges or on appeal. Kim Woo-chung pleaded that he had no knowledge of the bank account under the control of Roh and that in fact his subordinates had set it up without his approval. Accordingly, one of Kim's chief lieutenants at Daewoo, Lee Woo-bok, was forced to resign. Lee, a longtime personal friend of Kim, had exerted some moderating influence at Daewoo on Kim's inclination to expand at any cost; following his departure, this inclination was to go unchecked. Arguably, therefore, one unintended consequence of the anticorruption campaign was to set in train events that ultimately would lead to the complete collapse of Daewoo some years later (see chapter 5).

Kim Young-sam himself tried to set an example by disclosing his own financial assets and noting that he would accept no contributions during his term in office. He vowed to end the close relationship between government and business. All these gestures were to prove somewhat ironic in light of the scandals that involved his family and rocked his administration toward the end of his term.

---

1. The implementation of the real name requirement was largely the work of Soogil Young, who was then senior counselor to the deputy prime minister and who is quoted later in this book. The implementation of this plan was accomplished outside the aegis of the Ministry of Finance, which generally resisted reforms of this sort.

In 1994, Kim's government took steps meant to make Korea's economy more responsive to market forces and to further reduce the already rapidly diminishing role of industrial policy. The once all-powerful Economic Planning Board (EPB) was downgraded and placed in the Ministry of Finance, which was merged with the Ministry of Economics to create a very large Ministry of Finance and Economics. This reorganization was meant to signal the end of government playing the role of financial intermediation—that is, deciding how investment would be allocated.

The status of the Korea Fair Trade Commission (KFTC) was upgraded. This agency continued to investigate large numbers of violations of the Korean Antitrust Act (KAA), and the total number of cases under review increased from 622 in 1992 to 1,328 in 1997. And even though it continued not to attempt aggressive remediation of violations where these were found, it could keep the chaebol out of sectors if it believed that entry would have harmful effects, under its power to allow or disallow the groups to declare new core businesses. For example, the KFTC blocked an effort by Hyundai to enter the steel industry toward the end of the Kim Young-sam administration. The commission claimed that the move would have enabled Hyundai to become vertically integrated from production of steel to production of automobiles, and thus would have extended the group's market power. Some cynics, however, believe that the real reason for the action was to punish Chung Ju-yung further for entering the political fray in 1992.

These reforms were significant; but mindful of the fate of his predecessor, Kim Young-sam believed that that the top priority of his government should be to produce economic growth and not necessarily to promote reform. As noted above, he had been elected in 1992 during what has come to be known as the "growth recession" in Korea. Few other countries would have called 5 percent real growth per annum a "recession" of any sort. Even during the Roh years, according to Bank of Korea figures (*Monthly Economic Bulletin*, various issues), real growth in Korea had been very high by world standards: it was recorded as 12.0 percent in 1988, while real growth during the 1989 slowdown that resulted in the sacking of Cho Soon was 6.9 percent, a rate that would have delighted most countries. And as previously noted, 1990 and 1991 witnessed growth in the high single-digit range (9.6 and 9.1 percent respectively) but at the cost of renewed inflation. Thus, when measured growth fell to 4.7 percent (later revised to 5.0 percent) in 1992, this drop was seen throughout Korea as a major setback. Accordingly, three months into his administration, rather than implementing the second phase of the interest rate deregulation, Kim cut interest rates. In addition, regulations restricting the issuance of bonds by small and medium-sized businesses were eased in the name of economic stimulus.

Growth responded positively but weakly in 1993 (5.6 percent), and then headed toward 8 percent in 1994, despite the implementation in the fall of 1993 of the "Blueprint" for interest rate deregulation that executives of the chaebol had direly warned would harm growth. Real growth in 1994 in fact rose to 8.6 percent, followed by 8.9 percent in 1995. Moreover, unlike the growth spurt following 1990, the current growth was not accompanied by inflation. And perhaps the ease with which Korea was able to achieve this growth blinded both the government and large Korean firms to the problems that were mounting.

To a large extent, this growth was export-led. In particular, Korean exports benefited from the high Japanese yen, which gave Korean firms competing in export markets against Japanese-made goods a competitive edge. Especially in electronics (including semiconductors), automobiles, and ships, the effects of the high yen—the *endaka*—were spectacular.[2] These three sectors were, in the order just listed, the three largest exporting sectors of Korea in 1993, but all of them faced intense competition from Japanese firms in world markets. The three sectors were, of course, dominated by firms affiliated with the five largest chaebol. Stimulated both by growing world demand and enhanced competitiveness (courtesy of the *endaka*) relative to Japanese firms, in 1993 exports of finished electronics goods by the Korean "big three" (LG, Samsung, and Daewoo) increased by 37 percent over levels of a year earlier, with Samsung alone registering more than a 50 percent increase.[3] In 1993 dynamic random access memory chip (DRAM) exports were $7.7 billion, but they rose to $11 billion in 1994. Total exports of electronics goods by Korea in 1993 exceeded $20 billion. Accompanying this expansion of exports, Korean firms also undertook significant direct investment in overseas markets.[4]

Korean firms all added significant additional capacity to manufacture DRAMs in 1994. Samsung initiated more than $1.5 billion in new capital investment and LG more than $500 million. Some analysts at the time warned that international demand for DRAMs was highly cyclical in nature, that demand in 1993-94 was at the crest of the cycle (see, e.g., Ernst 1995, whose warnings were echoed in the electronics trade publications), and that a downturn was all but inevitable. The downturn in fact did come only 18 months later and helped to precipitate the 1997 crisis.

But in 1993 and 1994, all looked good. Indeed, this continued to be the case in 1995. Largely fueled by fast-growing exports of electronics products and automobiles, the Korean economy grew at an annual compound rate of almost 9 percent in 1995. Capital investment rates, already

2. However, Kang, Wang, and Yoon (2002), using vector autoregression (VAR) techniques, find that Korean industrial output before 1997 was only slightly affected by the yen/dollar rate. This assessment does seem contrary to the received wisdom expounded above that Korean firms in export sectors benefited substantially from the *endaka*.

3. Data from Korean International Trade Association, *Korea Trade Statistics*, various issues.

4. For explanations of this increase in direct investment, and also a review of literature pertaining to Korean FDI in electronics, see Perrin (2001).

high in 1994 (and themselves a major contributor to economic growth), jumped again in 1995. Gross domestic investment, which had hovered between 31 and 33 percent of GDP during the late 1980s, rose into the range of 35 to 37 percent of GDP during the 1993-95 period, a high figure even by Korean standards.[5]

Korea's second-largest export sector in 1993 was automobiles. Expansion in this sector also was rapid and, if one looked beyond the immediate future, arguably ill advised. Between 1992 and 1995, capacity to produce passenger cars in Korea grew by almost 30 percent, from 2.66 million units per year in 1992 to 3.35 million units per year in 1995.[6] But in 1992 domestic demand was only 1.27 million units, while exports totaled 456,000, so that capacity utilization was slightly less than 65 percent. To be sure, domestic demand had been growing rapidly for several years, and the number of automobiles in Korea per person, given per capita national income, was still low by international standards (Rhee 1996). However, as rapid as the growth of domestic demand was, capacity was added even faster, because Korean automotive executives anticipated continued growth of exports. In 1995, the gap between capacity and domestic demand was thus actually greater than in 1992. Domestic automobile sales in 1995 totaled 1.547 million units, while exports were 1.09 million units. Capacity utilization had improved to 78 percent. But whereas in 1992 domestic demand was 47 percent of total capacity and 74 percent of output, in 1995 domestic demand had fallen to 46 percent of total capacity and 58 percent of output. Improved capacity utilization was entirely the result of increased exports.

The largest market for Korean automotive exports was the United States, followed by western Europe. In 1993 and 1994, sales of Korean cars in the United States were helped immensely by the *endaka*, but not in western Europe, or at least not to the same extent. Other major export markets were Latin America and Southeast Asia, where despite high rates of protection and local overcapacity (Wonnacott 1994), Korean imports achieved significant market penetration. In the United States, most Korean cars sold were made by Hyundai, with Kia in a distant second position. Alas, market research done by J.D. Power during the mid-1990s (commissioned by Hyundai) showed that Americans considered Hyundai automobiles to be of low quality and low reliability, even though by objective measures the quality and reliability of these cars had improved sharply since the late 1980s when Hyundai first entered the US market.[7] Interestingly, the same

---

5. Bank of Korea, *Monthly Bulletin*, various issues.

6. Data from Korea Automobile Manufacturers' Association, *Monthly Automobile Statistics*, various issues.

7. The J.D. Power survey covered 38 makes of cars; Hyundai was ranked number 34 and Kia number 38. In 2002 these results were little different: of 36 makes, Hyundai had risen to 24th, but Kia remained in last place. By that time, Daewoo had begun to sell in the United States; it was ranked 34th.

market research showed that the quality of Hyundai cars was rated higher in the United Kingdom and Germany than in the United States. Hyundai entered Europe at a later date than the United States, and thus the research indicated the importance and persistence of reputation effects.

The main selling feature of Hyundai in both the US and European markets was low price, but beginning in early 1995 a falling yen and rising labor costs in Korea were jeopardizing the ability of Hyundai to maintain low prices in these markets. Also, Korean cars did not embody advanced technological features comparable to those found in Japanese-, European-, and US-made products; this deficiency was in fact the main motivation behind the XC-5 project. In spite of these difficulties, Korean manufacturers expected to double the volume of automobile exports between 1995 and 2000, with the growth necessarily coming from the US and European markets. One can wonder whether these projections were realistic even had the 1997 crisis never occurred. In fact, Hyundai's unit exports to the United States in 1991 proved to be the highest of any year during the 1990s, with unit sales unsurpassed until 2001. Hyundai Motor Company also served a number of smaller markets via foreign direct investment rather than export, mostly in Southeast Asia and Africa. These operations were typically small and, indeed, below what is generally recognized as minimum efficient scale. They survived only because of high tariffs on imported vehicles (Lautier 2001).

After it reentered the passenger car business, Kia recognized that it needed to sell cars at large volumes in order to be competitive with Hyundai. Thus, Kia also looked to the US market, establishing a sales network there. In its total worldwide sales, Kia quickly reestablished itself as the number two Korean automaker, displacing Daewoo, which had risen to number two after Kia's earlier exit. In 1993, Kia began selling its Sephia subcompact car in the United States. In 1995, well ahead of Hyundai and anticipating a trend, Kia introduced a sports utility vehicle to its US product lineup.

In 1995 Kia also announced that it would participate in what proved to be an ill-fated joint venture with the fourth son of Indonesian President Suharto to build automobiles in Indonesia. The project was touted by Suharto as one that would bring huge benefits to Indonesia and hasten that nation's progress down the road to becoming an industrial power; but, in fact, the project was designed mostly to further enrich Suharto's son. The project would start by Kia's exporting assembled vehicles and, later, knocked-down kits to Indonesia. But, over time, a full-scale assembly operation was meant to come on line. The project would also use ever-increasing local content. The undertaking overtly violated a number of World Trade Organization (WTO) commitments of Indonesia; a number of disputes formally were lodged against Indonesia at the WTO, all of which went against Indonesia. The project was canceled following the 1997 financial crisis and the subsequent fall of Suharto.

As noted earlier, Daewoo Motors was originally a joint venture with the US firm General Motors. General Motors in fact had exerted a moderating influence on Daewoo, refusing to go along with the plans of its chairman, Kim Woo-chung, to expand internationally. But, like Hyundai and Kia, Daewoo also had ambitious schemes for selling cars overseas. Unlike the others, Daewoo intended to do so largely via foreign direct investment rather than export from Korea, though its overseas operations would use components exported from Korea (Lautier 2001). Thus, in 1992 Daewoo used borrowed money to buy out GM's stake in its automotive subsidiary, which subsequently went on an overseas shopping spree. In particular, Daewoo bought and subsequently enlarged a number of plants in Uzbekistan, Poland, Romania, and Ukraine. Smaller operations were also established in India and elsewhere in Asia. The overseas expansion cost Daewoo on the order of $5 billion (Kirk 1999, 6). Chairman Kim's main goal seemed to be to displace Kia as the number two car producer in Korea. In 1997 Daewoo bought Ssangyong Motors, a small entry by the financially weak Ssangyong group into sport utility vehicles that was losing money.

Also seeking to become a major international car producer was Samsung, which had received permission from the Korean government to enter the automotive sector in 1992. After investing several billion dollars to this end in a joint venture with Japan's Nissan, Samsung chairman Lee Kun-hee hoped to open his factory near Pusan in February 1998—just as Korea was plummeting into the worst recession in its postwar history, as it turned out. Samsung would soon agree to sell the operation to Daewoo, but this deal was never consummated because Daewoo went bankrupt. Eventually, in May 2000 the French firm Renault along with the Japanese firm Nissan would take over Samsung Motors, with the Samsung group retaining a less than 20 percent minority interest; by then, Nissan itself would be under the control of Renault. Samsung Electronics had helped to finance the venture into the automotive industry, and one outcome was that Samsung Electronics realized substantial losses. These losses would become the basis for major disputes between minority shareholders of Samsung—including foreign mutual funds—and Lee Kun-hee.

The third major exporter in 1993 was the shipbuilding sector.[8] Probably even more than in the other two sectors, shipbuilding—which was, as we have seen, the first of the heavy and chemical industries sectors in which Korean firms emerged as world leaders, led by Hyundai and followed by Samsung, Daewoo, and several smaller firms—benefited from the *endaka* of the early 1990s. Thus, whereas in 1992 47.9 percent of all orders worldwide (by gross tons) for new ships went to Japanese producers and 17.3

---

8. Data in this paragraph are from Lloyd's Register, *World Shipbuilding Statistics*, various issues.

percent to Korean producers, in 1993 the orders for new ships going to Korea exceeded those going to Japan, 37.8 to 32.3 percent. However, because Japanese producers had more capacity than Korean producers, in 1993 the volume of ships under construction still favored Japan, 45.4 to 22.3 percent. Because there was worldwide excess capacity in this sector in 1992 despite growing world demand, competition was fierce and based almost entirely on price. Furthermore, demand in this sector was notoriously cyclical. There had been a cyclical low in 1988, when 11.8 million tons of new orders were placed, but 15.9 million tons were ordered in 1990 and 16.1 million tons in 1991. Then, new orders fell to slightly more than 12 million tons in 1992 but climbed to almost 24 million tons in 1993. This high demand was creating a heyday in the sector, but many expected that demand might fall substantially in the future.

Price competition in shipbuilding was the rule even though the technological prowess of producers varied widely around the world. In 1992 Japanese-built ships embodied more advanced technology than did Korean-built ones (Kim Doo-suk 1996), and this was true in spite of efforts by Hyundai during the 1980s to upgrade the technical capabilities of its shipyards. Korea was able to compete by offering prices low enough to offset Japanese technological advantages. Those prices in turn were possible in part because Korean steel was priced much lower than Japanese steel (and the quality of steel, especially from the Pohang Iron and Steel Company, or POSCO, was high). Also, as just noted, in 1993 the *endaka* became a major factor in Korea's favor. Together, these factors lowered Korean shipyards' costs to about 73 percent those of the Japanese for ships of similar design and comparable size (Kim Doo-suk 1996, 68). Kim Doo-suk estimates that technological factors favoring Japanese producers were such that Korean prices had to be 75 to 85 percent those of Japanese prices for Korean ships to be competitive, with the high yen of 1993 giving only a slight competitive edge to Korean shipbuilders. Thus, while the *endaka* put the Koreans into a position that was favorable, it was also precarious.

The shipbuilding sector in Korea was not a large employer, but it was Korea's third-largest exporter in 1993 and a sector on which large numbers of Koreans indirectly depended on employment (e.g., those in the steel industry). Only four years earlier, the Korean industry had been in such bad shape that in 1989 the government had ordered a halt to capacity expansion and had extended special assistance to the most afflicted shipbuilders, Daewoo, Halla (which then was a sizable seller of smaller vessels but did not build large ships), and Hanjin. Hyundai and Samsung by contrast were relatively well-off. This period had been characterized by a won valued high relative to the yen. Even so, Korean shipyards operated at about 80 percent of the cost of Japanese yards, but this cost advantage was not enough to offset Japanese technological advantages. Thus, the heyday of 1993 in this sector was a welcome relief.

Given the glut that had persisted for many years in the global shipbuilding sector, Korean firms did not add much capacity during the late 1980s or early 1990s. But then, at the height of the 1993 boom, the Halla group, controlled by a nephew of Hyundai chairman Chung Ju-yung, decided to do what Hyundai had done in the early 1970s—to enter the large-ship sector by building what Halla claimed would be the most modern and efficient shipbuilding operation in Korea, if not the world. But by the time the shipyard was ready to be opened, the bloom was off the boom, and the whole group, mired in debt, would have to declare bankruptcy.

This move by Halla helped to propel an effort at the Organization for Economic Cooperation and Development (OECD) to put some sort of limits on government subsidies to shipbuilding. Thus, in 1995 the OECD concluded a shipbuilding agreement in which Korea participated along with the nations of the European Union, the United States, Japan, and the non-EU Scandinavian shipbuilding nations: it was designed to eliminate or reduce subsidies given to shipbuilders and to prohibit "injurious pricing" (or, as some countries put it, "dumping") in this industry. Given that Korea was the nation that relied the most on low costs and low prices to compete in world markets, Korea was arguably the nation most affected by the agreement. One consequence was to cause Korean producers to take steps to improve the technology used in their product.

Expansion by the chaebol during the 1990s was not limited to the enlargement of existing operations or the entry by one group into activities already undertaken by other groups. Some chaebol entered into entirely new activities, one of which was aircraft manufacture. Samsung entered this business in a licensing arrangement with Lockheed Martin to manufacture F-16 military jets for use by the Korean air force, Hyundai established a subsidiary to produce light aircraft of its own design, and Daewoo produced training aircraft for military use (Kirk 1999).

The Second Half of Kim Young-sam's Administration

The first half of Kim Young-sam's administration may have been characterized by nominal reform accompanied by considerable optimism and expansion, but the second half was marked by growing indications that rough waters lay ahead.

These danger signs grew prominent even though reforms continued. Thus, in 1995 the second phase of the 1993 "Blueprint" for interest rate deregulation was implemented one year ahead of schedule (this was, of course, the third phase of the original 1991 four-phase plan). Then, in 1996 Korea became a member of the Paris-based OECD, an international organization often termed the "rich nations' club." OECD membership required that Korea adhere to the OECD Code on Liberalization of Capital

Movements, and to meet the obligations of this code Korea implemented a number of financial reforms, mostly pertaining to external accounts (see Noland 2000). Under plans that were to be phased in over a number of years, Koreans would be allowed to hold foreign bank accounts and to purchase foreign securities. Domestic firms could freely issue warrants denominated in foreign currencies (previously they could do so only with government approval). Non-Koreans could issue securities denominated in won, and limits on foreign purchases of Korean equities would be lifted. Foreigners would be allowed to purchase short-term won-denominated bonds; restrictions on purchase of long-term bonds would also be relaxed, but in an unspecified time frame. Foreigners would also be allowed to hold won-denominated accounts at overseas branches of Korean banks.

The overall effect of these liberalizing measures was that short-term capital accounts were largely opened, but long-term ones were not. This sequencing, most experts would agree, was wrong (Dobson and Jacquet 1998; Shin and Wang 1999), because short-term money could now flow into Korea to finance long-term investment. The result would be a mismatch between the term structure of liabilities (the short-term debt owed to foreigners) and assets (the long-term investments financed by that debt, if the foreign financing was direct; or, if the foreign funds were intermediated by banks, the loans of the banks to those who made the ultimate investments). Bankers generally see this mismatch as problematic because if investors who have funded the liabilities were to withdraw their funds, there likely would be no liquid funds available to pay the investors. Thus, withdrawal of funds would create a liquidity crisis. In fact, in late 1997 exactly such a withdrawal precipitated the biggest economic crisis in Korea since the time of the Korean War. Also, the OECD liberalization created a mismatch between currency denomination of liabilities and assets of Korean banks. Assets were held mostly in local currency (won), while liabilities were often denominated in foreign currency (mostly US dollars). Under these conditions, were the won to depreciate significantly against the dollar (as happened in late 1997), the banks would suffer losses as their liabilities, when expressed in won, would grow (or, equivalently, their assets, when expressed in dollars, would shrink), implying shrinkage of the banks' capital.

After liberalizing capital accounts pursuant to joining the OECD, Korea did experience a significant increase in the rate of inflow of short-term capital. Portfolio investment in Korea (including short-term bank loans) increased from 1.2 percent of GDP in 1993 to 3.2 percent in 1994, and then jumped to 4.2 percent in 1995. These inflows rose further to 5.4 percent of GDP in 1996. Because controls on capital outflows had also been relaxed, these jumps were partially offset by increased capital outflows, mostly on direct investment accounts; but, even so, the net international indebtedness of Korea grew. Sterilized intervention was employed to prevent the capital inflows from triggering uncontrolled domestic monetary expansion and hence inflation. Nonetheless, because the nominal exchange rate was fixed, the real exchange rate appreciated, reducing the competitiveness of Korean exports (Kwack 1999; Krueger and Yoo 2001; Warr 2000). Kwack Sung-yeung (1999) argues that with international capital mobility increasingly a fixture of the economic landscape in Korea during the mid-1990s, a move from a fixed exchange rate to a floating rate (which would have increased uncertainty about future exchange rates) might have discouraged at least the more speculative of the short-term flows and hence might have averted the crisis that followed. However, Korea did not choose to float the won. Peter Warr (2000) notes that as the 1990s unfolded, the won became increasingly overvalued as signaled by declining rates of growth of exports, declining terms of trade, and rising current account deficits (especially after 1995). He also suggests that capital outflows during the second half of 1997, leading to the currency crisis late in that year, might have been the result of expectations that the won would be devalued.

As foreign borrowing increased, so did the use of debt financing, especially in the manufacturing sector, where debt continued to rise faster than assets. At the beginning of 1994, the ratio of total borrowing to total assets in the Korean manufacturing sector was an already high 45 percent. By the end of 1997, this ratio had risen to almost 60 percent (Organization for Economic Cooperation and Development, *OECD Economic Surveys: Korea 1999*).

Following his legislative victory in 1996, Kim Young-sam stepped up his anticorruption drive by seeking indictments for corruption against his two immediate predecessors, Chun Doo-hwan and Roh Tae-woo, even though he had reason to be grateful to Roh at least for having essentially given him the 1992 presidential nomination. Kim Young-sam's hand was doubtless forced by the revelation of the account nominally held by Daewoo chairman Kim Woo-chung but actually held by Roh, described earlier. Chun was also to face capital charges for the 12/12 Incident and the slaughter in Kwangju.

The anticorruption trials drew enormous public support; they revealed that both men had received a total of more than $1 billion in bribes, most of which had been used to finance political slush funds.[9] Both were convicted and sentenced to long jail terms. Chun also was convicted on capital charges and sentenced to death. This latter sentence was commuted in late 1996 by an appeals court. As noted in chapter 3, in December 1997, both men were set free by Kim Young-sam, with the concurrence of then president-elect Kim Dae-jung.

As also noted earlier, Kim Young-sam sought to press charges against the leaders of the chaebol who had paid the bribes to Chun and Roh.

---

9. There is no evidence that either of these men gained exceptional personal wealth as a result of the bribes.

Indictments thus were handed down in 1996 against Lee Kun-hee of Samsung and Kim Woo-chung of Daewoo as well as the heads of a number of smaller groups. Both chairmen appeared unfazed by the indictments and no one expected that they would face any serious penalties. Both were convicted, but as noted earlier, Lee received a suspended sentence while Kim Woo-chung was sentenced to a jail term that was never served.

In January 1997, Kim Young-sam announced the formation of a presidential commission consisting of 31 members drawn from the industrial and financial sectors and from academia. Its mission was to prepare a comprehensive set of further reforms for the financial sector. Later in the year, the commission duly presented two sets of recommendations, one dealing with interest rate reform (essentially, implementation of the fourth phase of the earlier four-phase plan for interest rate decontrol) and the other with the reduction of entry barriers to the financial sector in Korea and with measures to address ailing financial institutions and to improve the central banking and supervisory functions of the government (Lee S. 1998). The Ministry of Finance and Economics subsequently drew up a plan that, according to the ministry, would implement 89 percent of the commission's recommendations. But these reforms proved to be too late and too little to head off the crisis that ensued six months later, though they were mostly pointing in the right direction. In fact, many of the commission's reforms were incorporated one year later into the conditions accepted by the Korean government in exchange for assistance by the International Monetary Fund.

In 1996 it became clear that at least some of the earlier capacity augmentation had been overzealous. In that year, domestic demand slackened and, affected by the high value of the Korean won, export growth came almost to a halt. As a result, Korean economic growth fell to 7.1 percent in real terms, from 8.9 percent in 1995, with a further drop expected in 1997. This spelled difficulty because, as noted in the previous section, during the prior five years so many Korean companies had made aggressive capital investments, their decisions based on what were proving to be overly optimistic projections about future growth. Moreover, most of these firms were leveraged to the hilt, to the point that even a modest slowdown could endanger their financial health and significantly increase bankruptcy risk.

Indeed, by 1996 earlier bankruptcies following periods of excessive debt-financed capital investment had faded in memory. The last such major cataclysm had been in 1985, with the failure of the Kukje group. But in 1997, even before the financial crisis broke out, bankruptcy struck a number of chaebol, including one in the top 10 (but not in the top 5, which have been the focus of most of the discussion in this book).

The first of these raised eyebrows, to say the least. This was the failure of the Hanbo group, already mentioned in connection with land speculation during Roh's presidency. Hanbo's main business was not real estate but steel, and it was in fact one of the least diversified of the groups identified by the KFTC as the top 30 groups in Korea. Hanbo, then number 14 on the KFTC list,[10] was the second-largest steel-producing firm in Korea. But Hanbo was far behind the largest steel producer, state-owned POSCO, by any measure (e.g., assets, output, or employment). Hanbo produced specialty steels that did not compete directly with POSCO's primary steel products and also performed downstream processing of primary steel. Hanbo had interests as well in construction, pharmaceuticals, and energy, but these were small compared to the steel operation. The group was extraordinarily highly leveraged even by Korean standards, as had been Kukje 10 years earlier. In January 1997, Hanbo declared that it was unable to service its debts of close to $6 billion and filed for bankruptcy.

Subsequent investigations revealed some sordid tales. Hanbo, in attempting to get banks to "evergreen" loans so that the firm might stay in operation, had bribed a number of influential persons to pressure the banks. One of those who had accepted bribes was Kim Hyun-chol, a son of President Kim Young-sam. It was alleged that some of the funds had been used to finance the 1992 campaign. Kim Young-sam worsened his own situation by refusing to release any records of these moneys, claiming that none had been kept. Kim Hyun-chol was convicted of accepting bribes and sent to jail, as was the CEO of Hanbo. President Kim's reputation as a corruption fighter was sullied and he fell into disgrace. Over the next year, he largely withdrew from the political arena; in July 1997, the nomination as candidate for president from the Democratic Liberal Party went to Lee Hoi-chang, and Kim played no role in the process. The scandal resounded to the benefit of Kim Dae-jung, who led the movement to force Kim Young-sam to disclose his campaign finances.

Possibly because of the scandal, Hanbo's crisis was not resolved in what had become the typical Korean style. The firm did not receive massive government aid, nor was it sold to cronies of the sitting president. Rather, it came effectively under government control, and the group's management was fired. As was typical of the earlier periods, however, funds were advanced to Hanbo to allow its operations to continue.

Further bankruptcies followed. The Sammi Steel Company, a specialty steel producer and the largest subsidiary of the 26th-ranked Sammi chaebol, declared itself bankrupt in March 1997, threatening the whole group.

---

10. As Noland observes (2000), this ranking was based on assets, which in Hanbo's case were considerably overvalued; had these been correctly valued, the firm would have ranked lower (Noland says 17th).

Hanbo, like other private steel companies in Korea, was largely a downstream producer of steel products. As noted earlier, the production of crude (unprocessed) steel in Korea comes almost entirely from state-owned POSCO, which supplies product for further processing to downstream firms, whose capacity in Korea was largely created during the 1980s and 1990s.

This triggered massive price declines for most stocks listed on the Korean Stock Exchange. The Jinro group, a large producer of beverages, defaulted on debt in April. The government's response to both these problems was more "classic" than its response to Hanbo: on April 18, 35 Korean banks, with government backing, announced an "antibankruptcy pact" whereby funds would continue to be lent to Sammi and Jinro to enable them to continue operations (Haggard 2000). The state-owned Korea Asset Management Corporation subsequently bought these loans from the banks, thereby injecting new liquidity into the banking system as well as removing what likely would be nonperforming assets.

The antibankruptcy pact was then extended to firms other than Sammi and Jinro. It called for the banks to continue to provide credit, and to suspend debt-servicing charges, to any of the large groups that could not meet these charges for a period of 90 days, but only if it was judged that the group was fundamentally sound and able to present a credible plan to restore itself to financial health.

This pact was soon to be tested severely, as the next card to fall was an important one: the Kia group, the big producer of trucks, buses, and motorcars. On June 23, 1997, the chairman of this group, Kim Sun-hong, approached the government for assistance because Kia's banks were unwilling to roll over loans that were coming due. The firm was made subject to the antibankruptcy pact, but Kim denounced this as inadequate and attempted to organize a "Save Kia" campaign. The campaign failed, and on October 22, the Kia group was nationalized and its management ousted. It has been reported that Kia's largest single shareholder, Ford Motor Company, was never notified of the nationalization.

Further problems erupted in October and November, as the financial crisis took hold. On October 2, the Ssangbang Wool Company, a textile producer, announced that it would likely default on debt. And in November, the Newcore group announced that 9 of its 18 affiliates faced imminent bankruptcy and would file for court protection. Two smaller bankruptcies, of the Kukdong and Hanil groups, also occurred in late 1997. Each of these owned assets that had formerly been in the Kukje group, which had been liquidated in 1985.

Thus, the warning signs were proliferating in 1997 that there were major problems in Korea that stemmed from the highly indebted chaebol and falling rates of return on capital, brought on in large measure by overexpansion of these groups. Even so, in the spring of 1997, Soogil Young, then president of the Korea Institute for International Economic Policy and a former top economic advisor to Kim Young-sam, seemed to believe that although long-term problems did exist, no crisis was imminent. Speaking before an audience in Washington, DC, Young stated:

> There is, in any case, no need for serious concern in the short term for Korea's foreign debt position. . . .

To say that there is no imminent crisis is not the same thing as saying there is nothing to be concerned about. There is indeed a crisis in progress in Korea —a longer-term crisis. The structure of high cost and low efficiency has become embedded in Korea's economy since the late 1980s, if not earlier, and has since been in place, largely intact, despite various efforts to ameliorate it. The result has been a gradual, but continual, loss of international competitiveness. This threatens the medium and long-term growth prospects of the Korean economy.

This problem of the Korean economy has been manifest since the late 1980s with the emergent supply inflexibilities in the markets for labor and land, and with the consequent spiraling of the costs of these factors of production. Korea's notorious supply-side inflexibilities in the financial market had been continuing unabated. In the market for goods and services, *chaebol* had been by and large resisting the pressure for the reform of their management and governance, and in this way failing to adjust to the emerging new realities of global competition[.] (Young S. 1997)

Young's worries about the long-term problems of Korea were certainly on the mark, but his soft-pedaling of short-term concerns was not. In fact, I was able to speak privately with Young at the function where the remarks cited just above were delivered, and found that he was, off the record, actually quite worried about the state of the Korean economy in even the short run. He was soon proven right.

5

The 1997-98 Crisis and Its Aftermath

The Crisis in Korea Unfolds

The 1997 Asian financial crisis, in which Korea figures importantly but not exclusively, has become one of the most written-about subjects in contemporary economics. Thus, I have no intention here of repeating in any depth what is covered well elsewhere; rather, only a summary of main events follows.[1] Views among analysts vary as to exactly why the crisis in Korea occurred. Steven Radelet and Jeffrey Sachs (1998), for example, argue that the crisis in Korea was almost entirely a result of volatility of international financial flows. They claim that the "fundamentals" of the Korean economy were sound and that there was no reason, apart from the withdrawal of funds from Korea by international investors, why the economy should have undergone the crisis that in fact did occur.

This interpretation is, of course, somewhat at variance with the story told here. Without question, the classical macroeconomic fundamentals of Korea appeared sound in the middle of 1997; inflation was low, there was a government fiscal surplus, overall growth was positive, and the balance of payments on the current account, while in deficit, was not seriously so

---

1. For more detailed descriptions and analyses of the crisis, the reader should see, e.g., Goldstein (1998) or Haggard (2000). Also, Nanto and Jones (1997) provide an excellent summary and analysis of the early stages of the crisis as it affected Korea in 1997. Warr (2000) gives an analysis of the macroeconomic aspects of the crisis, and Smith (2000) offers an account of how macroeconomic and structural factors interacted as the crisis developed. Kirk (1999) provides very detailed accounts of what happened in Korea between 1997 and 1999. Chopra et al. (2002) provide both a summary of various analyses of the crisis and a thorough analysis of their own.

and was, at any rate, improving. But at the same time, these indicators simply did not reveal the problems described in the previous chapter. Whether those problems that lurked below the positive fundamentals were so great that they could be wholly responsible for the economic crisis that ensued is nonetheless unclear. And thus it is almost certain that volatility at the international financial level played some role in creating the crisis. Also beyond question is that the deeper problems that existed in Korea prior to the crisis were revealed by the crisis. Whatever problems were largely buried beneath the surface in early 1997 were fully exposed by 1998.

But here we are less interested in the crisis per se than in its aftermath, when the Korean economy first went into a major recession and then underwent a rapid recovery, and in the subsequent policy changes that were meant to correct the problems that were exposed. The recession was abrupt and deep, but very short-lived. GDP growth was negative 6.7 percent in 1998, rebounded to positive 10.9 percent in 1999 and positive 8.8 percent in 2000, but dropped to 3.0 percent in 2001 (Bank of Korea, *Monthly Economic Bulletin*, various issues). Growth picked up somewhat during the first half of 2002, but there is quite a lot of uncertainty regarding growth during the second half and further out (for a summary of forecasts, see, e.g., Lowe-Lee 2001).

I have been arguing that Korean firms were particularly vulnerable to bankruptcy in the event of an economic downturn. And, indeed, widespread bankruptcy, in some cases involving very large firms, did occur in Korea following the crisis (see Krueger and Yoo 2002). Moreover, at the time of this writing Korean policymakers have yet fully to sort out the problems created by these bankruptcies and to address the problems that caused the bankruptcies in the first place. Even so, policies have been implemented that are likely to forever change how Korean firms do business; at the same time, the structure and conduct of many of Korea's largest firms have also changed.

But let's take up events from where we left them at the end of the previous chapter. Despite numerous indications of trouble in early 1997, Korean economic growth during the first six months of 1997 was quite robust. Thus, international lenders to Korea seemed to be confident that Korean firms and banks would encounter no barriers to repaying the short-term international loans that had been flowing to them. But the possibility of problems ahead began to register early in July, when Thailand was forced to ask the International Monetary Fund (IMF) for assistance to meet international obligations. On August 11, the IMF announced a "rescue package" to Thailand of more than $17 billion, some of it from IMF resources and some of it from other Asian nations, mostly Japan. Only a few days later, Indonesia floated the rupiah, which then plunged in value, signaling that this nation too was having severe difficulties in meeting international obligations.

The weakness of the rupiah affected Korea because Korean banks had lent significant sums to Indonesian banks. The Korean won began to depreciate, hitting a record low of 911 to the dollar on August 19. On October 8, Indonesia announced that it would have to join Thailand in seeking IMF assistance. Simultaneously, conditions elsewhere in Asia were deteriorating. In a surprise move, the central bank of Taiwan devalued its currency on October 18. The Hong Kong Currency Board raised interest rates on October 19 and, in response, the Hong Kong stock market plunged. In Korea the depreciation of the won hastened, despite Bank of Korea intervention on an increasingly large scale. On October 30 the won hit what had been declared as the value that would trigger massive intervention, but it kept depreciating. During November, the won repeatedly broke through levels that the Bank of Korea had very recently announced as ones that the currency would never be allowed to reach.

A climax of sorts was reached on November 17 when the Bank of Korea spent billions of dollars attempting to keep the won from falling through the level of 1,000 won to the dollar, to no avail. The next day the Bank of Korea recommended to the Ministry of Finance and Economics that the nation seek an IMF bailout loan; the day after that (November 19) the finance minister, Kang Kyong-shik, resigned and the Bank of Korea announced that it would stop defending the won. On the 25th, it became publicly known that an IMF team had arrived in Seoul and was examining the books of the Bank of Korea. Good news of continuing strong growth in the economy was ignored completely by markets on the 28th.

By this time, international lenders, especially Japanese banks that were heavily invested in Korea, were refusing to turn over short-term loans. According to Jwa Sung-hee and Huh Chan-guk (1998; cited in Noland 2000), 80 percent of loans coming due were refinanced, but this "rollover rate" fell to 50 percent in November and then to 30 percent in December. On December 2, the Korean stock exchange was forced to suspend trading on nine merchant banks.

After a number of false starts, on December 3 the IMF and the Korean government announced a package of about $57 billion in stand-by credits for Korea. Of this sum, $21 billion would be from the IMF itself, while the World Bank would contribute $10 billion, the Asian Development Bank $4 billion, the US government $5 billion, and several other countries $1 billion each. The package came with a large number of conditions attached, many of which were subsequently modified.[2] (Some of these conditions in fact were urged by reform-minded Koreans who were consulted by the IMF.) A news conference to announce the agreement that morning was postponed and the media informed that final agreement on the bailout

---

2. A summary of the IMF conditions under the IMF stand-by agreement (first letter of intent) with Korea is provided by Young S. and Kwon (1998). Detailed descriptions are found in Sohn and Yang (1998); see also Wang and Zang (1998).

would not come for several days; but then several hours later, the conference was reconvened to announce that the "stand-by agreement" had been reached after all.

Perhaps because of a carnival-like atmosphere surrounding the announcement of the stand-by agreement, markets remained unstable and the won kept falling even after December 3, reaching 1,790 to the dollar on December 12. On December 15 the Bank of Korea raised interest rates and simultaneously announced that the won would henceforth float freely, as per the agreement with the IMF. The won promptly appreciated to 1,400 won to the dollar. But then in the days that followed it plummeted again, possibly because of worries in the market over statements by presidential candidate Kim Dae-jung to the effect that if elected president, he would not adhere to the agreements with the IMF.

On December 18, Kim won the election, aided by the strong backing of Korean labor unions. He immediately indicated that he indeed would abide by the agreements. On December 23 the Bank of Korea, with the agreement of the IMF, raised the repurchase rate on won (the rate at which Korean banks could effectively borrow funds) to almost 30 percent. Also, a "standstill agreement" was reached between foreign banks and the Korean government whereby the former agreed not to withdraw further funds from Korea. The US Treasury helped to broker this agreement. The won subsequently stabilized at close to 2,000 won to the dollar—about 40 percent its worth in early July (in terms of the dollar). Thereafter, the won began to appreciate, albeit erratically.

Interest rates were held high for almost three months, well after it became clear that the free fall of the won was over. These rates were then allowed to fall, but only slowly. The IMF subsequently admitted that it had been an error to hold interest rates so high for so long, even if high rates were initially necessary to stem the depreciation of the won.[3] In particular, the prolonged high interest rates were seen as almost surely having induced the major recession that followed. The IMF also had stressed in December fiscal austerity on the part of the Korean government, so that the small public deficit would be turned into a fiscal surplus; the reasoning was that this would generate for the government the funds that would be needed to cover the costs of financial restructuring. Thus, both monetary and fiscal policy sought by the IMF as conditions for stand-by credit were contractionary. (See OECD, *OECD Economic Surveys: Korea 1999*, chapter 2, for an analysis of macroeconomic policies followed by the Korean government under IMF guidance during the early months of 1998.) The IMF initially forecast that even under these policies, real growth in Korea would be about 3 percent. Yet the real growth rate in 1998 was −6.7 percent

---

3. For three different views on this, see Chopra et al. (2002), Cho Y. (2002), and Chung and Kim (2002).

The severity of the recession in fact reflects the indebtedness of Korean corporations. Kim Se-jik and Mark Stone (2000) use econometric analysis to show that both falls in output and rises in rates of bankruptcy in all the afflicted East Asian nations in the wake of the 1997 crisis were positively related to corporate leverage. In other words, the higher the use of corporate leverage, the greater the fall in output and also the greater the number of bankruptcies, controlling for a number of other variables—exactly the result that a financial analyst would predict. And as the 1998 recession took hold, bankruptcies began to mount. By the end of the year, these included 11 groups on the Korea Fair Trade Commission's 1997 list of the top 30 (reproduced as table 5.1). The largest of these were Kia and Jinro, which had reported difficulties in 1997, and Newcore. Both groups filed for reorganization. During 1998 they were joined by Halla (founded by the younger brother of Hyundai founder and chairman Chung Ju-yung, and now run by Chung's nephews) and the Hanil Keopyung, and Haitai groups. The smaller Dongha, Shinho, Kohap, and Hanwha groups all were bankrupt as well but were kept running by means of syndicated loans under the antibankruptcy pact, as was also the case for four other small groups.

By the late fall of 1998, the won had reached an approximate rate of 1,200 to the dollar, and the exchange rate subsequently stabilized in this range. In 1999 growth turned positive, and this trend continued into 2000. The crisis and recession were over not much more than one year after the crisis first hit, but the problems that were revealed were many and deep.

Financial Sector Reform

Even if the short-term conditions imposed on Korea by the IMF for stand-by credit were, in hindsight, not wholly wise, the IMF did recognize many of the long-term weaknesses that had developed in the Korean economy that were responsible for the depth of the recession.[4] To correct them, the IMF focused in its stand-by conditions on four areas: financial sector reform, industrial sector reform, privatization of state-owned enterprises, and labor market reform.

At the top of the list was financial sector reform, which had already been recognized as a priority in the final year of Kim Young-sam's presidency. The IMF reforms, which in many aspects mirrored those suggested by the Presidential Commission on Financial Reform one year earlier, fell into three broad categories: those pertaining to the central bank (the Bank of Korea) and the financial supervisory system, those

---

4. Some of these weaknesses have been touched on in earlier chapters; additional aspects of financial sector weakness in Korea are discussed by Koh and Ji (2000).

Table 5.1 Top 30 chaebol in Korea, June 1997

Rank	Name	Debt-to-equity ratio[a]	Number of subsidiaries	Bankrupt in December 1998
1	Hyundai	5.8	57	
2	Samsung	3.7	80	
3	LG	5.1	49	
4	Daewoo	4.7	30	
5	SK	4.7	46	
6	Ssangyong	4.0	25	
7	Hanjin	9.1	24	
8	Kia	n.a.	26	X
9	Hanwha	12.1	31	X
10	Lotte	2.2	30	
11	Kumbo	9.4	26	
12	Halla	20.7	18	X
13	Dongha	3.6	19	X
14	Doosan	5.9	25	
15	Daelim	5.1	21	
16	Hansol	4.0	23	
17	Hyosung	4.7	18	
18	Dongkuk	3.2	17	
19	Jinro	37.6	24	X
20	Kolon	3.2	24	
21	Kohap	4.7	13	X
22	Dongbu	3.4	34	
23	Tongyang	4.0	24	
24	Haitai	15.0	15	X
25	Newcore	17.1	18	X
26	Anam	15.0	21	
27	Hanil	5.8	7	X
28	Keopyung	n.a.	22	X
29	Kiwon	n.a.	25	
30	Shinho	6.8	25	X

n.a. = not available

a. Nonfinancial subsidiaries only; last year available for bankrupt firms.

Note: This table excludes Hanbo, in the process of being liquidated in July 1997.

Source: Korea Fair Trade Commission; debt-to-equity ratios from OECD, OECD Economic Surveys: Korea 1999.

pertaining to opening up the financial sector, and those pertaining to restructuring the financial sector.

In the first category, pertaining to the Bank of Korea and the financial supervisory system, the IMF essentially wanted to carry out fully those reforms that had been called for by the earlier Presidential Commission but that had been only partially implemented in the final months of Kim Young-sam's presidency. Thus, for example, the Bank of Korea had already been made independent of the Ministry of Finance and Economics

(MOFE). Also, most financial supervisory responsibility had been removed from the Bank of Korea and those functions placed under MOFE, leaving the bank's focus on monetary management. Under the IMF reforms, all supervisory functions were transferred to a new Financial Supervisory Board (FSB) that was independent of MOFE and would report to the prime minister. Also, under the new arrangement, either the Bank of Korea or the FSB would be allowed to request bank inspections, which would be carried out jointly by the FSB and the Bank of Korea. The FSB would have full and final authority to determine what, if any, corrective actions would be taken.

The IMF conditions called for the passage of legislation to enable various financial institutions (banks, insurance companies, securities institutions, and other nonbank financial entities) to enter each other's lines of business in order to increase competition within the Korean financial sector. This change was sought because research findings indicated that financial stability in nations tends to be enhanced when different types of financial institutions are allowed to compete with one another. To this end, existing securities and insurance supervisory agencies in Korea were to be merged into the FSB. The merger was actually accomplished in April 1998, when the Financial Supervisory Commission (FSC) was created, taking over the functions of four different financial regulatory agencies (those covering banks, securities, insurance, and all other nonbank financial institutions). The FSB remained as the executive body of the FSC.

IMF conditions regarding the second category (opening up the financial markets) also largely followed the recommendations of the earlier Presidential Commission, though on a much-accelerated schedule for implementation. The main objective was to liberalize long-term capital accounts (as noted above, short-term accounts had already been liberalized following Korea's membership in the OECD). Accordingly, restrictions on foreign ownership of stock in Korean firms were first to be relaxed and then eliminated entirely, in order to enable foreign takeovers of Korean firms. The bond market was opened to foreigners, so that foreign investors could hold any type of Korean bond (private or government-issued), although a foreign investor was temporarily restricted to holding no more than 30 percent of the total of any one type of bond outstanding. This restriction was lifted at the end of 1998.

One result of these reforms was that foreign direct investment flow into Korea jumped considerably, from $6.97 billion in 1997 to $8.85 billion in 1998, even though 1998 was a recession year (FDI flow is typically sensitive to the business cycle). This increase was in accordance with efforts of the new administration to reverse what had been a de facto Korean policy to discourage inward FDI. In contrast to earlier years, about a third of FDI in Korea was of the form of acquisitions. There is some evidence that this FDI brought benefits to Korea (Kim June-dong 1999; Yun 2000). In spite of the large increase, however, the total flow of

FDI to Korea relative to the size of the economy remained minuscule; indeed, Korea's ratio of FDI to GDP remained among the lowest both in Asia and among the OECD nations.[5] Also, the jump in 1998 was not actually as great as that in 1997. As just noted, FDI flow in 1997 had been almost $7 billion; in 1996 the flow had been only $3.2 billion, and it had been $1.9 billion in 1995.[6] Thus, the 1998 figure represented, if anything, the slowing of a trend that had begun several years earlier.

Reforms in the third category, having to do with financial restructuring, were the most pervasive. With some exceptions, they were carried out with more vigor and determination than were seen in earlier efforts at financial sector reform. Three sets of reforms were called for. The first was to perform triage, identifying banks and other financial institutions that were unviable. The second was to define clear exit strategies for those institutions: these included complete closure; takeover of unviable institutions by viable ones, without unduly endangering the financial health of the latter; and restructuring plans for those institutions judged to be salvageable. The third was to establish a timetable under which all Korean banks would meet the so-called Basel capital adequacy standards as established by the Bank for International Settlements (BIS).

Importantly, in implementing these reforms, the FSC adopted what was termed the "prompt corrective action" (PCA) system. Under this system, bank supervisors were required to measure banks and other financial institutions against specific quantitative risk indicators and, where these indicators suggested inadequacies, to take prompt corrective action. As well as introducing new, specific quantitative indicators, the PCA system was intended to signal a new attitude on the part of the supervisory authorities: regulatory forbearance would no longer be practiced. At the same time, the FSC indicated that it would not attempt to micromanage banks, but rather would distance itself from internal operating decisions while insisting that high prudential standards be maintained, as verified by the quantitative risk indicators. Specific indicators included the BIS capital adequacy requirements and analogous requirements for nonbank financial institutions. Certain other quantitative measures were devised that were based on best practices as defined by international organizations of supervisory authorities.

Should an institution fail to meet the thresholds demanded by these indicators, FSC supervisors could issue three levels of corrective procedures: management improvement recommendations, management improvement requirements, and management improvement orders. (Details of these escalating procedures can be found in OECD, *OECD Economic Surveys: Korea 1999*, chapter 3.)

---

5. For possible reasons why, see Beck (1999) and Yong (1999).

6. International Monetary Fund, *International Financial Statistics*, various issues.

To help carry out the restructuring, the Korea Deposit Insurance Corporation (KDIC) was created; it was meant to provide bank depositors with limited deposit insurance that in turn was paid by the banks themselves. In fact, to prevent a run on the banks, the government in late 1997 had implemented an emergency measure to guarantee all deposits in the banking system until 2001; the limited deposit insurance scheme thus was to kick in after these blanket deposit guarantees expired, and it came into effect on schedule. The premiums paid for such insurance were to be based on the soundness of the bank as measured by prudential standards set by the FSB. In addition, the KDIC helped with the recapitalization of certain banks by purchasing new equity in them, and it reimbursed depositors in some nonbank financial institutions where those institutions were unsound or bankrupt and deposits were at risk.

In late 1997, before the IMF intervened, the Korean government had created the Korea Asset Management Corporation (KAMCO) to purchase nonperforming loans and other "impaired assets" from banks and other financial institutions when the viability of these institutions was threatened. The creation of KAMCO was one of the recommendations of the Presidential Commission. In early 1998, under the IMF reforms, the role of KAMCO was supplemented by the creation of a "bridge merchant bank" (Haneurum Merchant Bank) whose role was to resolve the insolvencies of merchant banks.

The Korean government in fact got off to what the IMF considered to be a slow start in carrying out the restructuring agenda: it refused to close two large but insolvent banks, Korea First Bank and Seoul Bank, that the IMF wanted shut down (Noland 2000). Instead, these were nationalized in the weeks before Kim Young-sam left office. Subsequently, however, the FSB required that all banks not already meeting the Basel capital adequacy requirement as of the end of December 1997 submit rehabilitation plans. Out of 25 banks operating in Korea at that time (not including the 2 that had been nationalized), 12 were required to submit plans. In June 1998 the FSB found that 5 banks out of 25, including 3 of the 17 banks that operated nationally, had submitted "infeasible" plans. These banks were suspended and acquired by other banks deemed to be sounder under programs that enabled KAMCO to buy the banks' nonperforming loans and other "impaired assets." Also, KDIC injected new capital funds into the banks, thereby becoming a major shareholder in these banks and thus effectively bringing them under government control. The remaining seven received conditional approval but were put under close supervision.

At the same time, negotiations were initiated to sell both Korea First Bank and Seoul Bank to foreign investors. The first sale was completed after protracted and often rocky negotiations with Newbridge Capital. But the latter deal fell through, largely because the FSB and the bidder (HSBC, formerly the Hong Kong and Shanghai Banking Corporation) could not come to agreement over the definition and resolution of non-performing loans.

Overall, there was much success in the restructuring of the banking subsector in Korea in the 18 or so months following the crisis (Organization for Economic Cooperation and Development, *OECD Economic Surveys: Korea 1999*). The number of commercial banks had been reduced to 17 by early 1999, largely as the result of unsound banks merging into more sound ones, and the number of employees had fallen by a third. Almost all of the surviving banks met the Basel capital adequacy requirements. However, as I shall argue shortly, less progress may have been made than the early claims for victory might suggest (see Park Y. 2000a). The main reason for skepticism concerns the assumption of non-performing loans by KAMCO and the acquisition of major equity positions in the banks by KDIC; the Korean government thus became the controlling agent holding the majority of the assets of the Korean banking system, which included huge amounts of "impaired assets."

By the end of 1998, the FSB had also shut down 16 merchant banks and incorporated their operations into Haneurum Merchant Bank; out of a total of 30 merchant banks in operation at the end of 1997, only 18 survived. Also, 2 securities companies out of 34 were shut down, as well as 4 insurance companies out of 50; however, 5 companies accounted for almost 80 percent of the assets of the industry, 3 of which were affiliates of the top 5 chaebol, and none of the top 5 was shut down. Finally, 2 investment trust companies (out of 31) were closed. By the end of 2000, there had been further consolidations: the number of commercial banks was down to 11, the number of merchant banks was down to 9, and the number of investment trusts was down to 8. In April 2001 a large financial holding company was created by the government—the Woori Financial Group—that was to own 4 commercial banks (including the large but troubled Hanvit Bank), 1 merchant bank, and 11 other nonbank financial subsidiaries. The plan was that it would be a "test case" for creating a more advanced and competitive financial institution in Korea.

During these 18 months and in spite of the consolidation reported above, there was much less progress in restructuring the nonbanking subsector than the banking subsector (Organization for Economic Cooperation and Development, *OECD Economic Surveys: Korea 1999*). The main problem was that certain of these institutions, especially insurance companies and investment trust companies, were able to use various accounting practices to hide their true losses and the extent of nonperforming assets. Related to this problem were ownership linkages between the financial institutions and the chaebol, ensuring that nonperforming assets in the former were mirrored by loss-making operations in the latter. Thus, by March 1999 the total amount of nonperforming loans held by nonbank financial institutions exceeded significantly the total of such loans held by the banks; in addition, nonperforming loans as a percentage of total loans were significantly higher in the nonbank institutions than in the banking sector. And, as just suggested, the full extent of nonperforming loans was less certain in nonbank institutions than in the banks.

Importantly, the financial sector reform judged successful by the OECD mostly entailed restoring the immediate health of financial institutions. Such restoration did not necessarily imply that full and adequate steps had been taken to ensure that the past practices of these institutions—the practices that had helped to create the problems in the first place—were corrected. Rather, steps had been put in place to strengthen the balance sheets of the institutions, often with conditions attached that were meant to improve the practices of the institutions. To achieve this strengthening, the government took equity and long-term loan positions in banks and also bought bad loans from the banks and then attempted to resell them, taking losses in doing so that ultimately would have to be borne by Korean society.

The main vehicle for buying the banks' bad debts was KAMCO. In its first months, KAMCO injected money into the banking system by purchasing subordinated debt issued by the banks (Claessens 1999); it also bought nonperforming loans, in some cases arguably throwing good money after bad (Noland 2000). As a safeguard, beginning in April 1998 the purchase of nonperforming loans by KAMCO and injection of new capital into the banks by KDIC were both conditioned on a number of actions being taken by the banks themselves, notably the carrying out of the mergers already described and the raising of new equity capital from nongovernment investors. KAMCO did buy "impaired assets" (mostly nonperforming loans) from the banks and, in some cases, nonbank financial institutions at prices well above the true market value of those assets (in most cases at face value). Given that the purchases conveyed an implicit subsidy to the banks, it was quite reasonable that conditions for bank improvement should be attached to them.

KAMCO in 1998 was largely unable to dispose of the assets it acquired, even by selling them at a considerable discount. The situation improved in 1999, when arrangements were made by which KAMCO was able to sell some of these assets to foreign firms. Marcus Noland (2000) notes that during 1999, KAMCO was able to sell about 22 billion won of the more than 55 billion won of "impaired assets" it had acquired, for which it only received about 12 billion won, or about 55 percent of their face value.

The difference between the price as paid for such assets (usually face value) and the price as received by KAMCO largely determined the cost of the cleanup of Korea's financial sector. The total cost also included any capital losses incurred by KDIC upon selling the equity it had acquired in banks and other institutions to the public and the costs of refunding any deposits that were guaranteed. Robert Aliber (1998) has estimated that the total cleanup cost would eventually be about 30 to 35 percent of Korean

Table 5.2 Public funds used for Korea's financial sector restructuring, January 1, 1998-June 30, 2001
(billions of won)

	Recapitalization	Deposit repayment	Asset purchase	Non-performing loan purchase	Total
Banks	44.3	—	13.2	29.0	86.5
Nonbanks	20.9	20.0	0.9	11.9	53.7
Total	65.2	20.0	14.1	40.9	140.2

Source: OECD, *OECD Economic Surveys, Korea, 2001*, table 38, as reported by the Korean Ministry of Finance and Economics, 2002.

annual GDP, a figure that clearly is quite high but one that Aliber calculated to be manageable.

In late 2001, the Korean government issued a report indicating the total public funds spent for financial restructuring from the crisis through June 30, 2001. This total was 137.5 trillion won, or about 26 percent of GDP for the year 2000 (though of course these funds were spread over two and a half years). The breakdown is indicated in table 5.2. It is important to note that these reported "costs" are in fact the realization of losses that have already occurred, and are not new costs imposed on the economy. More specifically, they result from losses borne by banks and other financial institutions being reallocated to society at large—that is, to taxpayers.

Ultimately, the effectiveness of the financial sector reform depends on resolving those problems that caused the situation in the first place— that is, taking steps to avoid the accumulation of nonperforming loans to the point that these loans can threaten the viability of the whole Korean financial sector. Such loans were largely made to firms in the industrial sector in Korea, specifically to the chaebol. Thus while a thorough reform of the financial sector has been absolutely necessary in Korea, the problem of nonperforming loans could recur even after the current portfolio of such loans has been wiped clean unless the industrial sector were to be reformed as well. But reform in that sector has progressed much more slowly after the crisis.

Erratic Reform in the Industrial Sector

The IMF in fact recognized that reform in Korea would have to encompass the industrial sector, and in particular the chaebol, if the overall effort to reform the Korean economy was ultimately to succeed. Thus, in the various "letters of intent" agreed on between the IMF and the Korean government, there was general agreement that reform in the industrial sector should take place. However, while reform measures pertaining to the financial sector were specific and concrete—for example, the creation of the FSC, KAMCO, and KDIC and the specification and implementation of explicit reform strategies that they should undertake—those specified for the industrial sector often tended to be rather abstract and nonspecific. For example, the IMF program called for more transparency, better corporate governance (including management that would be more accountable to shareholders), reduction of entry barriers to specific sectors, stock market revitalization, privatization of government-owned enterprises, and resolution of nonsolvent nonfinancial firms (by forcing them to exit the market, if necessary). All these reforms were necessary, but exactly how to implement them was left unclear in the letters of intent.[7]

Following the crisis, a number of reform measures were in fact attempted. But as time passed, meaningful progress toward implementing reform in the industrial sector was at best erratic and, at the end of the day, rather scant. The dire financial status of firms in the Korean industrial sector was not in fact fully appreciated until the spring of 1998, when the Hong Kong office of the US investment banking firm Goldman Sachs and Company released a study that gave pause in Seoul. The study included estimates of interest coverage ratios of the 30 largest Korean groups as identified by the Korea Fair Trade Commission (KFTC). This ratio is defined as the cash flow (i.e., earning before tax plus depreciation and amortization charges, which are noncash expense items allowed as tax deductions but which do not reduce cash generated by the business) divided by interest charges on both long- and short-term debt held by the group. The estimates were based on disclosed debt. Given that the groups typically had undisclosed debts, these published interest coverage ratio estimates likely overstated the magnitudes of the true ratios for many if not all groups. The ratios for the top 10 groups, along with the underlying data used to calculate these ratios, are given in table 5.3.

Financial analysts consider the interest coverage ratio to be an important measure of the financial health of a firm or group of firms. A ratio of 3.0 or greater is indicative of a financially healthy firm. As can be seen from the table, only 2 of the top 10 chaebol meet this criterion of health, Samsung and Lotte (the latter, as noted in chapter 1, is largely a retailer and hotel chain and not an industrial chaebol). A ratio of 2.0 or less is indicative of poor financial health, and 6 of the 10 failed to have

---

7. An indicator of this vagueness is that the text of Wang and Zang (1998) describing adjustment reforms in Korea in the wake of the financial crisis is 189 pages, excluding annexes. Of these, 75 pages describe the IMF programs but only 5 are devoted to programs pertaining to the nonfinancial corporate sector. The remaining 114 pages describe progress in the implementation of this program. Of these, 7 pages treat the nonfinancial corporate sector—mainly discussing future reforms not yet implemented.

Table 5.3   Estimated interest coverage ratios, 10 largest chaebol in Korea, early 1998

Group name	Sales	Operating profit	Cash flow	Interest expense	Coverage ratio
Hyundai	68.19	2.67	4.32	2.75	1.6
Samsung	61.35	3.03	5.49	1.81	3.0
LG	41.19	2.27	3.56	1.57	2.3
Daewoo	38.95	2.25	2.74	1.96	1.4
SK	21.44	1.44	2.67	1.02	2.6
Ssangyong	18.73	0.42	0.70	0.70	1.0
Hanjin	9.21	0.36	1.23	0.61	2.0
Kia	11.96	0.67	1.13	0.93	1.2
Hanwha	7.82	0.56	0.85	0.52	1.6
Lotte	2.62	0.24	0.45	0.12	3.9

Note: Sales, operating profit, cash flow, and interest expense figures are in billions of won; figures are for listed affiliates only.

Source: Goldman Sachs and Company (1998).

interest coverage ratios above 2.0. A ratio of less than 1.0 indicates that the firm or group is technically insolvent, not generating enough cash to meet interest payments. While none of the top 10 had an interest coverage ratio less than 1.0, a number of groups in the next 20 did—for example, the Shinho group, number 30 on the KFTC list, had an interest coverage ratio of 0.6. The Ssangyong group, one of the major winners during the HCI drive but a group that struggled throughout the 1980s and 1990s, showed a ratio that, at 1.0, placed it perilously close to insolvency. An interest coverage ratio above 2.0 but below 3.0 represents an intermediate case, neither financially healthy nor clearly sick. Two of the groups, LG and SK, had coverage ratios in this range. The low interest coverage ratios of the Hyundai and Daewoo groups might have suggested to financial analysts that neither of these groups could afford to take on additional debt. But as we shall soon see, this indicator was very much ignored in the months that followed the crisis.

A second report that appeared in 1998, this one prepared by the US management consulting firm McKinsey and Company (McKinsey 1998), also gave pause in Seoul. It examined the productivity of labor and capital in major Korean manufacturing and service sectors and compared Korean firms operating in these sectors with firms that were world leaders. Most of the analysis concerned the year 1995; in some cases, 1994 or 1996. The findings were stark: in most manufacturing sectors, productivities of both capital and labor (output per unit input) in Korean firms were shown to be only about half the levels found at the leading firms of the United States. That the productivity of labor was lower than in the United States was not really surprising, given that real wages in Korea (indicative, at least in theory, of the marginal product of labor) were also much lower than in the United States. Given lower wages, it in principle would be consistent with efficiency maximization that Korean factories employ more workers than equivalent factories in a higher-wage economy. However, the finding was that levels of staffing in Korean manufacturing operations were excessive when compared to equivalent US operations even after accounting for lower wages. This would imply that Korea could enjoy efficiency gains from reducing labor in such operations. In contrast to the conclusions regarding labor productivity, those regarding levels of productivity of capital—also significantly lower in Korea than in the United States—were surprising because, relative to the United States, in 1995 Korea was still a capital-poor country.[8]

Strictly speaking, the McKinsey findings pertained to average capital productivity and not marginal productivity, but it is a reasonable inference that if average productivity of capital was lower in Korea than in the United States, so too was marginal productivity. Thus, these findings tended to corroborate earlier empirical studies concluding that rates of return on capital in Korea had been falling since the 1970s. Moreover, the McKinsey results tended to confirm that bankruptcy risks in many Korean firms were rising.

The McKinsey report also noted that the relatively low productivity of capital in Korea was not, by and large, the result of Korea lagging other countries in terms of its technology. Because Korea had invested heavily in human capital development and in acquiring the best available technology, by 1998 technological lags were no longer much of a factor. The low productivities in manufacturing, according to McKinsey, were instead caused by poor governance of both industrial and financial institutions.[9]

As might be expected, the results varied considerably across industries.[10] Somewhat embarrassing perhaps to those who advocate private ownership of industry as a prerequisite to efficiency, Korea did very well in steelmaking, the sector dominated by then state-owned Pohang Iron and Steel Company (POSCO).[11] Labor productivity in this sector was 108 percent that of the United States and capital productivity 115 percent; thus, in steel Korean firms outperformed those of the United States. Interestingly,

---

8. In 1995, in the manufacturing sector, the amount of capital per worker in Korea was about 80 percent that of the United States.

9. In this regard McKinsey (1998) provides an interesting contrast to sectoral studies during the mid-1990s published by Koreans including Kim Y. (1995), Rhee (1996), and Kim Doo-suk (1996), who all see the main problem facing Korean firms as centered on technological backwardness.

10. The results that follow are largely based on case studies of individual firms.

11. However, McKinsey (1998) did identify numerous distortions in the Korean steel market that could be traced to government ownership of POSCO (e.g., subsidized production that reduced returns on investment to POSCO, discussed below).

and perhaps of comfort to the advocates of private ownership, return on capital invested in the largely privately owned downstream processing sector in Korea was shown to be even higher than in POSCO—in part, however, because POSCO delivered very low-cost crude steel to the processors. It seems to have been an unwritten rule in Korea that POSCO would not enter the business of the downstream "mini-mills," which in turn are largely blockaded from entry into primary steel production. As part of the IMF reforms, the Korean government agreed in 1998 to privatize POSCO by selling shares to the public. This process is now almost complete.

In automobiles, the productivity of labor in Korean firms was on average 48 percent that of US firms, and the ratio between the two for capital productivity was also 48 percent. In this sector, the international leader was not a US firm but rather the Japanese firm Toyota. McKinsey (1998) noted that Hyundai Motor Company's labor productivity in 1996, measured in terms of vehicles per worker, was barely half of what Toyota's had been in 1974. Furthermore, between 1954 and 1974 Toyota raised its labor productivity at a much faster rate than did Hyundai between 1976 and 1996. (According to McKinsey 1998, this comparison between two different 20-year periods was most apt, because in those spans of time Toyota and Hyundai each established itself as a major international producer.) Thus, McKinsey found not only that Hyundai lagged far behind the world's leading auto-producing firm in terms of productivity, but also that the gap was not being closed.

One finding of McKinsey was that the Korean automotive sector was still heavily sheltered from imports in 1995. Such sheltering apparently had a counterproductive effect on the Korean sector's performance. Because Korea had become the world's fifth-largest auto-producing nation, the case for infant-industry protection in Korea had long ceased to be valid by 1996 (if indeed it ever had been; see the discussion in chapter 2). Rather, high levels of protection seemed to coddle the sector, giving rise to perverse incentives for Korean auto producers not to make necessary efficiency-enhancing improvements in their operations. One of the elements missing in the Korean industry, for example, was lean production as pioneered in Japanese firms and adopted in large measure by American and European firms. The main symptom of its inefficiency was excessive labor. Thus, the study recommended that the government take measures to ensure that Korean automotive firms would be able to lay off workers, because "until Korean [automobile] companies can release workers, labor and capital productivity will be kept to low levels" (McKinsey 1998, 12). But as we shall see shortly, the actions taken in the Korean automotive industry in the aftermath of the crisis were, by McKinsey's reasoning, the very opposite of what was called for. While McKinsey indicated that Korean auto manufacturers did need to upgrade their technology, the recommended emphasis was less on the side of product design (the focus of the XC-5 program) than on the side of manufacturing and production technology.

In semiconductors, Korean firms' capital productivity was 54 percent that of their US competitors; labor productivity, 52 percent.[12] Most of the discrepancy was due not to differences in unit output per unit of capital or labor, but rather to a different mix of products. In particular, Korean firms' production was heavily concentrated (75 percent) in dynamic random access memory chips (DRAMs), which by the mid-1990s were becoming a commodity item. Much of the rest of the product mix was accounted for by standard logic chips, which were also becoming items of relatively low unit value. In the production of these chips, McKinsey (1998) found that Korean productivity levels in 1996 were comparable with the average of US manufacturers though behind those of the US industry leader (Micron). Assembly of chips was somewhat more labor intensive in Korea than in Japan or the United States, and there were some other residual operational differences. Unlike in automobile manufacture, however, the operational gaps between Korean firms and the best international firms were closing quickly. McKinsey suggested that one of the main weaknesses in the sector in Korea was a lack of design engineers who could devise products with higher unit value.[13]

Consistent with the analysis in chapter 4, McKinsey (1998) found that one of the main vulnerabilities of Korean firms in this sector was the highly cyclical nature of demand for semiconductor products, which creates a very volatile price trajectory. Indeed, as already argued, one reason for the slowdown in growth in Korea in 1996 and 1997 was a downturn in demand for these products. In 1999, rising demand (and rising prices) in this sector would play a substantial role in bringing Korea out of recession. Domestic demand also would prove to be a major factor in the decline in GDP growth in 2001 and the subsequent pickup in 2002 (Cashin and Liang 2002).

A further finding of McKinsey (1998) was that Korean firms lagged the world's leaders further in service sectors than in manufacturing. The reasons for this, by McKinsey's analysis, had much to do with regulations in Korea that limited competition for many services. One important result was the relatively high cost of many services, and these costs in turn reduced the competitiveness of Korean manufacturers.

The McKinsey study was largely prepared before the onset of the crisis, but toward its end it contains a section on the crisis that was clearly added after the main body of the report was complete. This section argued that the crisis was more than a result of a liquidity problem, as argued by Steven Radelet and Jeffrey Sachs (1998) among others. Rather, McKinsey

---

12. But note that the best Korean semiconductor firm, Samsung, apparently did not participate in the study.

13. Many of these same findings were also reported by Ernst (2000).

(1998) concluded that the crisis "was largely caused by low capital productivity, especially in capital-intensive manufacturing industries," and by the fact that "companies continued (in the face of declining returns on capital), with the support from banks, to make undisciplined capital investments in pursuit of growth."

The McKinsey results are buttressed by the findings of Kim Won-kyu, reported by Sri-Ram Aiyer (1999). Kim concluded that rates of total factor productivity growth in Korea in most sectors were slower during the period 1990-96 than in the period 1980-89. As explained in chapter 2, total factor productivity (TFP) is the residual factor left when growth of output cannot be accounted for by growth of measurable tangible factors such as capital and labor (and, in some specifications, human capital). It is generally thought to be (or to closely approximate) growth that results from technological change. Kim's finding thus was that the rate at which Korean output was responding to technological change was slowing during the 1990s, suggesting (consistent with other evidence) that overall growth during this time was being driven largely by simple expansion of capacity rather than by increases in efficiency, as technological progress would tend to bring. As noted earlier, findings by William Zeile (1991b) and others suggested that by contrast, during the earlier period 1970-85, TFP growth had been very rapid in many sectors.

Problems in the Korean industrial sector were well recognized even before the onset of the crisis, of course, and some efforts were made to address them in its immediate aftermath. Beginning very early in 1998, for example, the government, following the wishes of president-elect Kim Dae-jung, indicated that the chaebol (including the largest groups) should henceforth identify and concentrate on core businesses and should exit noncore businesses. Even before he was inaugurated, between January 13 and February 6, Kim had met and made agreements with chaebol chairmen that in order to achieve the necessary specialization, the groups would designate from three to six core businesses and that they would swap assets among themselves, in what came to be known as the "big deals." This was not the first time that such an approach had been tried; as discussed in the previous two chapters, elements of the same idea were present in earlier efforts to sort out the "unsound" companies that emerged during the HCI drive and its aftermath. Also, during the last years of Roh Tae-woo's presidency, mergers were attempted as a means of resolving weak businesses. The approach had been found wanting in the past, largely because even once the acquired firm was merged into a "sound" firm, insufficient action was taken to correct the causes of its "unsoundness." Instead, cash flow from strong operations generally was used in effect to subsidize the losses of the weak operations.

According to Yoo Seong-min (1999), who expresses open skepticism of the big deals, their main rationale was that through swaps, "excessive and duplicative" investments by the chaebol could be eliminated (but could this be accomplished without shutting down the least viable of these?) and scale economies could be achieved as well. Yoo also notes that an implicit element of the big deals was the creation of monopolies that would be protected from domestic competition. Given that in his book the president-elect had strongly criticized earlier government-enforced monopolies in Korea and the industrial policy that created them (Kim Dae-jung 1996), it seems curious that one of Kim's first acts when elected president was essentially to begin to implement exactly the types of policies he had written against two years earlier. Moreover, given the marked reluctance of chaebol chairmen to enter into these deals, it should have been apparent that they saw little benefit to their firms in carrying them out. There apparently was little benefit to be had even from gaining market power. Thus, as might have been expected, all the chairmen of the large groups dragged their feet when the time came to actually negotiate the big deals.

Although the big deals started as "voluntary" negotiations among the chairmen of the largest chaebol as per the agreement with Kim Dae-jung, when these negotiations failed to produce any of the desired transactions by the summer of 1998, the government stepped up the pressure for the deals to go forward. Under this pressure to produce a set of concrete actions, on October 7, 1998, the chaebol chairmen announced plans for a number of swaps, but only a few transactions actually took place thereafter.[14] These plans called for Hyundai and LG to consolidate their semiconductor operations into one operation, in the only one of the truly big "big deals" to take effect more or less as per the October plans. The October 7 plan did not specify whether Hyundai or LG would control the combined operation (or possibly run it as a joint venture); but when the deal was finally consummated in October 1999, one year after the deal had been announced, the combined operation came under the control of Hyundai Electronics Industries. As a result, Hyundai Electronics, for a time, became the world's largest producer of DRAMs, surpassing Samsung. In March 2001, as part of a general reorganization of the Hyundai group (discussed below), the name of Hyundai Electronics was changed to Hynix. Alas, size was to prove not to imply strength; Hynix began its existence as a highly troubled operation and remains so at the time of this writing; I discuss its misfortunes later in this chapter and in the next chapter as well.

The October 1998 plans also called for consolidation within the ship engine and power generation equipment sectors; there the main transaction was that Samsung Heavy Industries would be acquired by state-owned Korea Heavy Industry, which then would be privatized. The acquisition, a relatively minor one, in fact did occur in 2000. Small consolidations

---

14. Cho W. (2001) argues that this pressure in fact resulted in transactions that were "lose-lose," with neither party benefiting.

also occurred in the aircraft sector, where Korean firms were not major international producers, and in the railroad rolling stock sector. The October plans further called for consolidation of the petrochemical sector, where two mergers were envisaged. First, the operations of SK, LG, Daelim, Lotte, and Hanwha would be combined into one entity; and second, the operations of Samsung and Hyundai would be merged. Who would control the resulting entities was not specified and these deals were never completed. At the time of this writing, the petrochemical sector in Korea remains troubled.

Although not part of the October plans, a big deal announced shortly after this plan was made public was a proposed transaction in the automotive sector by which Daewoo would acquire Samsung Motors and Samsung would acquire, in exchange, most of Daewoo's electronics operations. This deal too never came to pass, largely because of the failure of the Daewoo group in mid-1999.

But another big deal of sorts did occur in the automotive sector in mid-1998, when the Korean government announced that it would seek to "denationalize" Kia by selling it to private interests. Ford Motor Company—which was, as noted earlier, a minority shareholder in Kia (directly and indirectly, Ford held a 17 percent share of Kia's equity)—expressed an interest in acquiring the firm, on condition that Kia's creditors write off 50 percent of its debt (Noland 2000). Noland notes that the deal as proposed would have made much sense for both parties, because Ford sought to strengthen its position in Asia while Kia needed the major injections of capital and technology that Ford could provide. But this was not happen. In September, the government rejected Ford's bid, reflecting the view of Korean auto executives that Kia should remain under Korean ownership—most likely because these executives feared that under Ford's control, Kia would emerge as a truly formidable competitor in the Korean auto market. (Arguably, this is just what Korea needed.) In October, control of Kia was instead awarded to the Hyundai Motor Company.

The Hyundai Motor Company had a debt-to-equity ratio of more than 5.0 and the whole group (including financial subsidiaries) a ratio of almost 6.0 in 1998. Nonetheless, Hyundai financed the purchase of Kia with debt that banks were somehow willing to advance to the firm despite the already very high levels of debt reflected in those figures. The acquisition of Kia came soon after Hyundai Motor Company had settled a prolonged and bitter strike by its labor unions that took place during the spring and summer of 1998. At issue was an effort by Hyundai to lay off workers. As noted above, Hyundai Motor Company employed far more workers than efficiency would dictate; to improve the competitiveness of the firm, a significant amount of labor shedding was unquestionably needed. However, during the strike, the government effectively sided with the unions and the workers and helped to broker a deal whereby Hyundai would not reduce its workforce except by attrition. The strike came at a time when unemployment in Korea was rising; moreover, Kim Dae-jung and his National Congress for New Politics (NCNP) party had received the backing of the organized labor movement in Korea during the 1997 election. But one long-term effect of the settlement may have been to render Hyundai Motor Company, already disadvantaged relative to international competitors because of its low rates of labor productivity, even less able to resolve its difficulties in the long run.

The Hyundai-Kia deal may have saved Korea from the ignominy of having one of its major groups come under foreign control. But the deal called into question a number of policies of the Kim Dae-jung administration, notably its commitment to being open to foreign direct investment, its commitment to transparency, and its commitment to getting the government out of the financial intermediation business (again, all of these were goals that Kim had set forth in his own 1996 book). Moreover, the deal was to prove to be one of several events that would push Hyundai to the brink of disaster, a story to which we shall return. Furthermore, the deal gave Hyundai a 95 percent share in the Korean truck market and more than a two-thirds share of the domestic auto market, undermining the government's stated commitment to increase effective competition in markets in Korea.

One possible reason why Hyundai received what amounted to favors from the government throughout 1998 and 1999 (albeit "favors" that were to have the cumulative effect of bringing the Hyundai group to the edge of complete collapse) was that Hyundai's chairman, Chung Ju-yung, strongly supported Kim Dae-jung's "sunshine policy" meant to ease tensions with North Korea (Noland 2000).[15] In particular, Chung reached an agreement in 1998 with the North Korean government by which Hyundai would undertake a number of projects in North Korea, most notably the development of a major tourist site (Mount Kumgang) to which tourists from South Korea would be transported on cruise ships operated by the Hyundai group (for descriptions of these projects, see Flake 1999).[16] Kim Dae-jung strongly favored and encouraged these undertakings. Among other things, Chung committed the Hyundai group to pay North Korea at the outset about $150 million, an amount that would rise eventually to as much as $1 billion per year, for the right to manage Mount Kumgang and other projects. Such a sum struck many analysts at the time as excessive in light of the group's financial condition (e.g., Noland 2000).

---

15. None of what follows should be interpreted as criticism of the sunshine policy per se. Although the subject is beyond the scope of this book, it does appear at the time of this writing that the sunshine policy has succeeded in some measure in reducing tension between North and South Korea. See Kim Sung-han (1999) for what amounts to a South Korean government perspective on the policy.

16. For detailed descriptions of Hyundai's efforts and the general state of relations between the North and South in 1998, see Kirk (1999, chapter 10).

A series of other measures passed by the government in 1998 were oriented toward reforming the chaebol. These included a requirement that the five largest chaebol submit Capital Structure Improvement Plans (CSIPs) under which their debt-to-equity ratios were to be reduced to 200 percent by the end of 1999. To this end, the ceiling on the total stock that a bank could hold in a single firm was raised from 10 percent to 15 percent in the hope that this change would encourage debt-for-equity conversions. Means by which the groups might have achieved the goal, in addition to debt-for-equity conversions, included selling affiliates and raising new equity capital. Some groups in 2000 did take advantage of rising equity prices to raise new equity; but this was most often in the form of "preferred" shares, which could be sold without diluting the control held by existing shareholders (i.e., the founding families). Yet another means to achieve the goal was "creative accounting." One such approach was to issue corporate bonds to replace bank debt. Oh Gyutaeg and Rhee Chang-yong (2002) find that the total amount of corporate debt in Korea, counting corporate bonds, was virtually unchanged during the years following the crisis, as industrial firms simply replaced bank debt with other forms of debt. They suggest that as a result, Korean firms would remain vulnerable to external shocks, as the discussion of the final section of chapter 4 indicated.

Another government requirement—one in fact designed to circumvent problems associated with creative accounting—was that the top 30 chaebol prepare consolidated balance sheets and income statements that would conform to internationally recognized accounting principles and that would cover all affiliates, including financial and unlisted ones. These financial statements were to have been prepared by the end of fiscal year 1999. Citing difficulties in meeting this requirement, including a lack of qualified accountants in Korea, the chaebol pleaded for (and received) an extension of the deadline until the end of fiscal year 2000. Also, the groups were required to end cross-guarantees of debts by the end of 2000; as discussed in chapter 3, these were the guarantees by one affiliate of a group to pay back the debt of another affiliate should the latter be unable to do so on its own. They were often used to transfer part of the risks associated with new start-up ventures of the chaebol to better-established chaebol affiliates. As noted earlier, these arrangements were favored because majority equity holders in the new ventures (usually the chaebol founding families) could pass on part of the risk to minority shareholders of established affiliates but appropriate the returns from the start-ups, if there were any, for themselves. The guarantees were most often made without the consultation or approval of the minority shareholders.

At the end of 1999, after examining statements submitted by the five largest groups, the government announced that four of the five had in fact met the goal of reducing debt-to-equity ratios to 200 percent. (Daewoo alone did not meet the requirement, but by then Daewoo was bankrupt

and in receivership.) Even then, it was clear that some creative accounting had been employed—most notably the upward revaluation of assets
in order to bolster the reported value of equity (Haggard 2000) and equity
swapping among subsidiaries (Beck 2000). Samsung met the requirement
in part by reclassifying some long-term debt as debt currently due (the
debt-to-equity ratio was calculated on the basis of debt with maturity of
one year or more; short-term debt, viewed as financing working capital,
was not included for purposes of calculating this ratio). Ira Lieberman
(1999) estimates that without asset revaluation, the debt-to-equity ratio
of Hyundai would have been close to 8.0.

These statements were not, however, the consolidated statements as
required, but rather statements that excluded nonlisted subsidiaries. There
were in fact many indications that the groups had not done much to
reduce debt-to-equity ratios (both Hyundai and Daewoo had indeed significantly increased their debt—Hyundai in order to absorb Kia and the
semiconductor operations of LG, and Daewoo to continue what amounted
to a helter-skelter expansion program, described in the next section). And
in April 1999 Kim Dae-jung had publicly expressed his frustrations over
failure of the groups to take more meaningful steps to meet the debt-to-
equity improvement goals such as selling assets or raising new equity
capital.

Had such new capital been aggressively pursued, one might have expected that the shares of founders and their families in the total equity
of the groups would have been reduced. However, Yoo Seong-min (1999)
calculates that between the onset of crisis and the middle of 1999, the
share of total equity held by the founders of the chaebol or their families
actually increased. Nor was there much evidence of the selling of assets:
although the five largest groups had reduced the number of affiliates
from a total of 232 at the beginning of 1998 to 167 at the end of 1999,
much of this apparent shrinkage had resulted from merging smaller affiliates into larger ones. Few affiliates were sold, and those that were
sold tended to be small. Peter Beck (2000), for example, notes that about
three-fourths of them employed 50 persons or fewer.

Moreover, the total assets of all of the big groups actually increased,
both in absolute terms and as a percentage of total assets of all Korean
corporations. According to the KFTC, the share of the top 4 chaebol in
the assets of the 30 top groups increased from 38 percent in 1996 to 48
percent at the end of 1999; these figures included assets acquired by the
top 4 from failed lower-tier groups (e.g., most significantly, Hyundai's
acquisition of Kia), most often with government blessing. In March 2000,
the FSC reported that the banks in Korea had advanced to the big four
chaebol more than 40 trillion won in loans in excess of what was meant
to have been legally permissible (Beck 2000).

In 1998 the case might have been made that new equity issues were
impossible to market, given the depressed state of the Korean economy

at large and the Korean stock market in particular. Indeed, the stock market crashed in 1998. But when in 1999 the market witnessed a sharp recovery, the chaebol still made no efforts to place major new common equity issues.[17] Rather, the evidence points to affiliates of the chaebol, in some cases offshore affiliates, buying back their own stock or the stock of affiliated firms in order to boost share prices, thus increasing the apparent value of equity (Mann 2000). During the run-up of the market there in fact appeared in the market new buyers dubbed "mutual funds." As Catherine Mann observes, mutual funds, at least in the United States, hold diversified portfolios of stocks. Their main function is to enable small investors to diversify their holdings of equity in order to reduce overall risk.[18] The Korean mutual funds, by contrast, seem to have held stocks only of one chaebol and in fact were managed by the chaebol. The holdings might actually have increased the risk to a holder of shares in the funds; in any case, there apparently was an effort to manipulate the stock market to the advantage of the chaebol. Mann notes that the stock price run-ups brought on by this effort were almost surely unsustainable, which would mean that small investors were vulnerable to being hurt. A longer-term victim likely would be the Korean stock market itself, which had never overcome the sullied reputation it gained during Roh Tae-woo's presidency. Moreover, the long-term development of Korea requires a well-functioning stock market, as will be argued further in chapter 6.

It is true, however, that foreign investors now hold about a third of the total value of shares listed on the Korean market, providing evidence that the market is not wholly unsound. But most foreign investment is concentrated in a relatively few firms regarded as "blue chip," such as POSCO (now largely privatized), Samsung Electronics, SK Telecoms, and so on. A better-functioning stock market might enable wider holding of Korean stocks by foreign shareholders, to the benefit of Korea.

Thus, when in August 2000 the consolidated statements of 16 chaebol were finally released, these showed that the debt-to-equity ratios of exactly

---

17. For a detailed analysis of stock and bond market behavior during the crisis and its aftermath in Korea, see Kim Sun-ho (2000).

18. According to financial theory pioneered by Harry Markowitz (1959), the risk associated with holding any security can be broken down into two components, one common to all securities (e.g., susceptibility to fluctuation in overall economic activity) and one specific to any given security. If the latter component is, on a security-by-security basis, statistically independent (i.e., one security's specific risk is not a function of the behavior of another security), then the statistical variance of a portfolio containing many securities will be less than that associated with a single security; in other words, diversification of holdings will reduce risk. The main barrier to such diversification by a small investor is lack of enough wealth to hold a sufficiently large number of securities to obtain the benefit of diversification. A mutual fund gets around this barrier by pooling the wealth of a number of such investors.

Table 5.4 Debt-to-equity ratios of the five largest chaebol in Korea, 2000

	Claimed debt-to-equity ratio, 1999 (percent)	Actual debt-to-equity ratio, 2000 (percent)	Interest coverage ratio, 2000
Hyundai	1.52	2.96	0.91
Samsung	1.46	4.43	3.15
LG	1.48	3.58	1.42
SK	1.33	2.55	1.47
Ssangyong	6.34	17.74	0.28

Source: Beck (2000); compiled by Beck from the Korea Free Trade Commission and other sources.

none of the large groups in fact had met the goal (see Park Y. 2000b). Table 5.4 indicates what the true ratios were for what were now the top five groups. (Because Daewoo was in receivership, the fifth-largest group was now Ssangyong, which had not met the goal even in the largely fictionalized accounts on which the government's end-of-1999 statement had been based.)

Table 5.4 also shows 2000 interest coverage ratios for the five large groups, which the new financial statements made it possible to calculate accurately. With the exception of Samsung, these ratios showed the groups to be actually less healthy than the earlier estimated ratios reported above as calculated by Goldman Sachs and Company (see table 5.3). Moreover, we must keep in mind that the Goldman Sachs calculations were for a year of economic downturn, whereas 1999 had witnessed strong growth. SK and LG, by this measure, were now in the unhealthy range. Hyundai seemed to be no longer unhealthy but rather critically ill: the interest coverage ratio for Hyundai was less than one, indicating that the group was technically insolvent. The ratio for the new entrant into the top five, Ssangyong, was less than 0.3, indicating even more severe financial problems than Hyundai. Unfortunately, because earlier ratios were based on incomplete and perhaps inaccurate information, it is not possible to tell whether the apparent deterioration in the condition of the major groups was caused by actual worsening of their financial condition or by an upward bias in the earlier estimates.

Other problems emerged in the industrial sector of Korea in 1998. In July 1998, for example, the FSC identified 55 firms that it considered to be nonviable. Most of these were affiliates of the chaebol; included were affiliates of Hyundai, Samsung, LG, and SK, four of the top five groups. (Curiously, especially in light of the bankruptcy of the whole group one year later, no affiliate of Daewoo made this list.) All of the afflicted firms and groups were subject to various "workout" programs—that is, they were reorganized, sold, merged, given new capital injections, and in a relatively few cases slated for liquidation. Most of these firms were in fact rather small ones; collectively, they were not at the crux of the problems in the Korean industrial sector.

The Collapse of Daewoo

One might have thought that when the brief but severe recession ended in Korea, as happened in 1999, and growth swung from negative 8.8 percent to positive 10.9 percent, the industrial bankruptcies would also have ended. But, in early 1999 the most spectacular bankruptcy in Korean history—that of the Daewoo group—still lay ahead. When the financial crisis broke out in late 1997, Daewoo had been, depending on exactly which measure one used, the second-, third-, or fourth-largest group in Korea. As we have seen, the group had been founded only in 1968, and its growth rate during the 1970s and 1980s had been little short of phenomenal.

During its entire existence, the group had been led by its founder, Kim Woo-chung, an energetic, charismatic individual possessed of, by most accounts, a rather flamboyant and outsized ego. (Daewoo, in fact, means "Big Woo," where the "Woo" is the first portion of the chairman's first name.) By 1997, the business empire of Daewoo was huge by any measure except perhaps true net worth. It consisted of 30 subsidiaries, of which only 10 were listed. The high number of unlisted subsidiaries itself should have elicited concern, particularly given that some of these were large firms (e.g., Daewoo Motors). Most of these were under the control of Daewoo Corporation, which operated as a de facto holding company. The affiliates included six nonbank financial institutions. The industrial subsidiaries of Daewoo participated in 26 industries as per classification of industry by the Korean Standard Industrial Classification at the three-digit level. The group was one of Korea's largest outward foreign investors: Daewoo held operations in literally dozens of countries around the world, and the name "Daewoo" had come to be recognized internationally. By the end of 1999, however, the group was defunct and chairman Kim was a fugitive from justice. At the time of this writing, in fact, Kim's whereabouts are not known to Korean authorities. He has been reported in exile in the south of France, in Switzerland, in North Africa, in Kazakhstan, and elsewhere.

Perhaps more than any single entity, Daewoo embodied what went wrong in Korea during its period of rapid growth. Using debt financing, the group expanded recklessly into activities in which it earned very low rates of return on capital invested. It and its chairman persistently used accounting gimmicks, nonlisted subsidiaries, and outright lies to hide the true extent of its borrowings and the poor performance of many of its operations. Even so, it was transparently clear that in many if not most of the activities in which it participated, Daewoo was a "me-too" entry, in that some other Korean group had pioneered or emerged as industry leader in that activity. Thus, for example, in shipbuilding, Hyundai was first entrant while Samsung via acquisition developed into the number two firm, leaving Daewoo as a distant and chronically troubled number three. In automobiles, Daewoo was the third firm to enter on a large scale, following Kia and Hyundai; but in this case, during the 1990s, Daewoo did emerge somewhat stronger relative to its Korean competitors than in most other sectors. Indeed, after the group's failure, Daewoo Securities and the Daewoo Motor Company emerged as the assets of the group were sought by other firms as a takeover target. In electronics and related products, Daewoo was well behind Samsung, Hyundai, and LG. In no core business that it undertook was Daewoo ever the Korean leader, nor was it ever ranked among the best companies internationally.

In spite of a generally mediocre return on investment record, however, Daewoo never seemed to have much trouble obtaining the finance needed to expand. Most observers credit the ability of Kim Woo-chung to ingratiate himself with Korea's presidents beginning with Park Chung-hee and including, it would seem, Kim Dae-jung. During 1998, in fact, a year of severe recession in Korea, Daewoo managed to increase its reported debt by 40 percent, or a total of $17 trillion won (Beck 2000).[19] It is not entirely clear how this was possible, and it is not even clear exactly what was done with the proceeds of the debt; the group has never released a financial statement that would indicate fully the uses of its funds. What was clear in 1998 was that Kim Woo-chung had no intention of reducing the rate of expansion of the group by cutting back on investment in what were widely recognized as low-return undertakings. Early that year, he announced in an interview that Daewoo would ignore Korean government pleas for reform and would continue to borrow to the hilt to finance expansion.[20] The big question thus becomes, Why did lenders, both inside and outside Korea, continue to lend to Daewoo during that year?

One theory is that banks in Korea during 1998, bereft of investment opportunities, saw Daewoo (along with the other big five chaebol) as subject to the "too big to fail" doctrine. This explanation seems inadequate, however, given government pressures for the chaebol to reduce debts and Kim Woo-chung's defiant attitude. Even if such a doctrine

---

19. In 2002, a scandal erupted in Korea regarding illegal campaign contributions to Kim Dae-jung in 1997 routed through a foundation controlled by Kim's third son. It was rumored that contributions had been received from Daewoo or from Kim Woo-chung. At the time of this writing, such allegations have not been established as fact.

20. Michael Schuman, "Daewoo Group Takes Expansionist Tack amid Crisis," *The Wall Street Journal*, April 22, 1998, A17.

was at work, Daewoo was the most likely candidate to be the exception. Also, much of Daewoo's borrowings were from foreign banks, and in 1998 it was not clear that foreign banks would be included in a rescue of Daewoo because it was too big to fail.

One standard explanation for the failure of financial markets to withhold funds from bad ventures points to informational asymmetry. Boiled down to its essence, this argument is that financial institutions lend because they do not know what is truly happening to the money they are lending; rather, they are acting on the basis of bad information and, indeed, are being misled by the borrower. But this explanation too seems inadequate: while Daewoo practiced something less than full disclosure (the total extent of the group's borrowings eventually proved to be significantly understated), Kim Woo-chung was quite open about his general strategy of borrow and expand. Moreover, his strategy was plainly reckless and should have been seen as such. In addition, that Daewoo was in deep trouble seems to have been well understood even before the onset of the crisis in 1997, and that the group was heading toward the rocks was widely acknowledged in 1998.

A third possibility is that even though financial institutions knew that the group's strategy was bad and that the group was in deep trouble, they believed—or perhaps hoped against hope—that the group could be turned around. If so, this would have been a misjudgment leading lenders to throw good money after bad. Moreover, it appears that foreign banks lent to Daewoo on terms more favorable even than those demanded by Korean banks. In particular, Korean banks typically demanded that loans to the group be collateralized, whereas most foreign loans were not collateralized. Exactly why this was so is not clear, or at least not to me.

Whatever the answer to this mystery, by December 1998 it was obvious that the group was in truly deep trouble, even though Kim Woo-chung vigorously denied it and indeed gave interviews at several times during 1998 both to claim that Daewoo was not in difficulty and to describe his ire at government efforts to rein him in.[21] Nonetheless, under duress, the group announced major restructuring plans in December, including an impending agreement on the terms of the big deal with Samsung by which Samsung would acquire Daewoo's electronics businesses in exchange for Daewoo taking over the fledgling Samsung Motors. Kim Woo-chung also suggested that once Daewoo had gained Samsung Motors, the group would reorganize its combined automotive operations into one subsidiary and sell a stake in it to General Motors. At that time, General Motors was mum about this possibility, but GM did later emerge as a

---

21. See, e.g., "Companies and Finance: Asia Pacific," *Financial Times*, November 24, 1998, in which Kim suggests that all affiliates of Daewoo were profitable with the exception of the recently acquired former automotive affiliate of Ssangyong.

bidder for the automotive subsidiary of Daewoo after the group went bankrupt. By that time, however, Samsung Motors had been sold to the French auto firm Renault and the Japanese automaker Nissan, the latter by then itself under Renault's control.

The restructuring plans also had overtones of desperation. Kim Woo-chung announced that Daewoo was talking with Japanese firms about a possible sale of its shipbuilding subsidiary. This subsidiary was highly troubled, and any sale would almost certainly have been on terms unfavorable to Daewoo. Daewoo was also negotiating with an American group (Newbridge Capital, which was at that time also negotiating a takeover of Korea First Bank; see above) to sell its telecommunications affiliate, and Kim was attempting to make a deal with the Japanese firm Nippon Electrical Glass to take over Daewoo's electrical glass operation. However, none of these proposed sales would yield enough cash to turn around Daewoo's losses. By the end of 1998, Daewoo's creditors were finally realizing that the prospects for Daewoo were very bad indeed (Noland 2000).

During early 1999, when the economic prospects for Korea in general were brightening, the financial problems of Daewoo intensified. Credit-rating agencies downgraded Daewoo's debt (in April, the US bond rating agency Standard and Poor's gave Daewoo a rating of B-). On July 17, the chairman was forced to pledge his personal assets in order to secure a rollover of corporate bonds and paper by domestic Korean lenders. It was not clear that those assets were adequate to guarantee this debt, however. With some encouragement and, more important, guarantees from the government, the creditors—which included financial subsidiaries of Hyundai, Samsung, SK, and LG—nonetheless extended the credit on July 19. The government also asked that foreign creditors roll over Daewoo's debts, but offered no guarantees. Foreign banks complained that there was no collateral behind the debts and, moreover, that they were receiving nonequal treatment from the Korean government, which had guaranteed the domestic rollovers. The head of the FSC replied that Daewoo would sell foreign assets to retire debt owed to foreigners (Noland 2000).

Matters deteriorated further shortly thereafter when creditors rejected Kim Woo-chung's restructuring plan and the government allowed creditors to take control of the restructuring process after foreign banks threatened to call Daewoo's foreign loans.[22] Days later, however, the restructuring was turned back over to Kim Woo-chung, possibly in an effort to cut foreign bankers out of the restructuring. Early August saw a soap-operatic conflict develop between the FSC and foreign banks over the handling

---

22. A somewhat more detailed description of the events described in the following four paragraphs is provided by Noland (2000), from which the description here is derived with additional facts from Beck (2000), Kirk (1999), Graham (2000), and Haggard (2000).

of Daewoo; one casualty was Hanvit Bank, which was forced to accept a large discount on an international placement of about $1 billion in bonds. Its losses sent a signal that there would be a price to pay if foreign banks were treated less favorably than domestic lenders in any disposition of Daewoo. The Korean stock market fell, and domestic sympathy for Daewoo was waning.

On August 11, creditors were allowed to sell off Daewoo's financial subsidiaries, without which the group could not meet its daily cash obligations; this act signaled the beginning of the end. In the days that followed, the breakup of Daewoo began, which ultimately left the flagship Daewoo Corporation with nothing except its automotive subsidiaries. In a speech delivered on August 15, the anniversary of Korea's liberation from Japan in 1945, Kim Dae-jung referred to the Daewoo crisis in calling for the restructuring of the Federation of Korean Industries (the industry association representing the chaebol, whose chairman had been Kim Woo-chung) and the breakup of the chaebol. (President Kim, however, soon retreated from the latter position.) In late August an agreement was reached whereby debt repayments of 12 Daewoo subsidiaries were suspended for three months in order to allow for an orderly workout procedure to be achieved; due diligence proceedings would be carried out by the FSC and findings reported.

In early November, creditors rejected restructuring plans for two of Daewoo's larger affiliates, prompting the resignation of Kim Woo-chung. At the same time, the due diligence investigation by the FSC found that Daewoo's total debt was not $49 billion, as had previously been reported, but rather $73 billion. The FSC also reported that the debts of Daewoo could not be resolved without some combination of public money and Daewoo's creditors taking "haircuts" (i.e., receiving less than face value for retirement of debts).

But would foreign and domestic creditors be treated the same in this resolution? During December, the Corporate Restructuring Coordination Committee of the FSC proposed a scheme whereby in principle each set of creditors would receive the same treatment but de facto foreign creditors would receive worse terms than domestic ones. The difference in treatment centered on foreign banks' heavy lending to the Daewoo Corporation, the headquarters of the group that for practical purposes had functioned as a holding company—loans that, as noted, were not collateralized. The domestic banks, by contrast, held relatively more loans to affiliates other than the Daewoo Corporation, which were mostly collateralized. The Daewoo Corporation had a particularly high debt-to-asset ratio, and thus the FSC proposed a higher discount for Daewoo Corporation debt than for affiliate debt.

But this proposal was undermined by a revelation on December 6, 1999, that the Daewoo Corporation had illegally channeled upwards of $8 billion to ailing affiliates; this disclosure forced Kim Woo-chung on the lam (he was, fortunately for him, in Europe at the time and hence out of reach of Korean authorities) and also opened up the possibility that criminal actions could be taken against Daewoo in Korea and elsewhere. With these possibilities in the background, in late January 2000 foreign creditors and the FSC mutually agreed to a 61 percent write-off of Daewoo debt, but the creditors received part of the payment in warrants that had some potential to appreciate in value if the fortunes of Daewoo Corporation were ever to turn around. In effect, the assets of Daewoo were nationalized.

The saga still was not over. As noted, the Daewoo crown jewel, albeit a rather small one, was the Daewoo Motor Company (DMC). In early 2000, the Korean government announced that this subsidiary was for sale. Two large US auto-making firms, General Motors and Ford, indicated an interest in DMC (General Motors had been co-owner of DMC less than 10 years before). There were also rumors that Hyundai might take over Daewoo in a deal similar to that by which it had already taken over Kia. Articles appeared in the Korean press contending that national interests argued for DMC remaining under Korean control; such control almost surely would mean that the firm would be merged with Hyundai. But this merger would have given Hyundai a virtual monopoly on passenger cars in Korea; moreover, the Hyundai group itself was facing mounting financial difficulties (see next section). In May, Hyundai announced that it would not seek to take over Daewoo, although rumors persisted that the government was attempting to find a means by which this takeover might happen.

After a protracted period of bidding, in June the Korean government announced that the winner was Ford, whose offer was in the range of $7 billion, contingent on completion of a due diligence report. General Motors had bid in the $4 billion range. But in September, the due diligence report indicated that DMC had liabilities in excess of those reported, especially in the overseas operations that it had added since it had parted ways with General Motors in 1992. In addition, Daewoo faced penalties from the government of India for failing to meet export quotas that had been imposed as part of Daewoo's entry into India. The Korean government indicated that in spite of these findings, it would not accept a reduced offer from Ford, and on September 15 Ford backed out of the deal.[23] The Korean stock index plummeted.

General Motors proved to be still interested in DMC, but not at the $4 billion price that had been offered in June 2000. In June 2001, General Motors was reported to be offering only about $1 billion for DMC; it had earlier also indicated that if it were to buy the firm, it would want to close an outmoded plant in Inchon unless public funds to keep the plant open

---

23. John Larkin, "For Sale, Again: The Collapse of Ford's Bid to Buy Daewoo Motors Will Slow Financial and Corporate Reform," *Far Eastern Economic Review*, September 28, 2000.

were forthcoming.[24] DMC's workers responded by declaring that if the Inchon plant were closed by GM, they would make it "very difficult" for Daewoo cars to be sold in South Korea; DMC's labor union in fact sent a delegation to GM's annual meeting in the United States to demonstrate opposition to any takeover of DMC by GM. In the meantime, the Korea Development Bank, the main creditor of DMC, indicated that the Inchon facility would have to be included (and kept open) in any sale of the firm.[25]

On May 1, 2002, the acquisition of DMC by General Motors was finally announced after more than a year of negotiations. GM was to pay $400 million for a 67 percent stake in DMC; this represented only 10 percent of the price GM had originally offered to acquire the Korean auto firm. Reasons for the reduced price included not simply the additional debt uncovered under the due diligence proceedings but also the loss in value suffered by Daewoo while the negotiations were under way. Thus, for example, during early 2002, when other Korean auto firms were reporting markedly higher sales than a year earlier, DMC's total sales dropped. Indeed, by the time the buyout was completed, Daewoo had fallen behind Ssangyong to become the number three automaker in Korea, far behind Hyundai (including Kia) and with Renault-Samsung closing ranks.

As part of the deal with General Motors, Daewoo's creditors, led by Korea Development Bank, acquired a 33 percent share in Daewoo at a price of $197 million. On June 29, it was announced that a new firm, GM-Daewoo Auto and Technology, would be created in September 2002 to take over Daewoo Motors' assets. GM also announced that all Daewoo employees under the level of vice president would be hired by the new firm. In addition, the Suzuki Motor Company of Japan would be buying a 14.9 percent stake in this new firm for $89 million; this stake would be sold by GM and hence would reduce GM's holding in Daewoo. Furthermore, in the future, GM would sell a 10 percent stake to its Chinese joint venture, Shanghai GM. Daewoo's bus operations were not part of the original deal with GM, and on July 1, 2002, a memorandum of understanding was signed by which an agreement in principle was reached to enable Youngan Hat Company to take over the assets associated with the bus operations.

The Near Collapse and the De Facto Breakup of the Hyundai Group

On March 21, 2001, Chung Ju-yung, founder of the Hyundai group, died at age 85. Starting virtually from scratch, he had in his lifetime assembled

---

24. Agence France Presse wire report, reported on the *Financial Times* Web site, http://www.FT.com, June 27, 2001.

25. John Burton, "Union Protests at GM Plans for Daewoo," *Financial Times*, June 4, 2001.

one of the largest business empires in the world, albeit with much help from Korea's public treasury. Late in life, he had placed much of the empire on the line in what amounted to an idealistic cause, an effort to help end the antagonistic and dangerous relationship between North Korea, where he had been born, and South Korea, where he had himself prospered (and, in doing so, without question helped to transform South Korea from quite a poor into quite a rich country). If Daewoo mostly represented much of what had gone wrong with Korea, Hyundai represented what had gone right as well as what had gone wrong. Hyundai was, of course, a much bigger group than Daewoo; and unlike Daewoo, Hyundai was a world leader, at least in size, in some of the many business in which it operated. In other businesses, Hyundai was far from being a world leader, and the huge variance in performance of the many affiliates that made up Hyundai was at the heart of the problems that the whole group was experiencing.

Indeed, in no small part because of the venture in the North, but for many other reasons as well, at the time of Chung's death the Hyundai group was on the verge of following Daewoo into failure. At the time of this writing, the ultimate fate of the remnants of the Hyundai group remains unresolved and cloudy.

One thing became clear following the death of Chung Ju-yung: the group would not continue to operate as one chaebol (see SaKong 2000-2001). Indeed, Chung Ju-yung himself launched a breakup of the group, for familial more than business or economic reasons: he wished to divvy up his empire among his three surviving legitimate sons. The sons could not agree among themselves how to share the wealth and power that would come their way when their father passed away. One son, Chung Mun-hoon, would assume control of the original firm, Hyundai Engineering and Construction Company, Hyundai Merchant Marine and Hyundai ASAN (which controlled the ventures in North Korea). His younger brother Chung Mun-joon would control Hyundai Heavy Industries. Hyundai Motor Company (HMC) and its acquired affiliate Kia (which was run as a quasi-independent unit) would go to the third brother, Chung Mun-koo, who reportedly did not get on with his siblings. Hyundai Electronics Industries would be spun off from the other units and an effort would be made to reduce this affiliate's debt and to raise new cash. Certain other affiliates would also be spun off.

Because of the complex cross-holdings among the Hyundai affiliates and the poor financial state of many if not most of them, the separation was to prove difficult. For example, Hyundai Merchant Marine, designated as part of Chung Mun-hoon's piece of the empire, was a major shareholder in Hyundai Heavy Industries (HHI), destined to be part of Chung Mun-joon's mini-empire. Thus, in June 2001, the former sold many (but not all) of its shares in the latter, and planned to sell the remainder in the indefinite future. One problem was that HHI shares were depressed;

in June they in fact were selling below book value. One cause for their drop in value was the revelation that HHI had advanced financial aid totaling about $1.2 billion to the distressed Hyundai Electronics Industries and other Hyundai units. As usual, this financing had gone forward without the consent of minority shareholders; indeed, the financing had been advanced without HHI even informing these shareholders of the transaction.

At the same time, HHI itself was a shareholder in other Hyundai units. It held stakes, for example, in Hyundai Corporation (the trading affiliate), Korea Development Corporation, Hyundai Oilbank, and Hyundai ASAN. It held 50 percent of Hyundai Petrochemical, one of the most troubled of Hyundai's units and one that was meant to come under Chung Mun-joon's purview. In addition, HHI was guarantor for debt for Hyundai Engineering and Construction Company and Hyundai Merchant Marine; these, as noted, were to fall to Chung Mun-hoon. Under post-1997 laws forbidding cross-holdings among firms, many of these connections had to be severed under any circumstance. At the end of fiscal year 2001, HHI in fact was operating at an overall loss, even though its main businesses, its shipyards, held a net backlog of orders and were turning substantial operating profits. The losses derived from its ties to other Hyundai affiliates, especially the petrochemical affiliate. Another major shareholder of this last affiliate—Hyundai Engineering and Construction Company, the flagship inherited by Chung Mun-hoon—was itself highly troubled. As already noted, then, HHI and other Hyundai units were beset with exactly the sort of problem that had come to plague most of the chaebol: bad operations had the potential to bankrupt good ones.

Thus, as spring turned into summer in 2001, the question in Seoul was: Could any of the Hyundai units survive as viable units once the separation occurred? As recently as early 2000, few financial analysts would have predicted disaster for the Hyundai group, though problems were known to exist. But as 2000 progressed—and, again, we should recall that this was a year of overall quite robust growth for Korea—the true scale of the problems began to surface. Although it seemed that these were everywhere (in large part because the cross-holdings of the group caused difficulties in one affiliate to affect the performance of other affiliates), two problems stood out as especially severe. One of these was the North Korean venture (or, rather, ventures), where payments pledged to the North Korean government were exceeding the ventures' revenues, let alone operating profits. The other was the combined semiconductor operation that had been created from the "big deal" with LG.

Hyundai Electronics Industries, as noted earlier, emerged from that deal as the world's largest producer of memory devices, displacing its Korean rival Samsung Electronics. But the operation also left HEI drowning in debt: when the merger with LG was completed in late 1999, HEI held a total debt of close to $10 billion. Not all of the debt, as was subsequently revealed, had been used to finance the business of the electronics firm; rather, HEI also invested in Hyundai Investment Trust, which was in turn pouring money into Daewoo. This investment was made despite HEI's own need for substantial capital investment to upgrade its production equipment; rather, debt servicing charges and the payments to HIT prevented HEI from making the needed investment in its own operations. At the time of the merger, both Hyundai and LG were losing money; but because the market for DRAMs was beginning to go into an up-cycle, in 2000 the combined firm was able to earn substantial operating profits. Then, in 2001 the bottom fell out of the DRAM market, and the firm lost close to a half billion dollars

In 2001 HEI became Hynix as Chung Mun-hoon announced plans to sell off his own shares and shares held by other Hyundai affiliates in the firm, so that the firm would cease to be part of the Hyundai group. In anticipation of this sale, these shares were placed on deposit at the Korea Exchange Bank. Hynix also announced that it would no longer be liable for any payment guarantees to other Hyundai affiliates. Thus, by June 2001 Hynix, the former HEI, was virtually an independent firm. But its problems were legion.

In June 2001, the firm raised more than $1.25 billion in an international sale of a "global depository receipt" (GDR) issue, which was required by Korean creditors in order to roll over about $4.4 billion in debts. The GDRs were sold to foreign investors, giving these rights to Hynix common stock at a discount of about 25 percent of the then-current market price. The firm announced restructuring plans, which included laying off excess workers as well as investing in new production equipment; however, apparently little action has been taken along these lines. Throughout 2001, in what has become one of the most controversial episodes of Hynix's checkered history, the Korea Development Bank underwrote a total of almost 3 trillion won of Hynix bonds. Several objections have been raised to this move, including threats by both the United States and the European Union to launch World Trade Organization complaints that the underwriting amounted to a subsidy to Hynix that is inconsistent with Korean WTO obligations. In October 2001, Hynix's creditors converted about 3 trillion won of debt into equity, agreeing in exchange to write off another 1.4 trillion won of debt.

Reports have emerged of alleged agreements whereby other former Hyundai-affiliated firms have agreed to help Hynix—for example, by buying semiconductor chips from Hynix at above-market prices. They raise suspicions that Hynix (and the whole former Hyundai chaebol) might be engaging in sub-rosa transactions that in effect continue the intra-group subsidization practices of the past, albeit in a somewhat altered form (Mako 2002a).

Whether in gaining its independence (if indeed it has become truly independent) Hynix had become so weakened that its survival was threatened was another matter; only time would tell. The big issue in 2001 was the price of DRAMs, which had fallen in mid-2001 to a price barely 10 percent that of one year earlier. Some analysts were predicting that without some recovery in DRAM prices, Hynix would almost surely fail.[26] Even with higher DRAM prices, the firm faced difficulties because it had failed to make capital investments between 1998 and 2001. During 2002, Hynix continued to teeter on the edge of bankruptcy and only the infusion of new capital by its creditors was keeping it afloat. In the spring of 2002, Hynix announced an operating loss of more than 84 trillion won ($7 billion) for FY 2001, the largest in the history of a Korean firm. Indeed, the magnitude of this loss was equal to more than 40 percent of the combined earnings of those Korean companies that reported profits. By early May, the market value of the firm had tumbled to 60 percent of its level of December 31, 2001.

On April 22, 2002, Hynix management announced that it had signed a memorandum of understanding (MOU) with the US firm Micron Technology whereby Hynix would sell its memory chip operations to Micron for $3.4 billion, on condition that these operations be infused with $1.5 billion of new cash. Tied to the MOU was a debt-rescheduling plan that would, in effect, require more than half of Hynix's debt to be written off by the firm's creditors. This would be a large hit on the creditors, as Hynix accounted for more than 20 percent of all corporate debt outstanding in Korea. Under this MOU, Micron would also assume a 15 percent stake in the remaining operations of Hynix for $200 million. The MOU was subject to approval by the boards of directors of Hynix and Micron, as well as the council of creditors of Hynix.

Almost immediately, on April 25, Hynix's labor union, with the backing of the Federation of Korean Labor Unions, adopted a resolution opposing the MOU and any sale of Hynix assets to Micron. The union proposed that Hynix instead "stand on its own feet," threatening to go on strike if the terms of the MOU were accepted by the Hynix board and creditors' council. However, on April 26 the chairman of the FSC, Lee Keung-young, urged the creditors' council to accept the terms of the MOU on the grounds that Hynix would likely fail entirely without the sale of assets to Micron. But some creditors expressed doubts about the sale, objecting to the large losses they would take if it were to go through. The creditors opposing the MOU were largely nonbank institutions, while the main banks (led by Woori, the new financial conglomerate centered around what had been the Hanvit Bank) generally were inclined to accept the proposed deal, fearing that loans to Hynix might otherwise be 100 percent nonrecoverable. Representatives of minority shareholders of Hynix also vocally opposed the deal.

---

26. See "When the Chips Are Down," *Far Eastern Economic Review*, July 19, 2001.

In what was something of a surprise vote, the Hynix board of directors rejected the MOU on May 1, 2002. Instead of the terms proposed under the memorandum, the board suggested that Hynix sell off its nonmemory chip operations and continue as an independent firm making memory chips only. Outside analysts, including those associated with Hynix's creditors, almost immediately questioned whether this scheme was feasible.[27] Following the vote, the share price of Hynix rose 6.1 percent, but the share prices of major creditors fell by as much as 8 percent. Micron on May 4 announced that it was "withdrawing" from the negotiations with Hynix; an official of the Korea Exchange Bank, the largest single creditor to Hynix, suggested that Micron might be open to restarting the negotiations in the future—but not in the near future. On May 9, the Hynix board of directors approved a plan whereby the firm would be broken into four different operations, three of which would be sold: chips other than memory, thin film liquid crystal displays, and other operations. By dividing the nonmemory operations into these three parts, Hynix management implicitly acknowledged that only one (thin film liquid crystal displays) was really viable; in particular, management explicitly acknowledged that the nonmemory chip operation was "a bit outdated." This plan was commented on favorably by FSC head Lee Keung-young on the day that it was announced.

During this period, there was considerable turnover in Hynix management, with the CEO being replaced in early May and 30 percent of all executives being laid off later that month in a bid to reduce costs and make management more effective. Hynix shares rose 13 percent over the month. In spite of these efforts, after the publication of due diligence reports prepared as part of the effort to break the firm into four parts as described above, FSC head Lee Keung-young announced on May 23 that even the core memory business would not be viable as an independent company and would have to be sold. Also, Lee hinted that further bailouts of the firm would not be forthcoming. During early June, creditors converted large amounts of convertible bonds into equity, giving them a large majority stake in Hynix's voting shares; some of these creditors also announced the creation of additional reserves against write-downs of remaining Hynix debt (e.g., the Woori group raised its reserves from 70 percent to 80 percent of Hynix debt held by the group). A minority shareholders' effort to gain a court injunction to prevent the conversions was rejected by the Seoul District Court on May 31.

During the second week of June, creditors began selling Hynix shares on the open market, precipitating a 15 percent drop in share prices. In early July, Woo Eui-je, an executive of the Korea Exchange Bank, became CEO of Hynix, and a new board of directors was selected. This

---

27. See "Hynix Seeking to Sell Off Nonmemory Unit for Survival as Memory Manufacturer," *The Korea Herald,* May 2, 2002.

board of directors was endorsed at an extraordinary meeting of share-holders on July 24, 2002.

On July 8, 2002, Micron publicly announced that it might still be interested in taking over the memory chip operations of Hynix. But at the time that this book was going to press, no new negotiations had begun. Only time will tell whether a deal might be struck and, if so, whether Hynix will suffer the same fate as Daewoo Motor Company—to be eventually sold for a sum far less than that originally offered but initially rejected.

Other former Hyundai businesses were also doing poorly. The losses on the North Korean ventures (Hyundai ASAN and Hyundai Merchant Marine) were clearly unsustainable. In February 2000, the accumulated losses of ASAN had exceeded its paid-in capital, and the firm unilaterally decided to halve the $12 million per month it had agreed to pay the North Korean government for the right to run the Mount Kumgang project. Hyundai had expected half a million tourists to visit that destination per year, but in the first two years of operation, fewer than 400,000 had actually come. Hyundai Engineering and Construction Company was contracted to build most of the facilities at Mount Kumgang (a large spa hotel, golf course, restaurants, etc.) as well as the necessary infrastructure. Hyundai Merchant Marine, which was the major shareholder of ASAN, was losing money on its passenger ship service to the project. In addition to Mount Kumgang, Hyundai had committed to a $5 billion industrial complex in North Korea near the town of Kaesong. In June 2001 the future of this project was in question.

In April 2001 Hyundai Merchant Marine, at the insistence of creditors, ended its passenger ship service to Mount Kumgang and handed over all operating responsibility to ASAN, which in turn negotiated an overland route to the project by which tourists could travel. In June, the South Korean government agreed to subsidize the undertaking through the Korea National Tourism Agency (KNTO). KNTO would provide up to $12 million a year to underwrite marketing expenses and also to pay the transportation costs of tourists going to the area. In return, it would receive the concessions to manage the duty-free shops and hotels at the site. There were rumors that the South Korean government had pressured Hyundai Motor Company to extend assistance to its sister companies involved in the North, but that Chung Mun-koo had refused on the grounds that such assistance could undermine the relatively good health of HMC (see below).

Losses in North Korea also affected Hyundai Engineering and Construction Company, which had its domestic problems as well, including a sharp downturn in its core construction business in South Korea. The finances of the former flagship company were complicated by its relationships with other Hyundai affiliates. HECC in November 2000 nearly defaulted on its debt, but agreement was reached with creditors on a rollover of bank credits that would last through the end of the year. This raised concerns about a possible bailout of HECC (Mako 2002a), because of the role of government in obtaining the agreement. Furthermore, during 2000 reports circulated that the FSC had pressured other Hyundai affiliates not to resist HECC's plans for a "self-rescue" (translation: other affiliates would come to HECC's aid). In January 2001 Chung Mun-hoon barely averted loss of control of the firm to creditors, but in June 2001 a consortium of these creditors, led by the Korea Exchange Bank, agreed to a massive debt-for-equity swap arrangement in exchange for a rollover of debt. This arrangement, carried out in 2002, effectively removed Chung Mun-hoon as the main shareholder of the firm; as a result, the former flagship was no longer in the hands of the founding family of Hyundai. The main shareholder became the Korea Exchange Bank, which is under government control. The firm in 2001 posted large losses, and its status at the time of this writing remains very unhealthy.

In 2002, in fact, the only one of the Chung brothers with much reason to smile was Chung Mun-koo. Somewhat remarkably in the eyes of many analysts, and in spite of the gloomy prognosis offered earlier in this chapter, both Hyundai Motor Company and its Kia affiliate were earning positive returns. This profitability was in good measure the result of upturns in their fortunes in the United States, where both the Hyundai and Kia brand names were selling reasonably well in spite of continuing quality and image problems. The turnaround there seems to have resulted from the aggressive pricing of popular models. In particular, Hyundai's Santa Fe sport utility vehicle and its relatively low-priced Sonata luxury sedan were both selling well, raising expectations that Hyundai would surpass its previous high point in unit sales in the United States, set in 1991.

One consequence of Hyundai Motor Company's improved fortunes in 2001 was a significant rise in its common stock price during the first half of the year. This might have reflected not just improved sales but also market perceptions that HMC was no longer tied to the Hyundai group.[28]

In the first quarter of 2002, however, exports of both Hyundai and Kia vehicles fell by a combined total of more than 6 percent, apparently because of a slowdown in the US economy. Largely offsetting this drop, domestic sales of cars in Korea picked up, so that total unit sales of the two Hyundai auto firms remained about constant. Even so, Kia's net profits fell about 14 percent in the first quarter. And while the Hyundai Motor Company's operating profit rose in that quarter, operating margin per vehicle sold fell in 2002 relative to 2001, an indication of the aggressive pricing strategy that Hyundai was following.

In the long run, however, it is unlikely that Hyundai Motor Company can become a major world producer of automobiles. Indeed, most forward-looking analysis of this sector suggests that the world industry will become increasingly dominated by a handful of firms, maybe as few as six

---

28. See "Hyundai Motor Group's Market Value up 76%," *The Korea Herald*, June 30, 2001.

but no more than eight. No analyst believes that Hyundai will be one of them. For this reason, perhaps, in September Daimler-Chrysler announced that it was purchasing a 9 percent stake in HMC. Because Daimler-Chrysler also held a position in Japan's Mitsubishi Motor Company (MMC) and because MMC had long held a small position in HMC (HMC, it might be recalled, originally produced vehicles of Mitsubishi design), Daimler-Chrysler's total holdings in HMC were about 12 percent. In June 2001 it was announced that a joint venture would be set up with HMC in Korea to manufacture engines for commercial vehicles. Nonetheless, perhaps to stave off nationalistic feelings such as those that were impeding efforts by the Korean government to sell Daewoo Motors to foreign investors (see the previous section), HMC executives indicated that HMC would never come under the full control of Daimler-Chrysler. Again, time will tell.

In the meantime, HMC, like other components of the disintegrating Hyundai empire, suffers from high debt (HMC in particular inherited the debt incurred to acquire Kia). Also, the problem of low labor productivity persists at HMC, as its factories remain overstaffed. Its unions remain intransigent on the question of any reductions in its workforce.

Thus, at the time of this writing, the Hyundai empire was in an advanced state of dismemberment. I argue in the next chapter that the de facto splitting up of Hyundai is almost surely to the good, as the group had become very dysfunctional. But the main issue now is whether the new units can survive, let alone prosper. This question, too, can be answered only in the future.

Will 1999 Be Remembered as a Repeat of 1990?

In an article published in 1999, You Jong-keun (1999), then governor of South Cholla province in Korea and an economic advisor to President Kim Dae-jung, admitted that during 1998 Kim had decided to place greater priority on bringing the Korean economy out of the deep recession it had fallen into than on achieving the structural and corporate reform that he and his advisors understood were necessary for the long-term health of the economy. However, You also indicated that the need for reform was understood, noting that reform of the top five chaebol was particularly important. In his words: "The success or failure of chaebol restructuring will determine the direction of Korea's paradigm shift" (You 1999, 18).

But as the year 2002 neared its midpoint, and this book was nearing completion, the job of corporate reform clearly remained unfinished. Indeed, by some measures the task seems more daunting today than it did in 1998. In 1998, one might recall, numerous firms were identified as nonviable and put into corporate workouts. But most of these firms—as well as other firms that are technically bankrupt, such as certain affiliates of Daewoo—are in fact still operating, in most cases by virtue of continuing loans that are little more than operating subsidies to cover the difference between operating revenues and operating costs (Noland 2001). Continuance of the status quo is expensive, particularly in terms of opportunity cost: because national savings are being expended to support loss-making operations, those same savings are not available to finance new investment in activities that could propel Korea out of the mire in which it is, for the moment, trapped. Many analysts thus now see a parallel between Kim Dae-jung's priorities of 1998 and those of Roh Tae-woo in 1990. In both instances, short-term growth was sought at the expense of needed long-term change. The growth in 1990 and ensuing years was a precursor to the calamity of 1997-98, and some Korean pessimists worry that the growth of 1999-2002 could be the precursor to a second calamity.

At the same time, there are major differences in the two periods. Unlike in 1990, the easing of monetary policy in 1999 did not lead to rising inflation; and this time there has not been a surge of expansion of capacity in industries already suffering from overcapacity (no new shipyards, no attempted entries into automobile production, etc.). Rather, the main problem now is what has failed to happen: closure of obsolete plants, reduction of workers in operations where there is clear excess of labor, and reduction of debt.

The main consequence is that Korea, in spite of reasonably strong macroeconomic performance in 2002, is failing to fully realize the potential that it clearly enjoys. Korea in fact remains a country with tremendous potential: the country possesses superb technology, an industrious and well-educated people, and, for all their woes, some of the world's best industrial companies, including chaebol-affiliated firms such as Samsung Electronics, SK Telecoms, and others.

So, where to go from here? This is the topic of the next and final chapter.

6

Conclusions

A Tale of Two Countries?

In the months prior to this book being completed in late 2002, the US press reported several of the biggest bankruptcies in US history. It indeed seemed almost as though there were a contest among certain large US firms to lay claim to being the biggest failure of all time. Thus, the energy services firm Enron briefly held the record, but its collapse was soon surpassed by the insolvency of the giant telecommunications services provider WorldCom. Each of these two fallen American firms made the bankruptcy of Daewoo in Korea two years earlier seem rather small in comparison. Moreover, the bankruptcy of these American giants largely caught the American public off guard. Whereas problems at Daewoo had festered for years, and the only surprise about its bankruptcy was how long it took for the firm to be declared formally insolvent, the failures of Enron and WorldCom were not at all anticipated.

As in Korea, in the United States the bankruptcies were characterized by substantial material wealth being acquired by certain company insiders, even as thousands of others lost wealth, their livelihood, or both. For example, Kim Woo-chung, the founder of Daewoo, is widely believed to be a very wealthy person. No one knows for sure, because his whereabouts are unknown and he remains subject to an arrest warrant should he return to Korea. But presumably, Kim is leading a life of considerable luxury in some nation that he has chosen for his exile. In the United States, former CEOs of bankrupt companies, along with other top executives, are out of jobs, but many of them are now exceedingly wealthy. Also, like Kim, executives of at least some failed US firms have been indicted on criminal charges, and the US press has speculated that further indictments involving executives of other firms might follow.

Problems other than executive misconduct have plagued those American firms that in 2002 have had to file for bankruptcy protection, and these problems often bore uncanny resemblance to those of the chaebol in the aftermath of the 1997 Korean financial crisis. Thus, for example, off-balance-sheet financing played a key role in the Enron debacle, just as similar financing figured heavily in the demise of Daewoo: in both cases, it was used to hide the true extent of the indebtedness of the respective organizations. Likewise, in both Korea and in the United States, "creative accounting" techniques were widely employed to distort earnings of business organizations as reported in income statements, so that revenues, earnings, or both were inflated and costs understated. Such creative accounting to distort the bottom line of income statements has been widely reported in the press as one factor in the suddenness of the downfall of WorldCom, as well as featuring in some lesser scandals in the United States (e.g., overstatement of profits by a number of firms, including Xerox and AOL-Time Warner); it also seems to have figured in the case of Hynix in Korea.

Similarly, in both countries, lax corporate governance helped to create the difficulties in their corporate sectors. Boards of directors of large companies seemed not to have played the role that, in principle at least, they should have—to evaluate dispassionately whether the management was steering the firms in a direction that served well the interests of their shareholders. Rather, in both countries, these boards often appeared to be the captives either of management in the case of the United States or, in the case of Korea, of the families of the founders of the firms (who, although no longer majority shareholders, nonetheless effectively retained control). Moreover, cronyism between senior officials in government and business leaders seems to have had deleterious effects. For instance, there seems to be little doubt that Enron, for a time at least, had friends in high places in Washington even during a period when the firm's excesses were getting out of hand; and the role of cronyism in Korea is described throughout this book.

But in the corporate insolvencies in Korea and the United States, we can see positive as well as negative similarities. In this regard, it is important to recognize that in both countries, during the very times when corporate malfeasance has been revealed to have taken place, the overall economic performance of the economy was often quite good. Strong economic growth occurred in both Korea and the United States during much of the 1990s (1998 in Korea is an obvious exception, but as noted in the previous chapter, the recession of that year was very short-lived). Furthermore, the fruits of this growth reached deep into the population.

Doubtless one reason for this growth was that investors were willing to take risks by investing in new activities, often based on new technologies.

Thus, while investment in information technology in the United States did lead to the "dot.com bubble" of the late 1990s (and to the related "telecommunications bubble"), it was also accompanied by unquestioned benefits for the US economy, which are almost surely very long-term in nature (see Baily 2002). And in Korea from the 1970s onward, while large-scale investment in new activities unquestionably created a large amount of wreckage, it also created one of the longest periods of sustained economic growth ever recorded by a single nation.

Thus, one challenge facing both Korea and the United States now is to implement reform that will curb the abuses yet not discourage risk taking where the potential returns are high but where there is significant downside potential for loss. Indeed, one hallmark of a dynamic economy is that business failures will inevitably occur, and some of these are likely to be spectacular. The development of new technologies that propel dynamic economic growth, after all, does entail significant risks as well as potentially high returns, and significant risk implies that some investments will not pan out. The objective of reform is, or at least should be, not to prevent business failure per se but to prevent malfeasance on the part of owners and managers that can lead to unnecessary failure.

It is also important to understand that the drawing of parallels between Korea and the United States in 2002 should be taken only so far. There are a number of significant differences between the bankruptcies and near bankruptcies that have occurred in recent years in the two countries. For example, in the United States, bankruptcies of large firms have historically been resolved rapidly. Some of the consequences have been harsh—workers at these firms have lost their jobs and investors in the firms have lost their shirts. But rapid resolution minimizes the drag on the economy caused by business failure, so that the costs associated with the failure are realized rapidly and do not last for years after the failure occurs. Certainly one reason why rapid resolution is possible is that the United States has in place a reasonably effective "social safety net"; for example, a worker that loses employment as the result of a bankrupt business shutting down is able to collect unemployment compensation and other benefits during a prolonged period without work. The current rash of failures in the United States is demonstrating that these safety nets could serve to be strengthened: for example, by pension management reform, so that no worker loses all or even most of his or her accumulated pension benefits because an employer fails; or by reform of the health care insurance system so that a worker who is forced into unemployment as a result of an employer's bankruptcy does not need to worry that personal health problems can lead to personal bankruptcy. Nevertheless, a safety net does exist. In Korea, by contrast, until the crisis of 1997 there was little or no safety net. One consequence has been that when a major firm failed or even tottered, a constituency was created to urge bailouts and subsidies for it. Moreover, the bankruptcy is resolved slowly if at all, making the "drag" from an insolvency greater than necessary. In this matter, Korea has improved in the years since the crisis, but most experts think that it still has a considerable way to go (Ahn 2001; Cho W. 2001; Chopra et al. 2002; Joh 2001; Kim Joon-ki and Lee 2001; OECD, *OECD Economic Surveys: Korea 2001*; Mako 2002a, 2002b).

The Need for Reform in Korea Has Not Ended

The parallels between the failure of large corporations in the United States and Korea underscore that new reform initiatives are needed in the first and that the process of achieving reform in the second has not yet been brought to a full and successful conclusion. The main difference between the two countries in this regard is that Korea has been implementing a whole series of reforms since the 1997 crisis, whereas reforms in the United States have yet to be fully formulated, let alone implemented. This is to be expected, given the relatively recent occurrence of the US corporate insolvencies. But even so, there is much to be learned by the United States (and by other nations) from the reform that has gone forward in Korea, despite the many differences between the two nations.

Indeed, perhaps the main lesson to be drawn from Korea is that quite aggressive reform there did not, as many might have feared, suppress recovery and economic growth. To the contrary, Korean economic growth following the recession of 1998 has been quite robust, as noted in the previous chapter. Kang Sam-mo, Wang Yun-jong, and Yoon Deok-ryong (2002) demonstrate that in fact the recovery from the 1997 crisis has been unusually rapid when compared with the rates at which other countries have recovered following a major financial crisis. It is probably not a stretch to argue that Korean recovery has occurred because and not in spite of the serious reform that has been implemented. Nevertheless, further reform is almost surely needed.

First, reform of the Korean financial sector must continue, so that the institutions in this sector not only intermediate savings into investment efficiently (something that has not happened in Korea as well as it should, as we have seen) but also monitor the performance of firms that receive funds and take steps, where necessary, to improve flagging performance. This development, as will be elaborated below, implies more than just further reform of existing financial institutions, as has been the post-crisis focus: whole new institutions must be created in the financial sector.

Second, still higher standards of transparency must be developed and implemented. Indeed, this is an area in which efforts in Korea have been somewhat lagging, though recent US experience demonstrates that it deserves priority. In fact, lack of transparency arguably has been the single factor most responsible for the difficulties in which much of corporate America now finds itself. Moreover, Americans have been largely blind to this problem until recent months, largely because most believed that standards of transparency in the United States were quite high—and have been shocked to discover otherwise. Koreans, by contrast, have long known that companies in Korea do not function under high standards of transparency, though some steps have been taken to raise them. The American experience might serve to convince Koreans that this particular bar needs to be raised yet higher.

Third, the reform of corporate governance in Korea has a long way to go. In particular, the incestuous relationships among the various affiliates of the chaebol should be further reduced, with the ultimate goal that major affiliates should operate entirely independently of one another. Indeed, one big issue facing Korea today is whether the remaining chaebol simply should be broken up. Because a breakup of what had been the largest of the groups, Hyundai, has largely already been achieved, one matter to be watched closely is whether the smaller groups that once constituted the Hyundai chaebol do, in fact, perform better as independent units than they might have been expected to perform within a larger group.[1]

Other issues involving corporate governance in Korea include the need for greater accountability of management to shareholders of firms, particularly to "minority" shareholders. In this case, "minority" is placed in quotes because so-called minority shareholders in Korea sometimes in fact have in total more funds invested in a firm than do the "majority" shareholders—most often members of the founding family of the firm—who have effective voting control over the company. One consequence is that in many Korean businesses minority shareholders and majority shareholders have divergent interests, but management serves the interests of the latter and not the former. (Similar divergences lie behind some of the problems in US firms as well.) Some way must be found by which the interests of minority shareholders are better represented in management decisions than currently is the case.[2]

Fourth, still better means for resolving bankruptcy must be implemented in Korea. As already noted, bankruptcy resolution in Korea remains extremely slow; and making this problem worse, many firms in Korea, in spite of the remarkable recovery of the economy as a whole, remain on the verge of bankruptcy. Nonresolution of insolvent firms creates considerable drag on an economy. How great this drag can be is evidenced by the experience of Japan, where the root of much of the current economic malaise is nonresolution of many firms that are bankrupt or close to it. The risk is high that without further reform of bankruptcy resolution, this drag could grow in Korea, slowing or even stalling future growth.

Fifth, the policy of "too big to fail" must be abandoned in fact as well as in rhetoric. Despite much lip service paid by the government, some of

---

1. For a thoughtful assessment of these issues, see Ehrlich and Kang (2002).

2. See Jang (2002) on this issue.

its actions have nonetheless revealed that this approach is not yet wholly dead in Korea. The big test in this regard surely will be how Hynix is resolved. At the time of this writing, the Korean government has pledged that it will not grant any further subsidies to Hynix. Sticking to this pledge would likely give credence to the proposition that the notion of some companies being too big to fail has indeed been discarded.

Sixth, and perhaps most important, Korea needs a social safety net better than what currently exists.

Further carrying out these reforms (which, in most cases, are already under way) will help Korea cope with other policy issues—for example, what to do about the falling off of foreign investment coming into Korea. This falloff, as argued below, has in large measure occurred precisely because the reform process in Korea has not proceeded far or fast enough.

Let's examine each of these areas of needed further reform in some detail.

Financial Sector

Exactly how much progress has been made in financial sector reform in Korea is, at the time of this writing, difficult to judge. Nonviable financial institutions have been shut down or merged into more viable ones, and weak institutions have been recapitalized and reorganized. In April 2001, a large financial holding company, the Woori Group, was created in an experiment to create a more advanced financial institution in Korea, but this was essentially a merger of a number of existing institutions.

Despite the progress made in this sector, there were some indications that Korea might slip back into its earlier practices that had gotten the country into trouble in the first place. As noted in the previous chapter, when Hyundai Engineering and Construction Company found itself in trouble in 2001, a consortium of financial institutions was formed essentially to bail HECC out. The bailout was not handled quite as it might have been some years earlier. It was centered around a debt-for-equity swap that, when fully carried out, would largely strip Chung Mun-hoon of control of the firm and give it to the consortium. In the past, in contrast, HECC might simply have received "evergreen" loans from its creditors, who would have acted under pressure from the government. Nonetheless, elements of the old system clearly persisted. According to newspaper reports, financial institutions that were reluctant were pressured into the arrangement by the government; among the unwilling was First Korea Bank, which is now under foreign control and which reportedly did not want to participate. Indeed, First Korea Bank was said to view this pressure as being in violation of an understanding between the government and the foreign investors that the bank could make its decisions free from government influence.

In the end, the refinancing of HECC departed significantly from "the bad old days" in positive ways. In particular, the resulting change of ownership control of the firm is almost surely a good thing for Korea, as it suggests that economic considerations, rather than political ones, might now play a greater role in decisions regarding such restructuring than they had in the past. Nonetheless, the heavy hand of the government in attempting to force all financial institutions with a stake in HECC to participate in a government-sponsored plan was disturbing.

The main issue in financial sector reform at the moment is how to reprivatize the banks, a question not yet decided in Korea. What clearly is needed is that banks, as well as other financial institutions, be independent of control both by the government and by the chaebol. But in March 2001 the finance minister of Korea suggested that to reprivatize the banks that had been effectively nationalized as the result of the banking sector recapitalization and reorganization undertaken in 1998, the government might lift limits on ownership of banks by nonfinancial companies. As noted in the financial press, this action would open the way for chaebol-affiliated firms to gain control of banks, and thus make possible exactly the same kind of abuses that got Korea into trouble in the first place—in particular, massive use of debt from captive financial sources to finance low-return expansion.[3] The finance minister who issued this trial balloon was surely well aware of the dangers of such backsliding, but he appears to have made the proposal for a purely pragmatic reason: no institutions in Korea other than the chaebol (or individuals other than owning families of these groups) have the means to buy the banks from the government.

One alternative might be to encourage foreign ownership of the banks. However, this approach is not sufficient in itself. While foreign participation in the banking sector would be desirable for many reasons (e.g., increased competition might force local banks to adopt best practices), foreign ownership of the entire banking sector in Korea almost surely would be unacceptable on political grounds alone. Another alternative might be to fashion a means by which banks could pass into broad-based private ownership. Korea now lacks institutions that might enable small investors to pool resources so as to become major shareholders in large organizations. Thus, the creation of such institutions could solve the problem of who can buy the banks.

Once the banking sector is privatized, the process of building the organizational capabilities of the banks must continue (and indeed one major objective of creating large financial holding companies such as the Woori Financial Group seems to be to foster greater organizational capabilities). As noted by James Rooney (2002), Korea's banks are still beset by poor lending practices, themselves the product of banking personnel's lack of relevant skills, particularly in the area of risk management. Also, banks in Korea remain undifferentiated. Thus, depositors in Korea generally do not

---

3. See the editorial "The Limits of Korea's Reforms: Will the *Chaebols* get Their Piggy Banks Back?" *The Asian Wall Street Journal*, June 21, 2001.

play what in other countries can be an important role: that is, to shift funds out of badly managed banks and into better-managed ones and thereby provide inducement to the former to transform themselves into the latter. Here we have come full circle, because much of the reason for lack of distinction among them is the extensive state control of the banks, which stifles innovation and actually discourages differentiation.

Apart from bank reform, a well-functioning equities market is a top priority, as Catherine Mann (2000) notes. In the case just cited, that of bank privatization, if the equity market were functioning better in Korea, the government could simply float shares of the banks on the market. One reason for the stock market's weakness, as suggested in previous chapters, is that it has historically been something of a casino; in particular, in a number of incidents equity prices have been manipulated in ways that damaged the interests of small investors to benefit large ones. The Korean stock exchange is thus not an institution in which Koreans have confidence. That is truly a shame, because the end result is to effectively deprive most Koreans of the chance to own equity in the large enterprises—both financial and nonfinancial institutions—that dominate their own economy, leaving ownership instead concentrated in the hands of very few. This situation also reduces the flexibility of the whole financial system, making it difficult for firms to raise new equity capital. But entry of new firms into the Korean economy and their expansion, which both require new equity, are essential if the economy is to achieve future growth (on this, see Yusuf and Evenett forthcoming).

Thus what is needed now is the creation of large institutional investors —for example, mutual funds and pension funds—that act on behalf of smaller investors. Although institutions that call themselves "mutual funds" have appeared recently in Korea, these have proven largely to be vehicles for stock market manipulation by large investors. In fact, in an article written several years ago (Graham 1999), I suggested that proper mutual funds and pension funds could play important roles in industrial sector restructuring. The idea was that banks and other lenders would engage in debt-for-equity swaps in order to reduce the overall indebtedness of the Korean industrial sector; the rate of exchange would be determined by independent assessment of the true worth of an individual company. But given the current institutional structure, such swaps would make banks and other lenders major shareholders in many chaebol-affiliated firms, a situation that seemed no more desirable than the chaebol being the major shareholder of the banks (in either case, an incentive is created for the banks to lend to the chaebol on preferential terms). Thus, I proposed that equity be bought by newly organized and wholly independent equity funds, both mutual and pension funds. They would be independent in the sense that they would not be controlled by the chaebol or the banks. In fact, such equity funds themselves could become the owners of banks as the banks are reprivatized.

These institutions would in no way be forced to buy any security that they did not wish to hold but rather would buy equities in open trading. The funds would receive their own funding from Koreans who wished to have somewhere to hold their savings other than the current institutions —the banks, investment trust companies, life insurance companies, and so on. This alternative might be attractive because a well-managed mutual or pension fund could potentially offer higher returns to small investors. Also, risk to the investor would be reduced by proper management: the portfolio held by the fund would be diversified so as to eliminate non-systematic risks to the shareholders.

In 1999, following publication of the article, I was informed by a very senior Korean government official that these ideas were too radical and "probably illegal" in Korea. But in 2001, two years after I was told this, at least one element of this radical and illegal scheme is actually beginning to be implemented in Korea: creditor institutions, which mostly are banks, are now requiring debt-for-equity swaps as a condition for any major loan renegotiation where the borrowing firm is in difficulty. But this in turn leads to a problem: what to do with the equity that the bank acquires? It probably is not desirable for Korea to become a bank-based economy such as Germany, where banks are the major equity holders in industrial firms. One answer is to sell the shares to the public, but in a form that allows the small shareholder to hold a diversified portfolio. And, once again, this implies the creation of new types of institutional investors.

Yet it might not be easy for institutional investors to establish themselves as credible alternatives to banks—as institutions to which small investors will entrust their funds. To address this problem, it might be possible to relax the stricture that current financial institutions not be allowed to control institutional investors, so that a financial group such as Woori could create and operate an equities fund. Such a fund would not actually be owned by the financial group; rather, ownership would reside in the shareholders in the fund, and the financial group would simply provide professional management and lend its name to the group for purposes of establishing credibility. If this sort of arrangement were to be permitted, it would be desirable for credible firewalls to be created between the equity and nonequity operations of the financial group so that decisions taken in one area would be independent of those taken in the other.[4] It might also be desirable that the groups be required to spin off their equities funds at some time in the future.

A key value of such institutional investors to Korea, beyond their potential to give households more alternatives for investing savings, is that they potentially can play a much stronger role than other financial institutions

4. The lack of such "firewalls" seems to be at the heart of problems at Citicorp, being reported in the US financial press just as this book is going to press.

in monitoring corporate performance. Such a role has in fact in recent years begun to be played by creditor institutions in Korea, meaning once again mostly banks. But this function tends to be carried out only after a firm whose debt is held by the banks gets into significant trouble. Institutional equity holders would have an incentive to monitor firms and correct incipient problems at an earlier stage, for the simple reason that they are shareholders in the corporations in which they invest. As shareholders, they hold voting rights and thus, unlike creditor institutions, have some say in the conduct of the corporation on a day-by-day basis. In countries where these institutions are strong, such as the United States, they have been known to force major changes in management of companies that have performed poorly (e.g., in the early 1990s, institutional investors played a major role in a management shake-up at General Motors Corporation).

Most often, this role is manifested simply by the investor selling the equity of firms in which there is no confidence, sending a negative signal to the management of such firms.

Thus if, for example, in the future some firm were to seek, Daewoo-like, to invest in a project with unpromising returns using borrowed money, an institutional investor might quietly suggest to management that the project be reconsidered. If management pressed ahead, the institutional investor might then send a strong signal to the market that something was amiss by selling its shares in that firm. As a practical matter, institutional investors monitor each other's behavior, and such a sell-off might trigger further sell-offs. Management might find, in these circumstances, that it indeed should reconsider its plans.

It should go without saying that institutional investors must be completely independent of the firms in which they invest in order to avoid conflict of interest. But in Korea, even in the post-crisis period, those nonbank financial institutions that have existed have mostly been chaebol-controlled mutual funds and other institutions that have functioned as piggy banks for the groups. This problem has been discussed in earlier chapters; here we need simply note that the creation of major institutional investors that are not under chaebol control remains a desirable but unfinished task in Korea.

Transparency

Financial transparency implies simply that financial and economic information pertinent to the operations of an enterprise is thorough, accurate, truthful, complete, and readily available to all interested parties. Transparency is important because if a market economy is to function well, all agents participating in the market must be well informed. (Market efficiency in fact depends on this fundamental premise; it is thus remarkable that in Korea but also in the United States and elsewhere, those political figures who profess a belief in the market economy have often sought to suppress regulations that would provide for more and better financial transparency.) If the contrary prevails—if, say, a lender believes that a borrower is earning profits when in fact that borrower is incurring losses, or the lender believes that the borrower holds only half the debt that is actually being held—then bad economic decisions can be made: good money might be thrown after bad by investors who act on the basis of what amounts to false information. The consequences of such bad decisions do not affect just the lender and the borrower. Rather, bad economic decisions adversely affect an entire economy and, indeed, an entire society.

In Korea, the failure of the sale of Daewoo Motors to Ford Motor Company illustrates this last point. The failure of this deal to be concluded derived in large measure from lack of transparency. "Due diligence" (itself essentially an effort to confirm the veracity of information presented by a firm, and to correct errors or omissions in that information) revealed not only that the entire group was deeper in debt than had been reported when the group failed in mid-1999 but also that the Daewoo Motor Company was subject to certain specific liabilities—some of these contingent liabilities (e.g., penalties in India for nonperformance)—that previously had not been disclosed. Following the cancellation of this sale, problems of transparency plagued the subsequent negotiations over the sale of Daewoo Motors to General Motors. In the end, the sale was completed in the spring of 2002, but by that time Daewoo Motors had lost most of its original value. As discussed above, the Korean firm was thus finally sold to General Motors for about $400 million; GM had two years earlier bid almost 10 times this amount.[5]

The specific loss of value of Daewoo Motors was not the only cost to Korea. Since the collapse of the Ford takeover of Daewoo, foreign direct investment in Korea has dropped markedly. One reason commonly mentioned in the financial press is, again, lack of transparency. In fact, the international accounting firm PriceWaterhouseCoopers in 2000 examined accounting practices in 35 major countries and found that Korean practices were the least transparent of the 35 (reported in OECD, *OECD Economic Surveys: Korea 2001*). When foreign investors examine an asset that might be for sale, they worry that the asset might somehow have a set of nondisclosed liabilities attached to it. Because meeting those liabilities would create costs, they of course diminish the true value of the asset. But, perhaps worse, the uncertainty regarding the value of the asset deters would-be buyers from purchasing it in the first place. Thus, uncertainty over the true value of Korean assets might very well be at this time the

---

5. Factors other than lack of transparency also contributed to this collapse of value.

biggest single obstacle to foreign direct investment in Korea, simply because foreign investors are wary that assets they seek to buy might come with nondisclosed, nontransparent liabilities.[6]

Obviously, an economy cannot function well if financial information pertaining to enterprises that operate in that economy is routinely inaccurate or fraudulent. Therefore, it is a legitimate role of government, even in free-market economies whose governments in principle largely avoid economic intervention, to enforce requirements for transparency. But unfortunately, there are numerous reasons why persons, firms, and even governments might seek to reduce rather than enhance financial transparency. Most of these reasons fall into two categories: to cover up mistakes or to hide dishonest or illegal actions that serve to benefit certain insider parties. Sometimes the reason boils down to the simple desire of an asset's seller—whether a private agent or a government—to realize as high a price as possible for the asset and thus to hide any bad news that might adversely affect that price. To be sure, such attempts at concealment can be shortsighted, at least from the viewpoint of the overall interest of investors in these assets. But as the recent corporate scandals in the United States make clear, persons whose job it is to manage an asset (a task that includes disclosing to investors proper information regarding that asset) can face conflicts of interest that lead them to hide bad news to benefit themselves. For example, management of several firms in the United States, where top managers often have been compensated by means of stock options on the common stock of the firm, discovered that by manipulating both reported earnings and balance sheet items, they could drive up the price of the common stock and cash in their options before the investor community at large realized that the reported financial information was bogus. In the case of Korea, as suggested above, the motivation for misreporting financial information has often been to try to obtain from a foreign investor a higher sale price than would have been paid had the information been correctly reported.

The enforcement of requirements for transparency has been more difficult in Korea than in many other nations precisely because of the structure of business. Following the practice in the United States, Korea long ago enacted laws requiring firms that are listed on the stock exchange to publicly report certain basic financial information, including balance sheets and income statements. Unlisted firms do not face similar requirements in either country. However, unlike large firms in the United States, Korea's chaebol evolved not as single corporate entities but as loosely affiliated groups of firms, where each affiliate was listed separately or not at all. Furthermore, because of various intricate connections among affiliates, information that was specific to one affiliate might have bearing on some

---

6. A recent assessment of FDI into Korea is provided by Kim June-dong (2002).

other affiliate's performance. If the former affiliate were unlisted, that information might be "opaque" to anyone but insiders who worked for the group, even if the latter affiliate were listed and hence financial information pertaining to it was in principle "transparent." Thus, for example, as noted in the previous chapter, the true debt-to-equity ratios of all of the chaebol, as publicly revealed during the summer of 2000 when the requirement for consolidated group information came into effect, proved to be significantly greater than what the groups had claimed up until that time. Banks lending to the groups therefore simply did not know their true indebtedness, though this information is highly pertinent to loan decisions. In addition, the lack of transparency often has served to benefit inside parties (e.g., the founding families of the chaebol) at the expense of outside parties (e.g., so-called minority shareholders, including foreign shareholders). One example of how such benefits arise has already been noted in previous chapters: loans or loan guarantees from an established chaebol affiliate whose stock is widely owned are used to finance the creation of a potentially high-return but risky affiliate whose equity is largely held by inside investors. The problem with this sort of arrangement is not that funds are put at risk; in fact, such risk might be a good thing, because it can create new activities that lend dynamism to the economy. The problem, rather, is that the minority shareholders of the established affiliate, without transparency, do not know that their money is being put at risk in such a way that there is (for them at least) no offsetting participation in what could prove to be a high-return venture.

The good news for Korea is that much progress has been made in achieving a greater degree of financial transparency than has prevailed generally in Korea. This includes the identification of out-and-out fraud and the impositions of sanctions on those who commit it. Thus, for example, in February 2001, as discussed in the previous chapter, a warrant was issued for the arrest of Kim Woo-chung, the former head of Daewoo who is currently a fugitive from justice, on grounds that he deliberately defrauded investors. In April 2001 the Financial Supervisory Service (FSS) was authorized to impose larger fines and penalties on accounting firms for improper audits, and these firms were made liable for damages that might be incurred by third parties (i.e., minority shareholders) as the result of such improper audits. In November 2001, the Financial Supervisory Commission (FSC) indicted the accounting firms that had audited Daewoo for collaborating with the firm to falsify accounts. In July 2002, the Korea Deposit Insurance Corporation announced that it would file suit against five of these firms to compensate for losses of public funds resulting from "improper accounting" of Daewoo and also of the Kohap group. Separately, the KDIC announced that it would sue the chairman of Kohap for inflating reported profits in a bid to receive public funds. Also during July 2002, the FSS appointed external auditors to 100 companies suspected of posting improper financial statements (auditors are customarily appointed by firms, not by government supervisory agencies). During the first seven months of 2002, a total of 27 executives from 10 different companies received jail sentences for accounting fraud or misuse of public funds, and investigations of similar fraud in 10 additional firms were under way.

The FSS had previously taken steps to strengthen the role of auditors by requiring that they notify the FSS of illegal transactions detected at financial institutions. This followed on a decision of the FSS in April 2002 to seek a new law that would ban auditing firms from offering management consulting services to clients. The FSS had already determined that about one Korean firm out of five received management consulting services from the same company that performed the firm's auditing services. A similar ban has, of course, been discussed in the United States following the Enron debacle, although at the time of this writing it has not been formally proposed by any agency of the US government. Nor has any such law actually been passed in Korea, though its enactment was expected by the end of 2002. Moreover, beginning in 2001, the FSS investigated 72 firms that failed to receive "satisfactory" ratings by their auditors for that year; in April 2002, it decided to force the delisting from the Korean stock exchange of 11 of these firms.

The release in the spring of 2001 of consolidated financial statements for the year 2000 by the 30 largest groups was a clear step in the right direction; the only shame here is that it was so long delayed. An earlier release might, for example, have enabled the emerging problems at Hyundai (discussed in chapter 5) to be identified sooner and thus have increased the odds for a favorable outcome. Consolidated financial statements were released for 2001 in May 2002, and these showed again that the consolidated debts of listed chaebol-affiliated firms were greater than reported on a nonconsolidated basis, as were the debt-to-equity ratios. But also, when compared with 2000, the debt-to-equity ratio of the large groups declined somewhat. In July 2002, the Korea Fair Trade Commission asked a total of 80 affiliates of Samsung, LG, and SK, and the three Hyundai successor groups to present detailed financial data on intragroup transactions. This move apparently was triggered by fears that a "borrow and expand" strategy among the big groups was beginning to reemerge.

As noted in previous chapters, in fact, reform to improve accounting and transparency standards began to be implemented in the wake of the 1997 financial crisis. Beginning in 1998, an independent body (the Korea Financial and Accounting Standards Committee) was appointed by the FSS to recommend appropriate standards for accounting practices in Korea. In 1999, the Korea Accounting Institute (KAI) was created to rewrite Korean standards. In July 2002, the KAI announced that new standards would be phased in from 2003 through the first half of 2004. These would be based on the International Accounting Standards (IAS) as formulated by the International Accounting Standards Board (IASB), a multinational group of experts.[7] The IAS are in the process of being adopted in most European nations. The KAI explicitly rejected the Generally Accepted Accounting Principles (GAAP) as widely used in the United States, noting that the GAAP contain many loopholes that have figured in the recent corporate scandals in the United States.

Progress to date in Korea, while in the right direction, is nonetheless arguably not yet adequate. Further improvement is especially needed in the performance of auditors themselves. One problem as identified by the KAI is lack of qualified personnel; Korea simply does not have enough trained financial accountants and auditors at the moment to do the job as well as it should be done.[8] Another problem is that even at the time of this writing, the need for more transparency is not fully acknowledged. For example, at a meeting held in late July 2002, the Federation of Korean Industries (FKI), the umbrella organization of the large chaebol, stated that "enterprises fundamentally cannot be transparent and any attempt to impose democracy on corporate management would kill the enterprises."[9] The immediate target of this declaration was the Korea Fair Trade Commission, which only a few days earlier had asked that details of financial transactions among affiliates of six large chaebol be disclosed. At the same meeting, Korean Deputy Prime Minister Jeon Yun-churi defended the KFTC request, noting that it had been undertaken in part to ensure that there were no "bookkeeping scandals" similar to those occurring in the United States.

But as several observers point out, it is not just private groups in Korea that could stand more transparency. In particular, transparency would benefit the government. Marcus Noland (2001) notes that the true costs of programs in North Korea should be identified. While agreeing that the government of South Korea "may well" have a strong and legitimate national interest in carrying through with such projects as a means of promoting integration with the North (or at least reducing hostility between the two Koreas), he stresses that more transparency might actually make this whole process more efficient and more effective.

Certainly greater transparency is still called for in the financial sector, where at least three missions are not yet wholly accomplished. The first is to identify remaining problem cases where, in effect, good money is being poured after bad; the second is to resolve these cases; and the third is to take steps to change behavior so that similar cases do not arise in the

---

7. Although the IAS is generally associated with the European Union, it is worth noting that of the 14 experts who constitute the IASB, 7 are US nationals.

8. In 2001, about 750 persons passed the accountancy exam in Korea to qualify as professional accountants. This number was probably not enough to meet needs, though it was up from about 350 in 1996 (OECD 2002, op. cit.).

9. "Conglomerates Facing Government Squarely on Intra-group Transactions," *The Korea Herald*, July 29, 2002.

future. Resolution of these cases almost surely will entail that investors suffer further losses on past investments. But the alternative is worse: to continue to pump funds into those troubled firms, in effect "evergreening" the loans, is necessarily to prevent those same funds from being available for more productive end uses (Krueger and Yoo 2002).

Improving transparency in the corporate sector goes hand in hand with further reform of the financial sector. Reform of the financial sector as discussed above implies that firms that are subpar simply must not be allowed to access credit on any but commercial terms. But, of course, this restriction requires transparency so that subpar firms can be identified as such. Denied access to credit on preferential terms, at least some subpar firms will go under, and these then become "mission 2" cases that must be resolved. It is to be hoped, however, that some large portion of currently subpar firms will be willing and able to take those steps necessary to turn themselves around. Noland (2001) uses the colorful term "zombies" to describe such firms. In 2002, the FSS reported that perhaps 15 percent of firms in Korea did not generate enough cash flow to cover debt service charges, thus almost surely qualifying as zombies. Noland believes that the future health of Korea depends on the zombies being killed off, but this position might be a bit extreme. In fact, in 2000 as many as 25 percent of Korean firms were zombies by the above definition, and most of the reduction of this percentage occurred because firms improved themselves enough to be taken off the "zombie list." The zombies must be eliminated, but killing them off is not the only option. They can instead be turned into more vital institutions: indeed, there are many cases of firms worldwide that have had near-death experiences but have been able somehow to "reinvent" themselves and emerge as healthy and useful enterprises. But for some firms a successful turnaround is unlikely. An honest triage to separate the incurable from the curable zombie is thus needed, and this requires transparency.

Corporate Governance

Closely tied to the issues of financial sector reform and improving transparency is that of corporate governance. In fact, two of the five reasons offered by Joh Sung-wook (2001) to explain why corporate governance has been weak in Korea are poor transparency and inadequate monitoring of the corporate sector by financial institutions. It follows that if one seeks better corporate governance, one must also seek more transparency in both the corporate and financial sectors and better functioning of financial institutions.

But other reforms in corporate governance might also be needed. In this regard, it is instructive to examine the other three reasons given by Joh for poor corporate governance. These are no "credible exit threat"—

that is, large failed firms in Korea do not leave the market (a problem addressed, according to Joh, by better resolution of bankruptcy, discussed later in this chapter); few legal rights or protection for minority shareholders; and negligent boards of directors. In this section, we concentrate on the latter two points.

At the moment the FKI seems to fighting to prevent minority shareholders from gaining legal rights and protection, which the government, in the final months of the Kim Dae-jung presidency, has stepped up its efforts to increase. The current moves should be seen in light of a long-term process by which, as Hugh Patrick (2002) notes, family control of large enterprises in many countries tends gradually to yield to public control; control is "public" when it is ultimately vested in shareholders and no one group of these shareholders either holds a majority interest or is able to block the majority in a shareholders' vote. Most of the Korean chaebol seem to be in some sort of middle ground between family control and public control. For example, the chairmen of the top 10 groups in Korea on average in 2002 owned only slightly more than 2 percent of the total equity of their groups; as reported in previous chapters, total family control for these groups is almost always below 30 percent. And yet, according to Lee Nam-ki, chairman of the Korea Fair Trade Commission, the chairmen of these groups remain "all-powerful."[10] Some evidence for his claim can be gleaned in reports that nepotism abounds in the Samsung group, reputedly one of the best-run of the top 10. For example, Samsung chairman Lee Kun-hee's first son was appointed in 2002 as assistant executive director of Samsung Electronics Company. This created consternation among a minority shareholder group, who feared, according to an unidentified spokesperson, that "slip-ups" by the junior Lee increased the risk of "inflicting losses on all the investors." Samsung Electronics vice chairman Yoon Jong-yong defended the move, stating that Lee was "one of the most competent people in the company and he just happens to be the son of the Samsung Group chairman."[11] Earlier, Lee's second daughter had been appointed general manager of Samsung Fashion Institute, an affiliate of Cheil Industries, the Samsung-affiliated textile firm that had performed so well in the 1960s during the first five-year plan under President Park Chung-hee. Lee's eldest daughter was the manager of the luxurious Shilla Hotel in Seoul, also affiliated with Samsung.

The dispute over whether Samsung chairman Lee's eldest (but still rather young) son is qualified to hold a high executive position at Samsung Electronics falls somewhat outside the scope of this study. But his appointment raises a key question: Does family control over the large chaebol

---

10. Quoted in "Tycoons Own Just 2 Percent of Top-10 Conglomerates," *The Korea Herald*, June 3, 2002.

11. Quoted in "Samsung under Fire for Appointing Chairman's Sibling to Key Post," *The Korea Herald*, June 17, 2002.

serve Korean interests, especially now that the founding families are minority shareholders of the firms that constitute these groups? There is clearly a constituency in Korea that feels that the answer is "no." However, defenders of the current system of corporate governance might note that the Samsung group, which appears to have continued family control more thoroughly than most other chaebol, is also overall the best performing of the top 10 groups (or at least this is true of Samsung Electronics). I shall address this line of defense in a moment.

A question closely related to that of family control is whether the large chaebol, or what is left of them, should simply be split up. The answer is "yes," for reasons that have been stressed throughout this book. The chaebol as presently constituted have acted to create the problems that have characterized the Korean economy in recent years, as their structure has helped to give rise to the perverse incentives that have encouraged overexpansion into activities with low rates of return. We have already delved into this matter in some detail, of course, but two main factors are responsible: the moral hazard created when the groups are considered "too big to fail" and the groups' willingness, rooted in the mechanisms of family control, to use high-return activities to subsidize low- or negative-return ones. Consequently, the groups still suffer from diseconomies of scale and scope. Strong evidence of their weakness is that listed chaebol affiliates that are well-run, high-return operations typically have total market values that are lower than indicators of performance would predict.

Thus, for example, as just noted, Samsung Electronics is consistently rated among the world's best-run companies, and it earns high profits; yet its stock price is low, as measured by the price-earnings ratio of its shares. This ratio, calculated by dividing the closing price per share of common stock on the last day of 2001 by earnings per share reported in 2000, was 2.6. The price-earnings ratio for listed US firms historically has been about 20 (rising during the recent bubble to about 30—but that figure, we can assume, was unnaturally high). So, accepting the P/E of 20 as "typical," the market value of the equity of Samsung Electronics seems to have been only about 15 percent of the value expected. To be sure, one reason for a low valuation of Samsung Electronics is that its earnings are heavily dependent on sales of dynamic random access memory chips; these, as noted in earlier chapters, are subject to very cyclical demand, which leads to volatility in earnings.[12] However, a bigger reason for Samsung Electronics' low valuation is that its earnings have been routinely used to prop up low-performing affiliated firms in the Samsung group.[13] Samsung Electronics was hit particularly hard in late 2000 when

---

12. See "Samsung Jitters," *Far Eastern Economic Review*, September 14, 2000; however, it should be noted that Samsung's earnings and its share price both have risen during 2002.

13. See "Lessons Unlearned," *Far Eastern Economic Review*, September 21, 2000.

newspaper reports revealed that substantial funds it generated had been used to support the stock price of Samsung Electro-Mechanics Company (SEMCO), which in turn had been using cash to cover the debts of Samsung Motors (now under the control of the French firm Renault). Thus, the best affiliate of Samsung has been penalized—severely—for feeding what had been one of the worst of these affiliates.

Such transactions have hurt the minority shareholders of Samsung Electronics, whose holdings of stock in this firm should be worth much more than they are. Indeed, one movement that gained strength in Korea in recent years advocates the stronger exercise of minority shareholders' rights. Yet one of the leaders of this movement, Jang Ha-sung, notes that most minority shareholders in chaebol affiliates are still reluctant to vote against the management, even when management acts against their interests (Jang 2001 and 2002).

Ironically, the low valuation arguably has adverse effects on the interests of the controlling family as well. The members of the Lee family who control Samsung are, of course, wealthy people by any measure. But they would be much wealthier if Samsung Electronics were valued 10 times higher by the market than it is—an increase within the realm of possibility were it not for the tangled connections between this firm and a host of other affiliates in the Samsung empire.

Though the stock market seems to penalize good firms in Korea because of their chaebol affiliation, it is also true that the stock market seems to reward such firms when they free themselves. The best example, discussed at length in chapter 5, is provided by the Hyundai Motor Company, whose sales have been rising and which has effectively declared its independence from the remainder of the Hyundai group: its common stock price rose 127.6 percent during the first half of 2001. The overall market value of the Hyundai Motor Group, which includes Kia as well as Hyundai Motor Company, rose more than 72 percent during that same time. In spite of some dilution of the holdings of chairman Chung Mun-koo because of increased foreign investment in the group (by Daimler-Chrysler) and some resulting loss of control, the value of those holdings (including stock both in Hyundai Motor Group and in Hyundai Motor Company) rose by 112 percent, increasing his personal wealth by almost $100 million.

In contrast, the combined market value of the SK group companies actually declined during the first half of 2001, despite good performance of the telecommunications affiliate. This might be because the consolidated financial statements required by the Korean government (as described in chapter 5) revealed that the total debt of the SK group was significantly greater than previously reported. Indeed, it has been reported that since 1998, the aggregate value of non-chaebol-affiliated firms on the Korean stock exchange has increased significantly more than the total value of firms affiliated with these groups (OECD, *OECD Economic Surveys: Korea 2001*).

Furthermore, and more important, for a profitable firm to subsidize the losses of some other firm is as harmful to society as for the government or for the banking system (by evergreening its loans) to subsidize a loss-making operation. In each of these cases, the net outcome is the same: financial resources that could be used to create high-return ventures that would boost marginal productivity of labor and capital (and hence contribute to rising real wages and growth) are instead used to "feed the zombies."

The answer to the question "should the chaebol be broken up?" is thus crystal clear: "yes, unequivocally." It only remains to be determined how this should be done.

One approach that does not seem to have worked is reforming the chaebol from the inside. For example, since 1999 firms affiliated with the chaebol have been required to appoint outside directors who are intended represent the interests of parties other than the founding families. This requirement has been met in principle, but apparently not in spirit. A survey by the KOSDAQ Listed Companies Association (cited in OECD, *OECD Economic Surveys: Korea 2001*) indicates that in 2000 about 80 percent of the supposedly outside directors in the major chaebol were in fact nominated either by the main shareholder (the chairman) or the group's management (under the control of the chairman). To be sure, the figure was down from about 98 percent in 1999, the year in which the requirement was put in place, but it nonetheless suggests that most of the outside directors are insiders' choices.

Also ineffective would be attempts to prevent continued expansion by invoking the Korean Antitrust Act, which is the wrong tool for the job. The KFTA is an antimonopoly law, intended to protect the economy from the ills that monopolization creates—specifically, abuse of market power. But the "chaebol problem" does not especially concern abuse of monopoly power, as has long been recognized (Chang 1996). Antimonopoly law in fact has little to say about diseconomies of scale or scope, even when those diseconomies are so large that they create significant costs that hamper an entire national economy, as has been the case in Korea. Thus, for example, antimonopoly authorities can (and do) block mergers where these are deemed to create the risk of abuse of market power. But the same authorities cannot block mergers that are just plain bad for the merging firms because some sort of diseconomy is created. We might regret their inability to do so, because diseconomies are probably created by mergers more often than market abuses. Nonetheless, it is not clear how antimonopoly law can be enforced effectively to break up a conglomerate that suffers from internal diseconomies.

To find approaches that will in fact work, it is instructive to see what actually is working. In particular, the Hyundai chaebol today is already partially broken up, with further separation of the Hyundai affiliates likely. This action is under way largely because the shareholders of Hyundai's different affiliates have realized that their interests are not served by the old way of doing business, in which one affiliate might be called on to lend some help to another affiliate without expecting a reward commensurate with the level of assistance given. In effecting this shift, it did not hurt that there was considerable divergence in views among the sons of the founder regarding where the interests of the various affiliates might lie. At the same time, it did not help that the Korean government more than almost any other institution in many ways resisted the breakup, or at least the most desirable aspect of the breakup—that one affiliate would no longer be liable to aid another affiliate in trouble.

At the moment, some of the successor entities of the old Hyundai empire are faltering. But the future of other Hyundai firms now is almost surely brighter than it once was. Thus if, for example, the Hyundai Engineering and Construction Company were to fail, its collapse would not bring down or otherwise punish the Hyundai Motor Company, as might have happened two years ago.[14]

In other cases, the assertion of rights by "minority" shareholders (e.g., those shareholders that do not belong to founding families but today most often collectively hold majority equity positions in chaebol-affiliated firms) is the likely means by which chaebol will be broken up. The shareholders of one affiliate simply have no interest in the transfer of resources, without any promise of commensurate reward, from that affiliate to other affiliates of the same chaebol. It is in their interests that each affiliate behave instead as an independent entity. Thus, the goal of chaebol breakup is closely linked to the movement to enable minority shareholders in Korea to force changes in corporate governance.

The creation of large institutional investors, who act on behalf of small investors on the basis of transparent financial information, therefore will hasten the breakup process. These investors will demand that well-performing affiliates of chaebol in which they hold equity interests not be used to finance losing operations. If, as should happen, significant amounts of debt held by the surviving chaebol are in fact converted to equity, these investors will come to hold substantial shares of the equity of affiliates—and, with these shares, voting rights.

The key to chaebol breakup is simply that the shareholders of these groups act in their own interests in an environment in which failure is not rewarded with a government-backed bailout. Of course, such an environment presupposes that the government fully jettison the "too big to fail" mentality that has been behind the various de facto bailouts (a point discussed below). Furthermore, only shareholders who can stand up to financially irresponsible management can ensure that the chaebol affiliates act in shareholders' interests. For them to succeed, progress must be made in the areas of reform already discussed. For example, for shareholders to

---

14. See Ehrlich and Kang (2001), op. cit.

be able to end financially imprudent practices, they need to be informed as to what imprudent practices have transpired; thus, continued improvement in financial transparency is essential.[15] But also, these shareholders must be sufficiently well organized to feel confident in asserting their voice. Forcing the chaebol to convert their excessive debt to equity, and then putting this equity in the hands of large institutional investors who act on behalf of smaller investors under the principle "united we stand, divided we fall," is a potentially effective way to achieve this level of organization.

Resolution of Bankruptcy

Korea's bankruptcy procedures are themselves bankrupt, according to a number of analysts (OECD, *OECD Economic Surveys: Korea 2001*; Chopra et al. 2002; Mako 2002a, 2002b). In fact, almost every major firm in Korea that has technically gone bankrupt since 1997 is still operating, including all large units of the failed Daewoo group. In the case of Daewoo, the continued operation of its constituent firms would not necessarily be a bad thing if those firms had been successfully turned around and put on a sound footing. But this does not seem to be the case. Of 12 Daewoo companies that were put into workout programs when the group failed, 10 remain in such programs, indicating that there has been no turnaround or resolution. In fact, rather than resolving the problems of failed firms, drawn-out bankruptcy procedures in Korea seem to impede resolution. One consequence has been to introduce new weaknesses into the financial system, because in most cases in which bankruptcies have failed to be resolved, the value of assets (mostly loans) held by financial institutions in bankrupt firms has dropped (OECD, *OECD Economic Surveys: Korea 2001*).[16] Thus, it would have been in the financial institutions' interests to have sold these assets quickly, even if in doing so they had incurred significant losses. Because they did not sell, their losses have been magnified.

---

15. In fact, shareholders' groups have become active in Korea in the years since the 1997 crisis, especially the group People's Solidarity for Participatory Democracy, headed by Korea University professor Jang Ha-sung. For an account of some of the work of this group, see Jang (2001). In 1998 it won a proxy battle against SK Telecoms and, in alliance with three foreign funds, was able to place outside directors on SK Telecoms' board of directors. Nonetheless, in spite of numerous reported actions of chaebol that would hurt shareholders (OECD, *OECD Economic Surveys: Korea 2001*, from KFTC reports), there have been only a small number of minority shareholder legal actions (OECD, *OECD Economic Surveys: Korea 2001*). Perhaps shareholders are dissuaded by the substantial legal costs of bringing such actions to court, which they might be unwilling to incur even in the expectation of net gain from bringing suit against management. Again, large institutional shareholders could help to solve this problem, as they would not be deterred by a large initial outlay to gain a financial reward in excess of the costs.

16. This statement appears to hold true for KAMCO as well as for other financial institutions.

That bankruptcy procedures in Korea have been rather ineffective is a legacy of Korean history, for traditionally bankruptcy was mainly handled not by formal legal procedures but rather by nonjudicial governmental intervention. Consider the resolution of Kukje, the largest bankruptcy in Korea until 1997, which took place under the authoritarian Chun Doohwan regime. As described in chapter 3, the method used—essentially, pieces of the Kukje group were sold to individuals with close ties to the regime—was arguably effective but highly unfair. In Korea today, such an approach to bankruptcy resolution is no longer acceptable, but no effective alternative has been found to replace it. The preferred route for resolution of large firms in trouble has been the nonjudicial "workout program": that is, nonlegal agreements between creditors and these firms. But by and large, these workout programs have not worked out. Thus, of 104 large impaired firms placed in the workout program under the government-instigated Corporate Restructuring Accord in 1998, as of the end of 2000, only 36 had "graduated," or been restored to some modicum of health; 34 remained in the program. Fifteen firms have been merged into other firms, without necessarily resolving the problems that brought them into the program to begin with (e.g., LG Semiconductors is now part of the distressed Hynix Corporation). Seventeen firms exited the program, similarly without any satisfactory resolution. Only four firms have entered into judicial bankruptcy proceedings.

In a word, the results have largely been paralysis. Unresolved bankruptcies result in situations where firms that are unviable are neither shut down nor subjected to measures needed to make them viable. Thus, of the two options mentioned at the beginning of this chapter to resolve an unviably high-cost firm (either exit the market or take steps, such as reducing costs, to become competitive), neither is exercised. The remaining option is that the firm continues in operation as a de facto subsidized entity. As Chopra et al. (2002) put it with some understatement, "in some respects, the difficult part of corporate restructuring still lies ahead—non viable firms need to be closed, and viable but distressed companies should be subject to rigorous workouts[.]" But of course, the whole point here is that nonjudicial workouts have failed—the companies that have entered into workouts have not, as it were, been forced to work out hard enough to lose weight as needed.

The alternative to workouts is more effective judicial procedures for the resolution of bankrupt or impaired firms. Breaking the bankruptcy logjam by instituting and implementing legal procedures that can actually resolve bankrupt firms thus is a major unfulfilled goal for Korea.

Some progress has been made, to be sure. In particular, a "prepackaged" bankruptcy system was introduced in March 2001 that enables creditors holding a total of at least half the debt of a distressed or bankrupt firm to negotiate an out-of-court settlement with the firm, which is then submitted to bankruptcy court for approval. Under earlier law, the votes of 80 percent of secured creditors and 66 percent of unsecured creditors were needed to approve a debt restructuring plan; thus the prepackaged system allows a smaller number of creditors, presumably the biggest ones, to negotiate such a plan without having to gain the approval of smaller creditors, who in the past often withheld approval in order to obtain special treatment. Also, under the new scheme, court procedures must be completed within five months. The limit is meant to break the judicial logjam in which cases often became embroiled, as they endured very long waits for court action.

The time limit on judicial procedures notwithstanding, if legal procedures for resolution of bankrupt firms is to be more widely employed in Korea, further improvements are necessary. In particular, corps of judges with experience in bankruptcy must be created. The Seoul District Court has handled about half of all bankruptcy proceedings, and two bankruptcy divisions have been established within this court. However, as noted by Ralph Carr (2001; reported in OECD, *OECD Economic Surveys: Korea 2001*), this court's work is hampered by the frequent rotation of judges. Carr observes that judges who handled the Kia and Hanbo bankruptcies no longer are involved in such cases. A start has been made: an experienced professional staff is now on hand in the court to assist judges (Oh S. 2001; reported in OECD, *OECD Economic Surveys: Korea 2001*). Nonetheless, it is clear that more needs to be done, as these procedures still lead to long delays in bankruptcy resolution.

The "Too Big to Fail" Doctrine

As has been stressed throughout this book, the government's implicit doctrine of companies being "too big to fail," with the moral hazard that it creates, has been at the heart of much of what has been wrong in Korea. In fact, this is the consensus view in Korea itself. "Too big to fail" thus was formally renounced by President Kim Dae-jung when he was inaugurated in 1998 and formally is no longer Korean policy.

The problem is that this renounced and denounced doctrine has not yet really disappeared. Indeed, judging not by what the Korean government says is policy but rather by what it is actually doing, the doctrine seems to be making a comeback. Thus, for example, the underwriting by the Korea Development Bank in the spring of 2001 of 1.6 trillion won in bonds for six firms (four of them Hyundai affiliates), accounting for about 80 percent of the value of bonds of these firms maturing during the first quarter of 2001, is widely perceived as intended to prevent the failure of these firms.[17] Without the intervention, it is unlikely that new

---

17. The underwriting of bonds to benefit Hynix has been challenged by the US government and the European Union as a subsidy to that firm's exports possibly inconsistent with the requirements of the World Trade Organization.

bonds could have been placed in private markets to finance the maturation of the outstanding bonds. The government argued that the underwriting was justified because the firms were viable but at risk of failure for two reasons: the bonds' maturation was concentrated in a narrow time window and Korea's bond market is underdeveloped, with no effective market for bonds below investment grade (such as the bonds in question). But were in fact the firms that benefited from this underwriting "impaired" (viable in the long run but facing short-run difficulties), or were they nonviable? The government in fact never demonstrated the former. Furthermore, such a rescue arguably reduces the pressure for corporate restructuring. Plainly put, in the past few years the government has seemed to be in the business of bailing out large firms that are high-cost suppliers to their markets, with the result that these firms neither exit the market nor take steps to make themselves competitive—despite numerous pronouncements that the "too big to fail" doctrine is now dead.

The bond underwriting is not the only example of the doctrine's reemergence. As discussed in the previous chapter, Hyundai Engineering and Construction Company (HECC) continued to be supported by financial institutions that, apparently under government duress, granted credits to cover massive losses during much of 2000. In the fall of 2001, this firm had negative net worth even as reckoned by Korean accounting standards and was incurring large losses. Yet it was set to receive financial assistance, including debt-for-equity swaps, equity injections, corporate bond purchases, and fresh loans. None of this would be bad, of course, if private financial institutions were advancing all of this assistance voluntarily. However, few analysts believed that such was the case.

The big test, as of the time of this writing, is how the Korean government will handle the continuing deterioration of Hynix. The signs thus far are promising. The government has repeatedly stated that no further bailout of Hynix is forthcoming and that the company's fate lies largely in the hands of its creditors, who are free to act without government direction or intervention. Of course, there still are those in Korea who believe that Hynix should receive further bailouts, arguing that a complete failure of the firm could put the country's entire economy at risk. But the risk of a Hynix failure is overstated; the Korean economy is large and could absorb even a series of big failures, let alone the demise of just one firm. In fact, the risk in the other direction is much greater: while the systemic risk created by Hynix failing is quite manageable, the risk of Korea becoming a stagnant economy in which noncompetitive giants survive only because of government support could be significant. The urgent priority facing Korea today is thus to end "too big to fail" as an operational policy of the Korean government once and for all, and to demonstrate that end by action as well as proclamation.

The Social Safety Net

As with other areas of reform, Korea has made significant progress in expanding the social safety net. Prior to the 1997 financial crisis, business enterprises themselves were the main vehicle by which benefits were provided to workers who lost their jobs. Indeed, within the chaebol workers who lost jobs because one affiliate contracted could often find employment in some other affiliate of the same group. But the high rates of corporate bankruptcy and of workers' unemployment accompanying the 1998 recession that followed the 1997 crisis brought a realization within Korea that some better form of safety net was required. Thus, the government significantly expanded public efforts to provide income support for workers who had lost their jobs. Additionally, new mechanisms were put into place to help laid-off workers find new employment (Chopra et al. 2002; OECD, *OECD Economic Surveys: Korea 2001*); these included wage subsidies to firms that hired new workers. The government also provided some wage subsidies to firms to retain workers that might otherwise be laid off. Finally, new schemes were introduced to provide some minimum income for the truly needy in Korea, including the aged and children of the unemployed. Expenditure on such social safety schemes went from 0.6 percent of GDP in 1997 to 1.6 percent of GDP in 1999. Not included in these figures were public works projects initiated by the government in 1998 that were intended to absorb laid-off workers. In late 2000 many of the new programs, which mostly had been introduced on an ad hoc and temporary basis, were made permanent under the Basic Livelihood Security Act, which also created a larger pool of resources on which the safety net can draw.

Thus, Korea has made substantial progress in expanding the social safety net. Nonetheless, there is more to be done. Further reform, including the revamping of some existing programs, should be directed toward making labor markets in Korea more flexible. To this end, a first step is to expand coverage of the present system of unemployment compensation, which currently covers only slightly more than three-fourths of Korean employees, regular and nonregular.[18] In particular, many categories of nonregular workers (i.e., those who are not full-time employees, where "full-time" is defined not only by hours per week employed but also length of employment) are not covered. But the use of nonregular workers in Korea is growing, and so the percentage of workers not covered by unemployment compensation is also growing.

The increasing number of nonregular workers might be seen as positive, because rules pertaining to regular workers employed by large firms

---

18. Given that the substantial numbers of individuals who are self-employed or who work in small family-owned businesses are not counted either as regular or nonregular employees, less than half the total workforce in Korea is covered by unemployment compensation.

introduce undesirable rigidities into the Korean labor market (Lee C. 2002). But at least some regulations pertaining to nonregular workers have created similar rigidity—for example, employers face restrictions in laying off such workers early; a reasonable step might be to combine an easing of regulations with greater participation of nonregular workers in unemployment compensation programs.

Wage subsidies directed to employers to retain otherwise unneeded workers might have been useful in 1998, when unemployment was rising faster than at any other time in Korea since the Korean War; but in the long run such a scheme, for obvious reasons, is likely to lead to labor market rigidity. Wage subsidies amounted to almost one-third of all subsidies granted in 2000, and they should be phased out and replaced by an expanded unemployment compensation scheme. Such expansion should entail both coverage of more individuals (as discussed just above) and longer duration of benefits. At the present, benefits last only from three to eight months, with the precise length for any one worker determined by strict eligibility criteria (OECD, *OECD Economic Surveys: Korea 2001*).

To Conclude the Conclusion

One problem that has not been touched on thus far in this chapter is corruption at the highest levels. In Korea, such corruption has been part of the scene throughout the years following the Korean War, and it has led to two former Korean presidents spending time in prison as well as the imprisonment of a son of the first fully democratically elected president, Kim Young-sam. Alas, the story of former presidents, or close relatives of sitting presidents, being indicted for corruption did not end with Kim Young-sam. In 2002, two of Kim Dae-jung's sons were convicted by Korean courts for illegal activities. One son is, at the time of this writing, serving jail time, while the second is under a suspended sentence. A third son (the eldest of the three) is a member of the Korean National Assembly and not likely to be indicted.

Corruption at the highest level is not a problem unique to Korea, of course; in one form or another, high-level corruption has broken out in almost all nations. Clearly, given its presence in Korea throughout the miracle years, this corruption has not drastically curtailed economic performance, although arguably it has contributed in the past to periods of political unrest. But corruption does have the potential to create economic problems, as is apparent from the experiences of many countries other than Korea (see, e.g., Tanzi 1998); indeed, there probably is some relationship between a nation's poor economic performance and its high levels of corruption, though the evidence on this is mixed and direction of causality difficult to determine (but on this, see Wei 2000). One thing is clear: a certain amount of disillusionment has set in among the Korean people as the result of revelations that close relatives of the two Kims who have been president—both of whom were pro-democracy advocates during the non-democratic years in Korea—have engaged in corrupt activity. Under such circumstances, Koreans might very well be asking themselves how different democracy really is from autocracy.

What to do about high-level corruption is a difficult issue at best; prison sentences for former heads of state of Korea who have proven corrupt has not, it would seem, acted as much of a deterrent. Perhaps this is then the place to conclude, by saying "this sort of thing simply must end."

References

Ahn Choong-yong. 2001. Financial and Corporate Sector Restructuring in South Korea: Accomplishments and Unfinished Agenda. *Japanese Economic Review* 52, no. 4 (December): 452-70.

Aiyer, Sri-Ram. 1999. The Search for a New Development Paradigm. *Joint U.S.-Korean Academic Studies* 9: 21-44.

Aliber, Robert Z. 1998. Transforming Korean Values. *Korea's Economy* 14: 28-32.

Amsden, Alice. 1989. *Asia's Next Giant: South Korea and Late Industrialization*. New York: Oxford University Press.

Arrow, Kenneth J. 1964. *Essays in the Theory of Risk Bearing*. Chicago: Aldine Press.

Baily, Martin Neil. 2002. Distinguished Lecture on Economics in Government: The New Economy: Post Mortem or Second Wind? *Journal of Economic Perspectives* 16, no. 2 (spring): 3-22.

Balassa, Bela. 1988. The Lessons of East Asian Development: An Overview. *Economic Development and Cultural Change* 36, no. 3 (April): S273-S290.

Beck, Peter M. 1999. From Exclusion to Inducement. *Joint U.S.-Korean Academic Studies* 9: 221-46.

Beck, Peter M. 2000. Korea's Embattled *Chaebol*: Are They Serious about Restructuring? In *The Two Koreas in 2000: Sustaining Recovery and Seeking Reconciliation*. Washington: Korea Economic Institute of America.

Cargill, Thomas F. 1999. The Need for a New Financial Paradigm. *Joint U.S.-Korea Academic Studies* 9: 111-30.

Carr, Ralph. 2001. That Sinking Feeling: Korea's On-going Bankruptcy Hangover. *American Chamber of Commerce in Korea Journal* 54, no. 2: 36-39.

Cashin, Paul, and Hong Liang. 2002. Key Features of Korean Business and Export Cycles. In *Selected Issue Papers on Korea*. Washington: International Monetary Fund.

Chang Seung-wha. 1996. Korean Competition Law and Policy in Transition. In *Competition Regulation in the Pacific Rim*, ed. Carl J. Green and Douglas E. Rosenthal. Dobbs Ferry, NY: Oceana Publications.

Cho Soon. 1994. *The Dynamics of Korean Economic Development*. Washington: Institute for International Economics.

Cho Won-Dong. 2001. Corporate Reform and Restructuring in Korea. Paper presented at meeting organized by Korea Economic Institute of America and the World Bank, Washington, DC (October 9).

Cho Yoon-je. 2002. What We Have Learned from the Korean Economic Adjustment Program. In *Korean Crisis and Recovery*, ed. David T. Coe and Se-jik Kim. Washington: International Monetary Fund; Seoul: Korea Institute for International Economic Policy.

Chopra, Ajai, Kenneth Kang, Meral Karasulu, Hong Liang, Henry Ma, and Anthony Richards. 2002. From Crisis to Recovery in Korea: Strategy, Achievements, and Lessons. In *Korean Crisis and Recovery*, ed. David T. Coe and Se-jik Kim. Washington: International Monetary Fund; Seoul: Korea Institute for International Economic Policy.

Chung Jae-shick and Kim Se-jik. 2002. New Evidence on High Interest Rate Policy during the Korean Crisis. In *Korean Crisis and Recovery*, ed. David T. Coe and Se-jik Kim. Washington: International Monetary Fund; Seoul: Korea Institute for International Economic Policy.

Claessens, Stijn. 1999. Korea's Financial Sector Reforms. *Joint U.S.-Korea Academic Studies* 9: 83-110.

Clifford, Mark L. 1994. *Troubled Tiger: Businessmen, Bureaucrats, and Generals in South Korea.* Armonk, NY: M.E. Sharpe.

Dobson, Wendy, and Pierre Jacquet. 1998. *Financial Services Liberalization in the WTO.* Washington: Institute for International Economics.

Ehrlich, Craig, and Kang Dae-seob. 2001. Independence within Hyundai? *University of Pennsylvania Journal of International Economic Law* 22: 709-36.

Ernst, Dieter. 1995. The Korean Electronics Industry under Pressure: Can Export-led Market Expansion be Sustained? *Korea's Economy* 11: 52-60.

Ernst, Dieter. 2000. *Catching–up and Post-Crisis Industrial Upgrading: Searching for New Sources of Growth in Korea's Electronics Industry.* Economic Series 2. Honolulu: East-West Center.

Flake, L. Gordon 1999. Inter-Korean Economic Relations under the "Sunshine Policy." *Korea's Economy* 15: 100-06.

Friedman, Eric, Simon Johnson, and Todd Mitton. 2002. Corporate Governance and Corporate Debt in Asian Crisis Countries. In *Korean Crisis and Recovery*, ed. David T. Coe and Se-jik Kim. Washington: International Monetary Fund; Seoul: Korea Institute for International Economic Policy.

Gleysteen, William H., Jr. 1999. *Massive Entanglement, Marginal Influence: Carter and Korea in Crisis.* Washington: Brookings Institution.

Goldman Sachs and Company. 1998. Asset Quality for Korean Banks: Bottoms-up Approach. Hong Kong: Goldman Sachs and Company.

Goldstein, Morris. 1998. *The Asian Financial Crisis: Causes, Cures, and Systematic Implications.* Policy Analyses in International Economics 55. Washington: Institute for International Economics.

Gomory, Ralph E., and William J. Baumol. 2000. *Global Trade and Conflicting National Interests.* Cambridge, MA: MIT Press.

Graham, Edward M. 1999. *A Radical but Workable Restructuring Plan for South Korea.* Policy Brief 99-2. Washington: Institute for International Economics,

Graham, Edward M. 2000. The Reform of the Chaebol since the Onset of the Financial Crisis. *Joint U.S.-Korea Academic Studies* 10: 83-104.

Guesnerie, Roger. 1992. Hidden Actions, Moral Hazard, and Contract Theory. In *The New Palgrave Dictionary of Money and Finance*, ed. Peter Newman, Murray Milgate, and John Eatwell. London: Macmillan Press.

Haggard, Stephen. 2000. *The Political Economy of the Asian Financial Crisis.* Washington: Institute for International Economics.

Hastings, Max. 1987. *The Korean War.* New York: Simon and Schuster.

Hong Won-tak. 1981. Export Promotion and Employment Growth in South Korea. In

Trade and Employment in Developing Countries, ed. Anne O. Krueger, Hal B. Lary, Terry Monson, and Narongchai Akrasansee, vol. 1, *Individual Studies.* Chicago: University of Chicago Press.

Hsieh Chang-tai. 1997. What Explains the Industrial Revolution in East Asia: Evidence from Factor Markets. Ph.D. dissertation, University of California at Berkeley.

Jang Ha-sung. 2001. The Role of Boards and Stakeholders. Paper prepared for the third OECD/World Bank Asian Corporate Governance Roundtable, Singapore (April).

Jang Ha-sung. 2002. Corporate Restructuring in Korea after the Economic Crisis. Paper presented at the 13th US-Korea Academic Symposium, University of Pennsylvania, Philadelphia, October 16-18.

Joh Sung-wook. 2001. Korea's Economic Crisis and Corporate Governance System. Korea Development Institute, Seoul. Photocopy.

Jones, Leroy P., and Sakong Il. 1980. *Government, Business, and Entrepreneurship in Economic Development: The Korean Case.* Cambridge, MA: Harvard University Press.

Jwa Sung-hee and Huh Chan-guk. 1998. *Risks and Returns of Financial-Industrial Interactions: The Korean Experience.* KERI Working Paper 9801. Seoul: Korea Economic Research Institute.

Kang Sam-mo, Wang Yun-jong, and Yoon Deok-ryong. 2002. *Hanging Together: Exchange Rate Dynamics between Japan and Korea.* Working Paper 02-06. Seoul: Korea Institute for International Economic Policy.

Kim Dae-jung. 1996. *Mass Participatory Economy: Korea's Road to World Economic Power.* Cambridge, MA: Harvard University Center for International Affairs; Lanham, MD: University Press of America.

Kim Doo-suk. 1996. The Korean Shipbuilding Industry. *Korea's Economy* 12: 65-70.

Kim Eun-mee. 1996. The Industrial Organization and Growth of the Korean *Chaebol*: Integrating Development and Organizational Theories. In *Asian Business Networks*, ed. Gary G. Hamilton. Berlin: Walter De Gruyter.

Kim Jong-il and Kim June-dong. 2000. *Liberalization of Trade in Services and Productivity Growth in Korea.* Korea Institute for International Economic Policy Working Paper 00-10. Seoul: Korea Institute for International Economic Policy.

Kim Joon-ki and Chung H. Lee. 2001. Insolvency in the Corporate Sector and Financial Crisis in Korea. University of Hawaii, Manoa. Photocopy.

Kim June-dong. 1999. *Inward Foreign Direct Investment Regime and Some Evidence of Spillover Effects in Korea.* Working Paper 99-09. Seoul: Korea Institute for International Economic Policy.

Kim June-dong. 2002. Inward Foreign Direct Investment into Korea: Recent Performance and Future Agenda. Paper presented at the 13th US-Korea Academic Symposium, University of Pennsylvania, Philadelphia, October 16-18.

Kim Lin-su. 1997. *Imitation to Innovation: The Dynamics of Korea's Technological Learning.* Boston: Harvard Business School Press.

Kim Se-jik and Mark R. Stone. 2000. *Corporate Leverage, Bankruptcy, and Output Adjustment in Post-Crisis East Asia.* Working Paper 00-06. Seoul: Korea Institute for International Economic Policy.

Kim Sun-ho. 2000. Capital Market Liberalization. In *Looking Forward: Korea after the Economic Crisis*, ed. Heather Smith. Canberra: Asian Pacific Press at the Australian National University.

Kim Sung-han. 1999. South Korean Policy Toward North Korea. *Korea's Economy* 15: 94-99. Korea Economic Institute of America.

Kim Tae-dong. 1991. *Economics of the Sixth Republic* (in Korean). Seoul: Purusan.

Kim Youn-suk. 1995. Korea's Science and Technology Development. *Korea's Economy* 11: 61-66.

Kirk, Donald. 1999. *Korean Crisis: Unraveling of the Miracle in the IMF Era.* New York: St. Martin's Press.

Koh Sung-soo and Ji Dong-hyun. 2000. Reforming Korea's Financial System. In *Looking Forward: Korea after the Economic Crisis*, ed. Heather Smith. Canberra: Asian Pacific Press at the Australian National University.

Krueger, Anne O. 1979. *The Developmental Role of the Foreign Sector and Aid.* Cambridge, MA: Harvard University Press.

Krueger, Anne O., and Yoo Jung-ho. 2001. Chaebol Capitalism and the Currency-Financial Crisis in Korea. Paper prepared for Columbia University conference in honor of Ronald Findlay, New York (February). Available at http://credpr.stanford.edu/pdf/credpr89.pdf.

Krueger, Anne O., and Yoo Jung-ho. 2002. Falling Profitability, Higher Borrowing Costs, and *Chaebol* Finances during the Korean Crisis. In *Korean Crisis and Recovery*, ed. David T. Coe and Se-jik Kim. Washington: International Monetary Fund; Seoul: Korea Institute for International Economic Policy.

Krugman, Paul. 1994. The Myth of Asia's Miracle. *Foreign Affairs* 73, no. 6 (November-December): 62-78.

Krugman, Paul R. 1998. What Happened to Asia? Available at http://mit.edu/krugman/www/DISINTER.html (January).

Kwack Sung-yeung. 1999. *Capital Inflows and Monetary Policy in Asia before the Financial Crisis.* Working Paper 99-12. Seoul: Korea Institute for International Economic Policy.

Kwack Sung-yeung. 2000. Total Factor Productivity Growth and the Source of Growth in Korean Manufacturing Industries, 1971-1993. *Journal of the Korean Economy* 1, no. 2 (autumn): 229-65.

Kwon Oyu. 1994. Financial Liberalization and the Prospect for US Investment. *Korea's Economy* 10: 19-23.

Lautier, Marc. 2001. The International Development of the Korean Automobile Industry. In *Going Multinational: The Korean Experience of Direct Investment*, ed. Frédérique Sachwald. London: Routledge.

Lee Chang-won. 2002. Reducing Labor Market Rigidity in Korea. *Korea's Economy* 18: 28-33.

Lee Jong-wha. 1996. Government Interventions and Productivity Growth. *Journal of Economic Growth* 1, no. 3 (September): 391-414.

Lee So-han. 1998. Korea's Financial Sector under Reform. *Korea's Economy* 14: 22-27.

Leipziger, Danny. 1998. *Public and Private Interests in Korea: Views on Moral Hazard and Crisis Resolution.* EDI Working Paper. Washington: Economic Development Institute of the World Bank.

Levine, Ross. 1997. Financial Development and Economic Growth: Views and Agenda. *Journal of Economic Literature* 35, no. 2 (June): 688-726.

Levine, Ross, and Sara Zervos. 1998. Stock Markets, Banks, and Economic Growth. *American Economic Review* 46, no. 1 (March): 537-58.

Lieberman, Ira. 1999. Korea's Corporate Reforms. In *Korea Approaches the Millennium.* Washington: Korea Economic Institute of America.

Lowe-Lee, Florence. 2001. Economic Trends. *Korean Insight* 3, no. 3: 2.

Mako, William P. 2002a. Corporate Restructuring and Reform: Lessons from Korea. In *Korean Crisis and Recovery*, ed. David T. Coe and Se-jik Kim. Washington: International Monetary Fund; Seoul: Korea Institute for International Economic Policy.

Mako, William P. 2002b. Korean Corporate Restructuring: Halfway There? *Korea's Economy* 18: 22-26.

Mann, Catherine. 2000. Korea and the Brave New World of Finance. *Joint U.S.-Korean Academic Studies* 10: 55-68.

Markowitz, Harry M. 1959. *Portfolio Selection: Efficient Diversification of Investments.* New Haven: Yale University Press.

Mason, Edward S., Kim Mah-je, Dwight H. Perkins, Kim Kwang-suk, and David C. Cole, with Leroy Jones, Sakong Il, Donald R. Snodgrass, and Noel McGinn. 1980. *The Economic and Social Modernization of the Republic of Korea.* Cambridge, MA: Harvard University Press.

McKinsey Global Institute (McKinsey). 1998. *Productivity-led Growth for Korea.* Washington: McKinsey and Company.

Moran, Theodore H. 2001. *Parental Supervision.* Washington: Institute for International Economics.

Nam Sang-yirl. 1999. *Total Factor Productivity Growth in Korean Industry and Its Relationship with Export Growth.* Working Paper 99-34. Seoul: Korea Institute for International Economic Policy.

Nanto, Dick K., and Vivian C. Jones. 1997. South Korea's Economy and 1997 Crisis. Library of Congress, Congressional Research Service, CRS Report for Congress 98-13E (December 29).

Noland, Marcus. 1993. Selective Intervention and Growth: The Case of Korea. Institute for International Economics, Washington, DC. Photocopy.

Noland, Marcus. 1996. *Restructuring Korea's Financial Sector for Greater Competitiveness.* Institute for International Economics Working Paper 96-14. Washington: Institute for International Economics.

Noland, Marcus. 2000. *Avoiding the Apocalypse: The Future of the Two Koreas.* Washington: Institute for International Economics.

Noland, Marcus. 2001. Economic Reform in Korea: Achievements and Future Prospects. Paper presented at the conference Peace and Democracy in the Korean Peninsula, Seoul (February 22).

Noland, Marcus, and Howard Pack. 2003. *Industrial Policy in an Era of Globalization: Lessons from Asia.* POLICY ANALYSES IN INTERNATIONAL ECONOMICS 69. Washington: Institute for International Economics. Forthcoming.

Oh Gyutaeg and Rhee Chang-yong. 2002. The Role of Corporate Bond Markets in the Korean Financial Restructuring Process. In *Korean Crisis and Recovery,* ed. David T. Coe and Se-jik Kim. Washington: International Monetary Fund; Seoul: Korea Institute for International Economic Policy.

Oh S. 2001. Bankruptcy Division and Commissioner. Paper presented at OECD Conference on Asian Insolvency Reform, Bali (February).

Pack, Howard, and Lawrence E. Westphal. 1986. Industrial Strategy and Technological Change: Theory versus Reality. *Journal of Development Economics* 22: 87-128.

Patrick, Hugh. 2002. Corporate Governance, Ownership Structure and Financial Crisis: Experience of East Asian Countries. In *The Financial Crisis and Beyond,* ed. Chiho Kim. Seoul: Korea Deposit Insurance Corporation.

Papanek, Gustav. 1988. The New Asian Capitalism: An Economic Portrait. In *In Search of an East Asian Development Model,* ed. Peter L. Berger and Hsin-huang M. Hsiao. New Brunswick, NJ: Transaction Books.

Park Seung-rok and Jene K. Kwon. 1995. Rapid Economic Growth with Increasing Returns to Scale and Little or No Productivity Growth. *Review of Economics and Statistics* 77, no. 2 (May): 332-51.

Park Yoon-shik. 2000a. The Asian Financial Crisis and Its Effects on Korean Banks. *Joint U.S.-Korean Academic Studies* 10: 69-82.

Park Yoon-shik. 2000b. Korea's *Chaebol* Issue Combined Financial Statements for the First Time. *Korea Insight* 2, no. 8 (August).

Patrick, Hugh. 2002. Corporate Governance, Ownership Structure, and Financial Crisis: Experience of East Asian Countries. In *The Financial Crisis and Beyond,* ed. Kim Chiho. Seoul: Korea Deposit Insurance Corporation.

Perrin, Serge. 2001. The Internationalization of Korean Electronics Firms: Domestic Rivalry and Tariff-jumping. In *Going Multinational: The Korean Experience of Direct Investment,* ed. Frédérique Sachwald. London: Routledge.

Radelet, Steven, and Jeffrey D. Sachs. 1998. The East Asian Financial Crisis: Diagnosis, Remedies, Prospects. *Brookings Papers on Economic Activity* 1998, no. 1: 1-74.

Raiffa, Howard, and Robert Schlaiffer. 1968. *Applied Statistical Decision Theory.* Cambridge, MA: MIT Press.

Rhee Du-whan. 1996. The Automobile Industry in South Korea. *Korea's Economy* 12: 55-64.

Rooney, James. 2002. Building Korea's Potential: Building Efficient Financial Markets. *Korea's Economy* 18: 13-21.

SaKong Il. 1993. *Korea in the World Economy.* Washington: Institute for International Economics.

SaKong Il. 2000-2001. Korean Economic Restructuring: Current Status and Prospects. *Korea Society Quarterly* 1, no. 4 (winter): 7-8, 55-54.

Shin In-seok and Wang Yun-jong. 1999. *How to Sequence Capital Market Liberalization: Lessons from the Korean Experience.* Working Paper 99-30. Seoul: Korea Institute for International Economic Policy.

Smith, Heather. 2000. Macroeconomic Policy and Structural Adjustment. In *Looking Forward: Korea after the Economic Crisis*, ed. Heather Smith. Canberra: Asian Pacific Press at the Australian National University.

Sohn Chan-hyun and Yang Jun-sok. 1998. *Korea's Economic Reform Measures under the IMF Program: Government Measures in the Critical First Six Months of the Korean Economic Crisis.* Policy Paper 98-01. Seoul: Korea Institute for International Economic Policy.

Sohn Chan-hyun, Yang Jun-sok, and Yim Hyo-sung. 1998. *Korea's Trade and Industrial Policies: 1948-1998: Why the Era of Industrial Policy Is Over.* Working Paper 98-05. Seoul: Korea Institute for International Economic Policy.

Steinberg, David I. 1985. *Foreign Aid and the Development of the Republic of Korea: The Effectiveness of Concessional Assistance.* Washington: United States Agency for International Development.

Tanzi, Vito. 1998. *Corruption around the World: Causes, Consequences, Scope, and Cures.* Working Paper 98/63. Washington: International Monetary Fund.

United Nations. 1952. *Report of the Agent General of the United Nations Korean Reconstruction Agency.* General Assembly, Official Records of the Seventh Session, supplement 19 (A/2222).

Wang Yun-jong. 1999. *Restructuring and the Role of International Financial Institutions: A Korean View.* Working Paper 99-06. Seoul: Korea Institute for International Economic Policy.

Wang Yun-jong and Zang Hyoung-soo. 1998. *Adjustment Reforms in Korea since the Financial Crisis.* Policy Paper 98-02. Seoul: Korea Institute for International Economic Policy.

Warr, Peter G. 2000. Macroeconomic Origins of the Korean Crisis. In *Looking Forward: Korea after the Economic Crisis*, ed. Heather Smith. Canberra: Asian Pacific Press at the Australian National University.

Wei, Shang-jin. 2000. Local Corruption and Global Capital Flows. *Brookings Papers on Economic Activity* 2. Washington: Brookings Institution.

Wickham, John A. 1999. *Korea on the Brink: From the "12/12 Incident" to the Kwangju Uprising, 1979-1980.* Washington: National Defense University Press.

Wonnacott, Paul. 1994. *The Automotive Industry in Southeast Asia: Can Protection Be Made Less Costly?* Working Paper 94-4. Washington: Institute for International Economics.

Woo, K.D. 1978. Wage and Labor Productivity in the Cotton Spinning Industries of Japan, Korea, and Taiwan. *The Developing Economies* 16: 182-98.

Yong Ahn-choong. 1999. Assessing Foreign Direct Investment. *Joint US-Korean Academic Studies* 9: 247-65.

Yoo Jung-ho. 1989. *The Korean Experience with Industrial Targeting Policy.* Seoul: Korea Institute for International Economic Policy.

Yoo Seong-min. 1995. *Chaebol in Korea: Misconceptions, Realities, and Policies.* Korea Development Institute Working Paper 9507. Seoul: Korea Development Institute.

Yoo Seong-min. 1999. Corporate Restructuring in Korea: Policy Issues before and during the Crisis. *Joint U.S.-Korea Academic Studies* 9: 131-85.

Yoo Seong-min. 2000. Industrial Restructuring and Corporate Governance: Policy Issues before, during, and after the Crisis. In *Looking Forward: Korea after the Economic Crisis*, ed. Heather Smith. Canberra: Asian Pacific Press at the Australian National University.

Yoo Seong-min and Lim Young-jae. 1997. *Big Business in Korea: New Learnings and Policy Issues*. Korea Development Institute Working Paper. Seoul: Korea Development Institute.

Yoon Bong-joon. 1998. The Nature of the Chaebol and the Korean Financial Crisis. Department of Economics, State University of New York at Binghamton. Photocopy.

You Jong-keun. 1999. Paradigm Shift in Korea. *Joint U.S.-Korean Academic Studies* 9: 9-19.

Young, Alwyn. 1995. The Tyranny of Numbers: Confronting the Statistical Realities of the East Asian Growth Experience. *Quarterly Journal of Economics* 110, no. 3 (August): 641-80.

Young Soo-gil. 1997. The End of Korea's Economic Miracle? The Korean Economy: Challenges and Prospects. *Korea Economic Update* 8, no. 4 (July): 1-3.

Young Soo-gil and Kwon Jae-jung. 1998. Korean Economy under the IMF Program. Presentation at the Institute for International Economics, Washington (January 12). Copies available from Korea Institute for International Economic Policy, Seoul.

Yun Mik-yung. 2000. Foreign Direct Investment: A Catalyst for Change. *Joint U.S.-Korean Academic Studies* 10: 139-74.

Yun Mik-yung and Sung-mi Lee. 2001. *The Impact of FDI ON Competition: The Korean Experience*. Working Paper 01-04. Seoul: Korea Institute for International Economic Policy.

Yusuf, Shahid, and Simon J. Evenett. Forthcoming. *How Can East Asia Compete? Innovation and IT for Global Markets*. Washington: World Bank.

Zeile, William J. 1991a. *Industrial Targeting through Government Credit Rationing: The Korean Experience in the 1970s*. Program in East Asian Business and Development, Working Paper 41. Davis: Institute for Government Affairs, University of California, Davis.

Zeile, William J. 1991b. *Productivity Growth in Korean Manufacturing Industries, 1972-85*. Program in East Asian Business and Development, Working Paper 38. Davis: Institute for Government Affairs, University of California, Davis.

Zeile, William J. 1993. Industrial Targeting, Business Organization, and Industry Productivity Growth in the Republic of Korea, 1972-1985. Ph.D. dissertation, University of California, Davis.

Zeile, William J. 1996. Industrial Policy and Organizational Efficiency: The Korean *Chaebol* Examined. In *Asian Business Networks*, ed. Gary G. Hamilton. Berlin: Walter De Gruyter.

Index

banking sector (*Cont.*)
  campaign finance scandal, 131*n*
  chaebol control, 153
  chaebol debt levels, 83-85
  chaebol restrictions, 64
  concentration, 83
  Daewoo loans, 131-32
  debt-for-equity swaps, 154-56
  default risk, 85
  deposit insurance, 113
  financial dualism, 59
  foreign ownership, 153
  insolvencies, 113
  Kukje group, 60-61
  liberalizing capital accounts, 99
  merchant banks, 62-63
  mismatches, 99
  moral hazard, 85-86
  nationalization, 113
  nonbank financial subsidiaries, 62
  nonperforming loans, 84, 84*n*, 113, 114
  PCA system, 112
  privatization, 59-60
  "real names" for accounts, 91, 91*n*
  reform needed, 153-54
  reprivatizing, 153
  restructuring, 113-14
  risky loans, 159
  roles and skills, 86
  shareholders, 84
  "too big to fail," 85-86
  See also names of individual banks
Bank for International Settlements (BIS), 112
Bank of Korea
  Asian financial crisis, 107, 108
  Cho, 75*n*
  IMF reforms, 110*t*
  Ministry of Finance and Economics, 110-11
bankruptcy
  corporate leverage, 109
  corps of judges, 170
  Daewoo group, 130-36
  debt restructuring, 169-70
  differences between Korea and US, 149-50
  earlier, 101
  judicial procedures, 169-70
  post-crisis, 106, 109, 110*t*
  pre-crisis, 101-03
  reforms needed, 151, 168-70
  social safety net, 149-50
  unsound firms, 151
  US firms, 147-49
  workout programs, 168
  paralysis, 169
bankruptcy risks, 62, 83, 101
  McKinsey report, 119
Basel capital adequacy standards, 112
  rehabilitation plans, 113, 114
Basic Livelihood Security Act (2000), 172
Baumol, William, 47-50

big deals, 122-23
  Daewoo, 132
  Hyundai-LG, 138
  Samsung, 132
BIS. *See* Bank for International Settlements
"Blueprint for Financial Liberalization and
    Internationalization," 90
  growth effects, 93
  third phase, 98
boards of directors, 66
bonds
  liberalization, 111
  market expansion, 75
  underwriting, 170-71
book, organization of, 8
bribes
  by chaebol leaders, 100-01
  Hanbo bankruptcy, 102
  See also corruption
bridge merchant bank, 113
bus operations, 136

campaign contributions, political parties, 18
campaign finance, bribes for, 100
capital
  marginal returns, 79-80
  real rental price, 81*n*
capital accumulation, during transformation, 8
capital controls, 99
capital formation, 23
"capital intensive," concept of, 2
capital investment
  chaebol regulations, 59
  debt financing, 8-9
  HCI returns, 30-31
  rates of return, 8-9, 93-94
capital markets, efficiency, 80
capital productivity
  compared, 119, 119*n*
  manufacturing, 122
  semiconductors, 121
  steel industry compared, 119
Capital Structure Improvement Plans (CSIPs),
  126
cartels
  cotton weaving and spinning, 20
  See also chaebol
cement plants, 31
centralized planning of economy, 15
chaebol
  accounting requirements, 126
  antecedents, 18
  asset shares, 127
  asset swaps, 122-23
  big deals, 122-23
  bribes to leaders, 100-01
  Chun and Roh eras, 51
  concept of, 4
  control of banks, 153
  credit, evergreening loans, 83

exchange rates (*Cont.*)
  short-term capital accounts, 100
  unitary rate established, 19
exit strategies, 112
"Export Day," 21*n*
export expansion
  diplomacy with Japan, 24
  growth figures, 18
  higher priority, 18
export growth
  decline, 43-44, 44*t*
  slowdown in 1990s, 101
Export-Import Bank of Korea, 64
export-led growth policies, 25
export policy
  current, 2-3
  early, 2
exports
  auto, 94
  auto projections, 95
  economic growth, 93
  subsidies, early, 16
  textile industry, 20-21

factor inputs, HCI drive, 45
failure, business, 149
family control over chaebol, 65-66
  Hyundai, 66
  LG group, 66
  nepotism, 163
  public control versus, 163
  Samsung, 164
Federation of Korean Industries (FKI), 25,
  134
  transparency issue, 161
Federation of Korean Labor Unions, 140
fertilizers, 38
financial dualism, 59
financial information issues, 158-61
financial restructuring, 112
financial sector
  cleanup costs, 115-16
    public funding, 116, 116*t*
  competition, 111
  curb market, 24
  Daewoo, 132
  default protection, 23
  development disparity, 3
  equities funds, 155
  HCI drive, 29
  IMF reforms, 112
  missions (three), 161-62
  nationalized under Park, 23
  need for, 86-87, 87*n*
  OECD entry, 98-99
  OECD reforms, 115
  reform, 109-16
    effectiveness, 116
    needed, 150, 152-56
    reform commission, 101

regulating, 58
transparency, 161
Financial Supervisory Board (FSB), 111
  standards for banks, 113
Financial Supervisory Commission (FSC), 111
  corrective procedures, 112
  Daewoo, 133-34, 159
  PCA system, 112
Financial Supervisory Service (FSS)
  auditing, 159-60
  role of auditors, 160
five-year plans, 16
  EPB on comparative advantage, 22
  first, 17
  HCI drive, 27
  heavy industry, 26-27
FKI. *See* Federation of Korean Industries
Ford Motor Company, 37, 38
  big deals, 124
  Daewoo Motors, 135, 157
  Kia bankruptcy, 103
foreign aid
  Korean textiles barred, 20
  Korean War, 1, 1*n*
  post-Korean War, 13
Foreign Capital Inducement Deliberation
  Committee, 22
foreign debt, 6
  government guarantees, 30
  preferential guarantees, 7
foreign direct investment (FDI)
  by Korea, 93
  Daewoo Motors, 96
  Hyundai Motor Company, 95
  IMF reforms, 111
  migration of activities, 48
  semiconductors and computers, 67
  transparency, 157-58
  volumes, pre- and post-crisis, 111-12
foreign finance
  control over credit, 22, 22*n*-23*n*
  dependence in 1950s, 22
foreign firms, regulating, 58
foreign investment
  ceilings lifted, 90
  Daewoo, 130
  declining, 152
  liberalized, 90
  stock market, 128
freedom of the press, 77-78
free trade equilibriums, 47-48
FSB. *See* Financial Supervisory Board
FSC. *See* Financial Supervisory Commission
FSS. *See* Financial Supervisory Service
Fujitsu, 69
fundamentals, Asian financial crisis, 105-06

GAAP. *See* Generally Accepted Accounting
  Principles
garment industry, 49

GDP
  postwar, 1
  quintupled, 2
GDP deflator, Roh era, 74, 75
GDP growth
  post-crisis, 106
  wages and inflation, 42-43, 43t
GDR. *See* global depository receipt issue
Generally Accepted Accounting Principles
    (GAAP), 161
General Motors, 38
  Daewoo Motor, 135
  institutional investor role, 156
  joint venture, 96
George A. Fuller, 31
global depository receipt (GDR) issue, 139
GM-Daewoo Auto and Technology, 136
Goldman Sachs and Company, 117, 129
Goldstar, 36
  electronics, joint ventures, 37
Goldstar Investment and Finance, 63
Gomory, Ralph, 47-50
government role, as "entrepreneur-manager," 16
gross domestic investment, 94
growth recession, 3, 76, 78, 92

Habib, Philip, 26
Haitai group, 109
  debt-to-equity ratio, 110t
  number of subsidiaries, 110t
Halla group, 35
  bankruptcy, 109, 110t
  debt-to-equity ratio, 110t
  number of subsidiaries, 110t
  shipbuilding, boom, 97
  subsidies, 97
Hanbo group
  bankruptcy, 101-02
  corruption scandals, 77
Haneurum Merchant Bank, 113, 114
Hanil group, 61, 103
  debt-to-equity ratio, 110t
  number of subsidiaries, 110t
Hanjin group, 35
  asset growth, 7t
  debt-to-equity ratio, 110t
  interest coverage ratio, 118t
  number of subsidiaries, 110t
  shipbuilding, boom, 97
  subsidies, 97
Hansol group
  debt-to-equity ratio, 110t
  number of subsidiaries, 110t
Hanvit Bank, 114, 134
  replacement, 140
Hanwha group, 109
  debt-to-equity ratio, 110t
  interest coverage ratio, 118t
  mergers, 124
  number of subsidiaries, 110t

HCI drive. *See* heavy and chemical industries
    (HCI) drive
health care insurance, 149
heavy and chemical industries (HCI) drive,
    26-38
  concentrating wealth, 39
  end of, 44
  evaluation, 45-46
  "HCI period" concept, 2
  inflationary rates, 55
  policy loans, 40, 40t
  problems, 38
  progression, 30
  rates of return, 45
  retainable industries, 49
  Samsung expansion, 7
  subsidies
    in loans, 40-42
    rates of return debated, 42
    subsidy/income ratio, 41-42, 41t
  tax breaks, 56
  "too big to fail" doctrine, 86
  "unsound" firms, 35
Heavy and Chemical Industry Declaration
    (1973), 27, 28, 29
Heavy and Chemical Industry Planning
    Council, 29
heavy industry, 21-22
  comparative advantage, 28
  five-year plans, 26-27
  locating, 53
  Park ambitions, 25, 28
HECC. *See* Hyundai Engineering and
    Construction Company
HHI. *See* Hyundai Heavy Industries
holding companies, 57, 58
Hong Kong, Asian financial crisis, 107
Hong Kong and Shanghai Banking Corpora-
    tion, 113
households, curb market, 24
HSBC, 113
human capital, 119
  concept of, 2
  shipbuilding, 32-33
human rights, 52
Hynix, 71
  creation of, 123
  creative accounting, 148
  management turnover, 141-42
  MOU with, 140
  problems, 139-42
  subsidies challenged, 170n
  too big to fail policy, 152, 171
Hyosang group
  debt-to-equity ratio, 110t
  number of subsidiaries, 110t
Hyundai ASAN, 137, 142
Hyundai Construction and Engineering
    Company, 67
Hyundai Corporation, cross-holdings, 138

inflation rates, 43, 43t
informational asymmetry, 132
information technology, 72
institutional investors
    chaebol breakup, 167-68
    potential of, 154-56
insurance companies, shut down, 114
Intel, 69
interest coverage ratios, 117-18
    defined, 117
    five largest chaebol, 129, 129t
    ten largest chaebol, 118t
interest rates
    deregulation, Kim Young-sam, 90
    deregulation plan, 75, 78
    IMF policy, 107
    policy loans, 40, 40t
    reform of, 101
intermediation, 6
International Accounting Standards Board
    (IASB), 160-61
International Accounting Standards (IAS),
    160
International Monetary Fund (IMF)
    contractionary policy, 108
    devaluation, 24
    financial reforms, 101
    financial sector reform, 109-10
    industrial sector reform, 117
    Korean bailout, 107-08
    stand-by conditions, 109
    structural reform, 112
    Thailand bailout, 106
investment
    Asian financial crisis, 99-100
    new activities, 148-49
investment trust companies (ITCs), 63, 64t, 77
    Cho on, 75n
    infusion, 75
    shut down, 114
ITCs. See investment trust companies

Jang Ha-sung, 165, 168n
Japan
    auto sector, 136
    as colonizer, 11-12
    competition, 93
    diplomatic relations normalized, 24
    DRAMs, 70, 71
    Kim Dae-jung abduction, 26
    shipbuilding, 96-97
    shipbuilding competitiveness, 34
    steel industry aid, 28
    technology transfer, 24
    textile exports, 20-21
    yen rate, 93
J.D. Power survey, 94, 94n
Jeon Yun-churi, 161
Jinro group, 103
    bankruptcy, 109, 110t

debt-to-equity ratio, 110t
number of subsidiaries, 110t
job loss, 6
joint ventures
    auto, 95
    electronics, 37
    semiconductors and computers, 67-68

KAA. See Korean Antitrust Act
KAI. See Korea Accounting Institute
KAMCO. See Korea Asset Management
    Corporation
Kang Ki-dong, 68
Kang Kyong-shik, 107
Kawasaki's shipyards, 33
KCIA. See Korean Central Intelligence Agency
KDIC. See Korea Deposit Insurance
    Corporation
Keopyung group
    debt-to-equity ratio, 110t
    number of subsidiaries, 110t
KFTC. See Korea Fair Trade Commission
Kia group, 38
    bankruptcy, 109, 110t
    big deals, 124
    debt, 144
    debt-to-equity ratio, 110t
    failure, 103
    Hyundai
        competition, 95
        takeover, 124-25
    interest coverage ratio, 118t
    monopoly, 72, 73
    number of subsidiaries, 110t
    US sales, 94, 94n, 95, 145
    See also Hyundai Motor Company
Kim Dae-jung
    abduction, 26
    background, 52
    campaign finance scandal, 131n
    chaebol core businesses, 122-23
    corruption charges to sons, 173
    Daewoo crisis, 134
    debt-to-equity ratios, 127
    election, 108
    exile and return, 55
    labor movement, 125
    monopolies, 123
    North Korea, 125
    opposition to Park, 15
    recession and reform, 144-45
    Roh compared, 145
    sunshine policy, 125
    too big to fail policy, 170
Kim Hyun-chol, 102
Kim Il Sung, 12
Kim Jae-ik
    credit supervision, 62
    death, 60
    heading economists, 56

Kim Jae-kyu, 39
Kim Jong-pil
  background, 52
  KCIA head, 15
  military coup, 14
  Kim Mahn-je, 61
  Kim Sun-hong, 103
  Kim Tu-bong, 12, 12*n*
  Kim Woo-chung
  borrowing strategy, 132
  corruption charges, 91, 101
  Daewoo debt burden, 61
  described, 130
  international expansion, 96
  KSEC shipyard, 34
  resignation, 134
  ties to presidents, 21*n*, 131
  wealth, 147
Kim Young-sam
  aligned with Roh, 89, 90
  anticorruption campaign, 91
  anticorruption drive, 100
    disgrace, 102
  background, 52
  debt levels of chaebol, 83-84
  economic growth, 92
  economic reforms, 92
  elected president, 89
  end to martial law, 54
  industrial policy, 72
  opposition to Park, 38-39, 53
Kiwon group
  debt-to-equity ratio, 110*t*
  number of subsidiaries, 110*t*
KNTO. *See* Korea National Tourism Agency
Kohap group, 109
  debt-to-equity ratio, 110*t*
  sub, 110*t*
  auditing, 159
Kolon group
  debt-to-equity ratio, 110*t*
  number of subsidiaries, 110*t*
Koo family, 66
Korea, history, 6
Korea Accounting Institute (KAI), 160-61
Korea Asset Management Corporation, 103
Korea Deposit Insurance Corporation (KDIC),
    113, 114
  Daewoo auditing, 159
  Kohap group auditing, 159
Korea Development Bank, 64, 136
  Hynix bonds, 139
  Okbo shipyard, 34, 35
  preferential loans, 40-41
  too big to fail policy, 170-71
Korea Exchange Bank, HECC debt swap, 143
Korea Explosives, asset growth, 7*t*
Korea Financial and Accounting Standards
    Committee, 160
Korea First Bank, 113

Korea Heavy Industry, 123
Korea Land Development Corporation, 77
Korean Airlines, 35
Korean Antitrust Act (KAA), 56-59
  enforcement, 92
    chaebol breakup, 166
Korea Asset Management Corporation
    (KAMCO), 113
  asset disposal, 115
  buying bad debts from banks, 115
  impaired assets, 113, 115
Korea National Tourism Agency (KNTO), 142
Korean Central Intelligence Agency (KCIA),
    15-16
  Chun named, 54
  Kim Jong-pil, 52
Korean Express, 63
Korea Fair Trade Commission (KFTC), 57-58
  transaction reporting, 161
  intragroup interactions, 160
  upgraded, 92
Korean stock exchange
  Asian financial crisis, 107
  delisting due to audits, 160
  non-chaebol affiliated firms, 165
  weakness, 154
Korean War, 12
Korean Workers' Party, 12
Korea Semiconductor Company, 68
Korea Shipbuilding and Engineering
    Corporation (KSEC), 32
  Daewoo takeover, 34
Korea Trade Promotion Agency (KOTRA), 25
KOTRA. *See* Korea Trade Promotion Agency
KSEC. *See* Korea Shipbuilding and
    Engineering Corporation
Kukdong group, 103
Kukje group, 60-61
  asset growth, 7*t*
  failure, 101
Kukje Securities Company, 63
Kumbo group
  debt-to-equity ratio, 110*t*
  number of subsidiaries, 110*t*
Kwangju, 54-55
Kwangyang Bay, 29
Kyongsang province, 53
Kyongsong Spinning and Weaving, 19-20

labor
  disputes, 74
  infant industries, 18
  nonregular employees, 172-73
  unemployment compensation, 172, 173
  wage hikes, 42, 43, 43*t*, 44
  See also social safety net
labor productivity
  compared, 118-19, 119
  Hyundai Motor Company, 120
  marginal, 75

Mount Kumgang project, 125
   outcomes, 142
multiple exchange rate system, 19
mutual funds
   Korean vs. US, 128
   needed, 154-55
   security risk, 128n

names, conventions for, 4n
National Congress for New Politics (NCNP), 125
nationalism, 15
neoclassical trade theory, challenged, 47
nepotism, 163
Newbridge Capital, 113, 133
Newcore group, 103
   bankruptcy, 109, 110t
   debt-to-equity ratio, 110t
   number of subsidiaries, 110t
Nippon Electrical Glass, 133
Nissan
   Samsung joint venture, 96
   Samsung Motors, 133
Nixon, Richard, 27
nominal exchange rates, 43, 43t
nonbank financial institutions
   credit expansion, 75-76
   as financing sources, 78
   reforms, 112
   restructuring, 114-15
   role, 65
   shares of deposits and loans, 64, 65t
nonferrous metals, 29, 38
nonfinancial corporate sector, IMF reforms, 117n
nonregular employees, 172-73
nonretainable industry, 49
North Korea, 11
   after Park's assassination, 53, 53n
   Chun assassination attempt, 60
   Chung Ju-yung venture, 137
   project transparency, 161
   tensions eased, 125, 125n
   threat, 16
   venture outcomes, 142
NTT, 69

October 7 plan, 123
office of the chairman, 57
oil shocks, 44-45, 56
opportunity cost, 145
Organization for Economic Cooperation and Development (OECD)
   Code on Liberalization of Capital Movements, 98-99
   Korean entry, 98-99
   membership, 2
   subsidies to shipbuilding, 98
overcapacity, concept of, 79-80
overinvestment, shipbuilding, 36

Park Chung-hee
   access to subsidies, 30
   assassination, 15, 38-39, 51-52
   background, 14-15
   Daewoo shipbuilding, 34
   dictatorship, 15
      authoritarianism, 26
      discontent, 26
      popularity waning, 24
   heavy and chemical industries, 2
   heavy industry, 21-22
   Hyundai relationship, 32
      special ties, 7
   succession, 51-52
   theatrics against entrepreneurs, 19
Park Tae-joon, 28
PCA. See prompt corrective action (PCA) system
pension funds, needed, 154-55
pension management reform, 149
People's Solidarity for Participatory Democracy, 168n
Petrochemical Industry Promotion Act (1970), 28
petrochemical sector, 124
Philippines, income levels compared, 2
Pohang Iron and Steel Company (POSCO), 4, 28-29
   blue-chip, 128
   Hanbo steel, 102
   high productivity, 119-20
      distortions, 120n
   labor productivity, 119
   quality, 97
   steel for ships, 32
Poland, 96
policy loans
   replaced, 68
   streamlining plan, 90
political parties, Kim Young-sam era, 89
portfolio investment, 99
POSCO. See Pohang Iron and Steel Company
power generation equipment sector, 123
preferential loans, 75
   equipment of export industry, 70t
   semiconductors, 69, 70t
   "preferred" shares, 126
Presidential Commission on Financial Reform, 109, 110
price competitiveness, 21
PriceWaterhouseCoopers, 157
privatization
   banking sector, 59-60, 153
   steel industry, 120
productivity, Korean versus world leaders, 118-19
prompt corrective action (PCA) system, 112
protectionism, United States, 27
public control, 163
public enterprises, 16

SEMCO. *See* Samsung Electro-Mechanics
    Company
semiconductor industry
    cyclical demand, 121
    labor productivity, 121
semiconductor products, 67
semiconductors, evaluation, 71
Seoul Bank, 113-14
Seoul District Court, 170
Seoul National University, 19
service sectors, 121
Shanghai GM, 136
Sharp, 69
Shilla Hotel, 163
Shina group, 35
Shinho group, 109
    debt-to-equity ratio, 110*t*
    number of subsidiaries, 110*t*
Shinjin, 38
Shipbuilding Promotion Act of 1967, 28
shipbuilding sector, 31-36
    cyclical, 97
    Daewoo, 133
    Daewoo entry, 131
    employment, 97
    export expansion, 96-98
    HHI, 32
    Hyundai, 31-32
    major shipyards, 35
    price competition, 97
    smaller operations, 35-36
    subsidies, 97-98
        dumping, 98
        OECD halt, 98
    support continued, 38
    technological range, 97
ship engine sector, 123
shipping lines, 33
Short-Term Agreement on Cotton Textiles
    (1964), 27
short-term capital accounts, 99
    exchange rates, 100
SK (formerly Sun Kyung) group, 5, 7
    asset growth, 7*t*
    debt-to-equity ratio, 110*t*, 129*t*
    electronics, 37
    founding entrepreneurs, 19*n*
    history, 6
    interest coverage ratio, 118, 118*t*, 129,
        129*t*
    intragroup transactions, 160
    mergers, 124
    nonbank financial services, 63
    number of subsidiaries, 110*t*
    Park favoritism, 19*n*
    stock prices, 165
SK Telecom
    blue-chip, 128
    shareholders' groups, 168*n*
SK Telecommunications, 5

social safety net, 172-73
    reform needed, 152, 172-73
    risks of bankruptcy, 149-50
So Sok-jun, 60
South Cholla province, 53, 54
Southeast Asia, 31
Soviet Union, Korean War, 12
Ssangbang Wool Company, bankruptcy, 103
Ssangyong group, 96
    asset growth, 7*t*
    debt-to-equity ratio, 110*t*, 129*t*
    interest coverage ratio, 118, 118*t*, 129,
        129*t*
    number of subsidiaries, 110*t*
Ssangyong Motors, 96
standard logic chips, 121
standstill agreement, Kim Dae-jung election,
    107
steel, compared to Japanese, 97
steel industry, 28
    Hanbo bankruptcy, 102, 102*n*
    "minimills," 120
    privatization, 120
Steel Industry Promotion Act (1970), 28
steel sector, support continued, 38
sterilized intervention, 99-100
stock market crash, 128
stock market, Korean
    Roh era, 76-77
    weakness, 154
stock prices
    Hyundai Motor Group, 165
    run-ups, 128
    Samsung Electronics, 164-65
    SK (formerly Sun Kyung) group, 165
strategic alliances, with international
    producers, 69
structural reform, IMF, 112
subcontracting practices, 57
subpar firms, 162
subsidies
    bad debts of banks, 115
    citizens underwriting, 48*n*
    default risks, 85
    early Park years, 16
    electronics sector, 36
    elite wealth, 39
    favoritism, 8
    HCI drive, 29
    infant industries, 18
    large and front-ended, 30
    long-term credit allocation, 23, 23*n*
    policy loans, 40-41, 40*t*
    policy revised, 29-30
    scale economies, 48-49
    semiconductors, 70
    shipbuilding, 33
    textile exports, 20-21
    US aid to textile sector, 20
Suharto, President, 95

Other Publications from the Institute for International Economics

* = out of print

POLICY ANALYSES IN
INTERNATIONAL ECONOMICS Series

Who's Bashing Whom? Trade Conflict in High-Technology Industries   Laura D'Andrea Tyson
November 1992   ISBN 0-88132-106-0
Korea in the World Economy* Il SaKong
January 1993   ISBN 0-88132-183-4
Pacific Dynamism and the International Economic System*
C. Fred Bergsten and Marcus Noland, editors
May 1993   ISBN 0-88132-196-6
Economic Consequences of Soviet Disintegration*
John Williamson, editor
May 1993   ISBN 0-88132-190-7
Reconcilable Differences? United States-Japan Economic Conflict*
C. Fred Bergsten and Marcus Noland
June 1993   ISBN 0-88132-129-X
Does Foreign Exchange Intervention Work?
Kathryn M. Dominguez and Jeffrey A. Frankel
September 1993   ISBN 0-88132-104-4
Sizing Up U.S. Export Disincentives*
J. David Richardson
September 1993   ISBN 0-88132-107-9
NAFTA: An Assessment
Gary Clyde Hufbauer and Jeffrey J. Schott/ *rev. ed.*
October 1993   ISBN 0-88132-199-0
Adjusting to Volatile Energy Prices
Philip K. Verleger, Jr.
November 1993   ISBN 0-88132-069-2
The Political Economy of Policy Reform
John Williamson, editor
January 1994   ISBN 0-88132-195-8
Measuring the Costs of Protection in the United States
Gary Clyde Hufbauer and Kimberly Ann Elliott
January 1994   ISBN 0-88132-108-7
The Dynamics of Korean Economic Development* Cho Soon
March 1994   ISBN 0-88132-162-1
Reviving the European Union*
C. Randall Henning, Eduard Hochreiter, and Gary Clyde Hufbauer, editors
April 1994   ISBN 0-88132-208-3
China in the World Economy Nicholas R. Lardy
April 1994   ISBN 0-88132-200-8
Greening the GATT: Trade, Environment, and the Future Daniel C. Esty
July 1994   ISBN 0-88132-205-9
Western Hemisphere Economic Integration*
Gary Clyde Hufbauer and Jeffrey J. Schott
July 1994   ISBN 0-88132-159-1
Currencies and Politics in the United States, Germany, and Japan
C. Randall Henning
September 1994   ISBN 0-88132-127-3
Estimating Equilibrium Exchange Rates
John Williamson, editor
September 1994   ISBN 0-88132-076-5

Managing the World Economy: Fifty Years After Bretton Woods   Peter B. Kenen, editor
September 1994   ISBN 0-88132-212-1
Reciprocity and Retaliation in U.S. Trade Policy
Thomas O. Bayard and Kimberly Ann Elliott
September 1994   ISBN 0-88132-084-6
The Uruguay Round: An Assessment*
Jeffrey J. Schott, assisted by Johanna W. Buurman
November 1994   ISBN 0-88132-206-7
Measuring the Costs of Protection in Japan*
Yoko Sazanami, Shujiro Urata, and Hiroki Kawai
January 1995 ISBN 0-88132-211-3
Foreign Direct Investment in the United States, 3rd Ed. Edward M. Graham and Paul R. Krugman
January 1995   ISBN 0-88132-204-0
The Political Economy of Korea-United States Cooperation*
C. Fred Bergsten and Il SaKong, editors
February 1995   ISBN 0-88132-213-X
International Debt Reexamined* William R. Cline
February 1995   ISBN 0-88132-083-8
American Trade Politics, 3rd Ed. I.M. Destler
April 1995   ISBN 0-88132-215-6
Managing Official Export Credits: The Quest for a Global Regime* John E. Ray
July 1995   ISBN 0-88132207-5
Asia Pacific Fusion: Japan's Role in APEC*
Yoichi Funabashi
October 1995   ISBN 0-88132-224-5
Korea-United States Cooperation in the New World Order*
C. Fred Bergsten and Il SaKong, editors
February 1996   ISBN 0-88132-226-1
Why Exports Really Matter!* ISBN 0-88132-221-0
Why Exports Matter More!* ISBN 0-88132-229-6
J. David Richardson and Karin Rindal
July 1995; February 1996
Global Corporations and National Governments
Edward M. Graham
May 1996   ISBN 0-88132-111-7
Global Economic Leadership and the Group of Seven   C. Fred Bergsten and C. Randall Henning
May 1996   ISBN 0-88132-218-0
The Trading System After the Uruguay Round*
John Whalley and Colleen Hamilton
July 1996   ISBN 0-88132-131-1
Private Capital Flows to Emerging Markets After the Mexican Crisis*   Guillermo A. Calvo, Morris Goldstein, and Eduard Hochreiter
September 1996   ISBN 0-88132-232-6
The Crawling Band as an Exchange Rate Regime: Lessons from Chile, Colombia, and Israel
John Williamson
September 1996   ISBN 0-88132-231-8
Flying High: Liberalizing Civil Aviation in the Asia Pacific*
Gary Clyde Hufbauer and Christopher Findlay
November 1996   ISBN 0-88132-227-X

Australia, New Zealand,
and Papua New Guinea
D.A. Information Services
648 Whitehorse Road
Mitcham, Victoria 3132, Australia
tel: 61-3-9210-7777
fax: 61-3-9210-7788
email: service@adadirect.com.au
http://www.dadirect.com.au

United Kingdom and Europe
(including Russia and Turkey)
The Eurospan Group
3 Henrietta Street, Covent Garden
London WC2E 8LU England
tel: 44-20-7240-0856
fax: 44-20-7379-0609
http://www.eurospan.co.uk

Japan and the Republic of Korea
United Publishers Services, Ltd.
KenkyuSha Bldg.
9, Kanda Surugadai 2-Chome
Chiyoda-Ku, Tokyo 101 Japan
tel: 81-3-3291-4541
fax: 81-3-3292-8610
email: saito@ups.co.jp
For trade accounts only.
Individuals will find IIE books in
leading Tokyo bookstores.

Thailand
Asia Books
5 Sukhumvit Rd. Soi 61
Bangkok 10110 Thailand
tel: 662-714-07402 Ext: 221, 222, 223
fax: 662-391-2277
email: purchase@asiabooks.co.th
http://www.asiabooksonline.com

Canada
Renouf Bookstore
5369 Canotek Road, Unit 1
Ottawa, Ontario KlJ 9J3, Canada
tel: 613-745-2665
fax: 613-745-7660
http://www.renoufbooks.com

India, Bangladesh, Nepal, and Sri Lanka
Viva Books Pvt.
Mr. Vinod Vasisht'ıa
4325/3, Ansari Rd.
Daryaganj, New Delhi-110002
India
tel: 91-11-327-9280
fax: 91-11-326-7224
email: vinod.viva@gndel.globalnet.
ems.vsnl.net.in

Southeast Asia (Brunei, Cambodia,
China, Malaysia, Hong Kong, Indonesia,
Laos, Myanmar, the Philippines, Singapore,
Taiwan, and Vietnam)
Hemisphere Publication Services
1 Kallang Pudding Rd. #0403
Golden Wheel Building
Singapore 349316
tel: 65-741-5166
fax: 65-742-9356

Visit our Web site at:
http://www.iie.com
E-mail orders to:
orders@iie.com